WAITING FOR THE

To Hugh
Best wishes
Roger

Waiting for the Rains

by

Roger J. Barton

DOVETAIL PRESS

2012

Published by **Dovetail Press**
105 Littlemoor Road, Pudsey,
Leeds LS28 8AP
www.dovetailpress.co.uk
info@dovetailpress.co.uk

All text pages designed and assembled by the author
All photographs taken by the author on film
and digitally converted
Composed in 10 on 12 pt Palatino
Printed by Dolman Scott
www.dolmanscott.com

ISBN 978-0-9572274-0-8

Acknowledgments

I WOULD like to thank the following for their assistance: my wife Kathy for editing the text, helpful suggestions and tolerance during my many hours on the computer; Barry Fox for reading and editing the text; members of the Pudsey Library Writing Group for their support and encouragement.

'Diana's Vow'. Ancient rock painting, Zimbabwe

Contents

Preface

EVERYWHERE IN Africa, south of the permanently dry Sahara Desert, the rains govern life. They arrive, hopefully, at pretty much an exact time every year. Too much rain is a catastrophe, washing away fields and flooding the countryside. When rains fail, or do not produce the necessary amount of water, life may fail too. The rural areas, where most of the population still lives, cannot grow their crops and life in these communities becomes precarious as crops whither and water holes dry up. The wisdom of the spiritualists is consulted to appease the forces of other worlds by giving offerings and to have mercy on their people. It is not only the rural poor who suffer, but insufficient rain produces food shortages and makes life harder for the urban poor as well. Several countries of southern Africa produce cash crops to sell and without rain these too are ravaged and the economic structure of the country dries up like the river-beds.

When the rains arrive on time and in sufficient quantity, the heavens are praised and the prospect of a good harvest ensured. The economy will prosper with water oiling both the large and small enterprises that depend on it. Waiting for the rains to arrive is like waiting for life to be renewed.

Perhaps Africa is accustomed to waiting. Queues form for a government official to issue a document, where possibly only a bribe will reduce the waiting time. Crowds linger in the shade of trees for the intercity bus, invariably late. People wait on the side of a rutted road while an overladen bus is repaired before resuming more miles of jarring travel. And all is performed peacefully without complaint, as if it were all in the nature of things. The waiting time is filled with valuable meetings, conversing with neighbours or attending to children's needs. It is not a wasted time.

For anyone new to Africa, used to the efficiency of western life, waiting assumes the proportions of a nightmare. But after he or she starts to become accustomed to 'Africa time', they too start to wait patiently for bureaucracy to work or transport to arrive. Maybe this is dangerous, as it won't do, back in the west. Waiting appears to become endemic the more southerly one goes. Even the southern Europeans have a more relaxed attitude. Possibly we have something to learn from Africa that the rushing around which seems so necessary in the western world is an institutionalized madness. Waiting could well be what we need to reclaim some quality of life.

Africa is huge, with a terrain that varies from desert to tropical rain forest and snow-capped mountains. There are enormous variations between its numerous cultures, many which are infused with mysterious customs. It is a land with modern cities and an urban elite, but the majority of its population still live a traditional life in small villages with age-old values. There are still enormous differences of wealth, with the rich living only miles away from those in poverty.

Africa is also a diverse place, where one would expect extraordinary things to be happening on an everyday basis. And that's how I found it to be. Africa has rules of its own and it guards them jealously. It will take a long time for them to change. The rules that apply to the western world still have little relevance here. I discovered a way of life with many contradictions – even after some conditioning to the African way of doing things. This affected the expatriate community who were caught in something of a no man's land between the indigenous population and the life they had left behind in their home country.

There was a confusion of values, some borrowed from their African hosts and some made up to suit the circumstances. With few guidelines and not much accountability, it was not surprising some went off the rails. This after all was a land part traditional, part with a colonial inheritance attempting to find its own unique future. There was bound to be a unique concoction of outcomes.

Expatriates are a diverse group, perhaps more so in the 1970s, when the world was a larger place than it is now. They were accustomed to living away from friends and family, even children, for most of the year. Their children voyaged across the skies two or three times a year to visit a place remote from their home. They clocked up thousands of miles over the years as they followed their distant family across the world. Even now, serial expatriates often spend a greater part of their career in this seemingly endless search for a new posting. In doing so their outlook on life is different.

The lifestyle of the local people they have come to manage, or manage the organizations they work in, could not be more different. Theirs is a close-knit community, with young and old learning to live together. There is a respect for the elders and family support for those in need. But even this is breaking down as a search for work draws crowds into the cities. Black and white are finding they can learn from each other. It is a tribute to the human condition how coexistence flourishes with understanding and tolerance.

Some African countries have progressed to stable democracies, while others appear to be in a permanent state of ethnic strife. To travel overland, for even short journeys, can still be an adventure not suited for the timid. The news reports from Africa will often be difficult to understand and are as varied as the continent itself. Added to its tendency for bizarre politics, it is not surprising that the newcomer is baffled, yet at the same time fascinated by the confusion of it all. In many ways, not much has changed since the 1970s; there are still local wars, but these are now between ethnic clans and with political rivalries. No sooner than one score is settled, than another flares up. This gives Africa the appearance of always being in a state of turmoil and this is often true, with little predictability of what is going to happen next. It is a strange and ever changing place where a unique sense of adventure is still to be found.

Several years after leaving Africa I have decided to write about what I saw and experienced. The advantage of perspective made me realize the 1970s and 1980s were a pivotal time that I had lived through, with colonial wars ending and new leaders taking charge. This era is now history. I was an expatriate while some conflicts were still raging and others had ended with their new black leaders in honeymoon mood. My story is about this post-colonial period with the day-to-day details of life both in a small community and in one of the largest cities on the continent.

I lived in Africa for ten years between 1970 and 1980. The countries I describe are Malawi and Zambia, but they could be almost anywhere else in the vast continent south of the Sahara. Boundaries are a political divide, not a cultural one. Malawi is relatively small and at that time little known, land-locked in south-east Africa, surrounded by Mozambique, Zambia and Tanzania. Zambia, by contrast is enormous, covering an area of nearly 300,000 square miles and again land-locked. There are a total of eight countries surrounding its borders and at that time conflicts were raging in several. They were all about who was to gain power.

This was a period of post-colonial times when the guardian home rule from several European countries had just been handed over to a local popular leader. But in others, a bitter campaign for independence was still raging. It was a turbulent time for the new leaders, as those recently ousted in the leadership contest were still around and waiting in the wings for any opportunity to take over.

Travelling through much of Africa was then, and can be now, a step into the unknown. For many it was going where few had gone before. Travel to remote destinations was a serious affair for the novice explorer. The wars against the colonial powers did make travel hazardous, but even so, Africa was probably a safer continent to cross then, than thirty years later. Tourists were an exception on long and expensive flights. Those were the days when the migrant mail liners made luxury sea journeys to the southern cape or onwards to boost the much-requested need for white migrants to Australia. The passengers on both the mail sea liners and flights were essentially travelling for serious reasons. There was a steady stream of business and sales staff, missionaries, expatriates and school children coming to join parents for boarding school holidays. Added to the mix, were just a handful of seasoned travellers, getting ahead of the tourist competition who were to discover Africa in the following two decades.

Africa demands a change of attitude and this can take time and experience. Situations that would be impossible to live with in the western world of organized living have to be viewed from a different perspective. This change will be necessary, because if you don't, then you will not survive in this part of the world. But make the effort and it is possible to accept the people and their culture, often much different to your own. This does not mean accepting everything you see in Africa, any more than in your home country. I came to Africa to make a contribution and change some things hopefully for the better. I made the attempt, not always successfully. But I had to know what the limits were and when to step away. This is something only time and experience taught me.

I have considered this story closer to a historic memoir and what I lived through as a piece of recent history. It is a personal account of my experience of these times. This is different to the viewpoint of an armchair academic or war correspondent sent in to file reports. I was living and working there and it was my home for over ten years. Perhaps this story will help in providing a background to the Africa seen through news reports.

The chapters are divided into subject areas, so it is possible to target a particular subject, i.e. travelling by road, or the effects of the climate, without having to follow any particular order. This is an account of what the country felt like to live in, not only during the post-colonial era, but what can very often apply to recent times. A lot does not change in Africa and much remains the same today as it was decades ago. It is an extraordinary mix.

There are too many images of disaster from Africa, often used to encourage the western donor to contribute to the aid budget. Today, Africa is poised to become a success story, with its mineral wealth and under-utilized agriculture. Many positive images occur in ordinary day-to-day situations. They can be the most memorable ones about a situation or a place and more than anything else can summarize an image. There are the children who run out from a village school to greet you as a visitor; the sharing of the rural bus with maize sacks and chickens; the fascination of seeing the African way of repairing broken bicycles; or the drinking of shake-shake beer in a grass-roofed bar in the bush as the fiery sun merges into the horizon. I have tried to provide a picture of the period just a few years after independence. I hope this account will capture some of that atmosphere.

CHAPTER 1

Welcome home

IT WAS June 1977 and I was in the first class compartment of a Zambian Airways 707, heading for Lusaka, the capital city. It did seem surprising to climb into this rather grand and spacious area, which as far as I knew was not a perk of the job I was being sent out for. I was pretty sure it was the chaotic seating plans. The airline regularly overbooked, relying on last minute cancellations to ensure no seats went unoccupied. This planning strategy rarely worked out and so there were passengers with boarding passes looking for seats, which were already filled. It was common practice on Zambian Airways to ask for volunteers to get off and spend another week lounging around their departure city, while more persistent passengers were found seats. I'm sure, had it not been for international regulations, fold-up chairs would have appeared down the aisle. I found myself ushered into a plush seat a few steps away from the pilot's station. It was already early evening when the plane took off from Heathrow, the main airline hub in London.

At this time anywhere in Zambia, the setting sun would be a signal for drinks to flow, whether in a small thatched bar in the bush or a city centre hotel. It was in fact 'sundowner' time. I was on a little bit of Zambian territory, albeit in the sky and the tradition was not going to be interrupted. As the plane banished the grey clouds and headed through the gloom into an azure sky, the formality of anything western was left behind. An African world was an intrinsic part of the flight arrangements. The air-hostess was now a conveyor of the best concoctions available. There appeared to be limitless quantities of Zambian drinks still left over from the previous flight. Glasses were filled or bottles replaced with a smile and no refusal was accepted. The notion of fluid intake to counter dehydration was applied only to alcoholic content. I wondered whether the idea of replacing booze capacity with space for another passenger had ever occurred to those zealous full-seating planners.

The lady sitting next to me was a seasoned Lusaka dweller and insisted on giving me advice about the city - in between the whisky chasers. As far as I can remember, she never mentioned anything about Lusaka being under a night curfew. The story about a possible coup attempt from some disgruntled elements within the military just didn't seem worthy of mention. But perhaps she just didn't know. My earlier recruitment meetings at the Zambian High Commission in London did not think it worth mentioning either.

The drone of the engines had a sort of hypnotic effect as the flight progressed. Perhaps this is why I found it difficult to assess her warnings about hold-ups with automatic pistols and organized criminal gangs operating out of the townships. I had just spent six years working in Zambia's next door neighbour Malawi, under the autocratic rule of President Banda. He had ways of clearing dissent from the streets and countryside, although by dubious methods. I mused about how Lusaka, just six hundred kilometres away across the border, could be so out of control? But this was Africa where revolutions were supposed to be commonplace; where order and disorder sit uncomfortably side by side. You are expected to be experienced in these things. It's as important as knowing about the job you are going to do and you just work around the local political dilemmas. The lady with the drinks just smiled and asked,

"Please sir, which kind of Carlsberg would you prefer?"

At Lusaka Airport the sun was glaring through a sky of vivid blue. It was the coolest time of the year and with the city sitting on the top of a 1,000 metre plateau, there was a vitality of mountain freshness in the air. Airport arrivals and departures had not yet declined into the anomalous tunnel structures leading to and from the lounges we are now all acclimatized to. Our 707 had taxied to within a couple of hundred yards of the airport viewing platform. Arrivals could take that magnificent tarmac walk to the entrance doors, with all the grandeur of a celebrity, with possibly a few greetings shouted up to those waiting on the viewing gallery. This was the weekly flight from England; it did not need placard-waving tour operators to identify their clients. It was easy to tell who was who. These included elderly missionaries, returning residents, business seekers and sales executives, boarding school children visiting for the holidays, a smattering of seasoned travellers. An expatriate member from my department knew who I was too; perhaps there was some indelible identification attached to expatriate migrants.

On the drive into the city the familiar sights of savanna Africa became real again. I had been away from this territory for ten months now, but the images of people and vehicles shimmering through swirling dust clouds appeared as though it was yesterday: the fearless highway walkers impervious to traffic; bicycles with four people holding on; head loads of firewood; buses blasting on shrill horns and overtaking on the wrong side. The roads represented the life here: few rules and colourful confusion. The road was a human tide of movement; vehicles shared their environment with people, animals, bicycles, buses and trucks. Africa is a place of people, their numbers dwarf vehicles and they all intermingle, finding their own space. The road has yet to be the sole abode of the car. And then suddenly they all disappeared and were replaced by the dual highway

2

running down the centre of the region's largest city. The multi-storey buildings and their broad pedestrian walks seemed unreal from the rural images only minutes past. The conversation with my colleague turned to reality.

"There is a dusk to dawn curfew on," he announced, as though it was merely a routine occurrence. It was easy to forget. He knew only as much as anyone else in the city - except perhaps those involved.

"Something serious about to happen?" I queried.

"Don't ask me why! But keep off the streets at all costs after dark. It's dangerous enough at the best of times . . . but now you can be shot on sight."

After I was located in my apartment close to the city centre, I watched the lights go out and heard the police sirens wail. This was Africa with its own unique rules and a special way of dealing with everyday life.

CHAPTER 2

Going to Africa can be a slow process

I WAS not looking for a posting to Africa. But an inconspicuous advertisement in one of the Sunday papers caught my attention. It was in Malawi, possibly one of the furthermost extremities of the old empire. A place few knew anything about, including myself. I had no idea exactly where the country was or my ultimate suitability for what could be a perilous experiment in a tropical wilderness. The more I thought about it, the more the prospect of a possibility of going to Africa became a focus. It was for a post as a Training Officer with the Government Printing Office in the administrative capital of Zomba. It was a long step from an advertisement to an acceptance. But the idea grew and became something of an exotic preoccupation. It was not something I had planned for, or even consciously thought about, but going somewhere exotic had always been a tantalizing, if somewhat remote prospect from an early age. I never had any idea of how it could be achieved, but as they say, 'it's the stuff dreams are made of'. It is so often just a momentary glance in a newspaper or a chance meeting with someone, that changes one's whole life direction. A crossroads as it were.

Lake Chilwa from Zomba Plateau

I had acquired atlases from an early age and found out for myself where the most remote territories were. The only tangible benefit as I can recall was that my knowledge of geography became exemplary as I poured over routes of early explorers and found places with incredible names, places worthy to get lost in. I placed circles around place names that had nothing more significant about them other than they were remote and seemed exotic. It was like an explorer searching for an indescribably difficult place to reach in a jungle outpost. Perhaps this was one of those tantalizing opportunities, which only appear when they are not being sought and have to be seized upon then and there. It's about waiting and seizing the right moment and the right opportunity. There is rarely a perfect time and risks are part of it all.

A romantic vision

In the late 1960s there still existed a romantic vision of Africa, even if it was not wholly real. It was a product of an age where distance really did exist and stories came by geographic magazines. Illusions were enduring and made believable by a mixture of part myth, with stories often exaggerated by reporters eager to sell to their client newspapers. This was still a time of colonial influence in Africa where large areas of the continent were under white rule, or only just handed over, much to the relief of the home country. The reports of infighting and corruption that were later to make up so much of the continents tragic future were still at least a decade away. Africa still had several years to prolong the image of romance and allure. For all I knew there were still explorers hacking a path through the jungle or negotiating deals with ragged villains shipping exotic goods across desolate trails up-country. Possibly there were still river-side hotels with teak stained bars and slowly whirling fans attempting to dispel clammy night air and biting insects, with rain pounding for hours and clattering onto wide palm leaves. It's all exotic, remote and so far away.

In the late 1960s and 70s, travelling was an extraordinarily daunting affair, which had not seized the imagination of the population at large. Or if it had, the opportunity of serious travelling had not penetrated as far as the ordinary working person. Travel for most people was an exclusive affair, reserved for once a year holidays and usually not very far from home. It was the reserve of the rich and famous and generally only read about in glossy magazines and travelogues. The inaccessibility of it all only enhanced the sense of distance and made such locations even more exotic and mysterious.

The start of the process

It was the summer of 1970 and I had just finished my one-year Certificate of Technical Education course at Garnet College in London. My wife

Kathy and I were living in Rotherfield, just over the border of Sussex, amidst gentle rolling hills and quiet country lanes. As the advertisement started to take a serious hold of my attention, I remember having to retrieve those same old atlases and relive some of those childhood fantasies, but this time with an element of serious intent.

As I started to penetrate the mystique of the inland kingdom of Malawi, I started to discover how remote and isolated the place actually was. In an age before the instantaneous information of the Internet generation, recent information was hard to come by and took great powers of detection to retrieve. Malawi was small and land-locked, with few large towns and poor communications with its neighbours. The very sparseness of information was intriguing and this alone invoked a sense of mystery about the place. I was later to find much of this was a conscious endeavour by its notorious President Banda to keep what were considered undesirable visitors and foreign journalists out. This was an action, which both kept an innocent way of life intact and an almost total news blackout of what was going on in the country.

Kathy and Lloyd by the Zambezi River

Surviving the interview

My application went through the recruiting body, which was the Crown Agents. At the time they acted as a sort of head-hunter for all personnel requirements and purchasing specialists on behalf of the newly independent crown territories. As independence matured it was a short time before these responsibilities were taken over by the Malawi Buying and Trade Agents. It was the body to whom I was to form a long-term relationship.

Interviews are singularly strange affairs. They are places, maybe they should be called situations, where dreams come true or are dispelled. It is an atmosphere somewhat akin to a quiz show, where the panel fires questions to which you either know the answer or not. Alone and without back-up, it is often only your wits, quick thinking, or experience and confidence that will carry the day. I felt confident about the interview, possibly because I did my homework and came prepared with some knowledge of the country and some sensible questions to ask. The panel sat in the London offices of the Crown Agents behind a huge desk in an oak panelled room. It would equally well have suited a reception area for visiting dignitaries. It was quiet, as though all extraneous sound was absorbed into the walls. The large desk had neat writing pads and typed lists. The chairs were heavy with a feel of age. My application was somewhere in the organized pile of files.

There were representatives from the Crown Agents and a Malawian from the High Commission, plus a miscellaneous assortment of what I can only describe as observers. Although I'm sure each one must have had some input into the proceedings, it appeared I was under scrutiny of the kind necessary to ensure candidates were suitable for the extreme outreaches of the old empire. After what seemed an inordinate period of time, I was eventually invited to give my own questions to the panel. I remember asking about the strict conservative culture that the country portrayed to the outside world. This was often referred to in any literature about Malawi as a warning to all western newcomers. It must have struck some kind of a chord, as the panel head swung back in his chair and gazing towards the ceiling seemed to despair of modern society.

"Well yes," he mused, "it is a conservative place, but judging by the way this country is going, we could well do with something of their kind of standards over here." It seemed a good point to finish on.

In the anteroom immediately afterwards, I recalled a loud voice from beyond the oak panelled door stating I had answered everything to his complete satisfaction. It must have been an extremely rare situation to be within earshot and hear glimpses from the conclusions of an interview board. However, some two weeks later it appeared I had indeed convinced them and was awarded the post. From that moment on, the process began that would suck me into the impenetrable procedure of both the British Government's recruitment campaign, on this side of the equator and the Malawi Government's equivalent on the other side. It was a process that would take several months from the initial signed agreement to arrival in the country. It proved to be as organized as a military campaign or the planning routines of an espionage placement.

The first documentation appeared in the form of lengthy foolscap (A4 was not a popular format yet) pages breaking down the pay structure. There were sixteen pages of conditions in what resembled an initiation procedure. Documents and information packs took over my postal deliveries. There was a feeling that once started it could only lead to an irrevocable final conclusion - the dispatch of another expatriate. The momentum did not accelerate as the days and weeks passed, but ground on at a pace consistent with the old empire itself.

As the news of my intended career move infiltrated through my colleagues, their initial impression seemed to indicate I was embarking upon something akin to a geological expedition, with some doubt as to whether I would ever be seen again. I had to convince them the country was not only accessible by a log raft over raging rapids, but had a regular air service. No one I knew at the time had done anything like it; they had settled for work and careers, which were certain (certainty in careers really were possible in those days) and predictable. It seemed an inexhaustible conversation piece.

Analysing the package

The detailed information packs, which arrived with regularity, unearthed both the complexities and simplicities of life in this far flung and to me, mysterious part of the continent. I began to realize just how different the life-style I was embarking on really was. The conditions of the appointment were as detailed as any legal document - which in fact they were.

. . . The officer undertakes that he will comply with and act in all respects according to the conditions set out in the Schedule to this Agreement and will diligently perform the duties assigned to him . . .

I was a *bona fide* civil servant to the Ministry of Overseas Development, a division somehow intertwined with the Foreign and Commonwealth Office, under the Overseas Aid Scheme. But many of the operational strategies had the invisible arm of the now defunct colonial service. I was to sign on for a minimum of two years, which could be extended to three and a half years, if all parties agreed. As the document detailed:

. . . if the Government so desires and the Government Medical Officer certifies that the officer is physically fit for such extended service . . .

All conditions from now on were to be associated with the civil service and its African institutions, all of whom were steeped in decades of obscure procedural practices. The remuneration package itself was more than just a statement of salary. It was not structured in a way to purposely confuse, but would relinquish just a little at a time and provide enough details for the potential employee to calculate what the sum total could be, provided relevant conditions were met. It was first divided into two sections. Part was to be paid in Malawi, the same as anyone at my civil service level would receive. Then a second, so-called inducement package, that was by far the largest component, was to be paid by the British government in the UK, which was tax-free. This amazing add-on benefit, in the days of prohibitive personal taxes, should have been enough to induce anyone to leave these northern shores.

References to baggage allowance included not just the usual personal effects, but household equipment and even items of furniture. There were local holidays too, at least just enough to allow for sojourns into the countryside. As long as the expatriate stayed the course, an entitlement to a 25% gratuity upon completion of the contract was an extra inducement to stay. At the end of the contract, a six month leave period was added on, not only on full pay, but also qualified for a gratuity payment, again tax-free. Such an extensive period, must again have been a legacy from an era when it was considered a necessity to recover from whatever bouts of jungle fever had laid the intrepid expatriate low. But however exotic this may be, it probably had more to do with a modern necessity of an enhanced time to re-settle and to make up for the absence of pension entitlements.

Further scrutiny of this document revealed a plethora of allowances and entitlements, which although of obvious importance, revealed themselves only by careful reading. It was as if they were secrets, not to be given up lightly. The pages slowly released their details, like a journey through a computer game, until eventually all of its secrets were revealed. Return flights were naturally part of the package, but also included all members of one's family and holiday flights for children. There were also allowances for children to continue their education at boarding school within the UK. This was an enticement that would allow for a private boarding school education, part paid by the government. Revered by some parents as the icing on the cake of inducements. Having children absent for much of the year, often at boarding school, was the price often accepted for a quality education. I was to discover, this was part of the conditions accepted by many parents living an expatriate life-style.

Last but not least was a tropical clothing outfit. My 'kit' as it was referred to in my introduction guide, would be of my own choosing. But a lengthy description detailed what would be suitable for all kinds of necessities, from city office to expeditions. Descriptions followed on not only suitable styles, but detailed the type of fabrics and how both they and the wearer would be affected by the climate. Whereas today tropical clothing is even advertised in many specialist shops, in 1970 some searching was necessary among the local tailors to find the right outfit.

I found local outfitters had little in the way of suggestions or advice. They were not often called upon to suggest what could be suitable for expeditions into the African bush. The inclusion of a dress allowance must have epitomized an association with a colonial past. Apart from the climate dictating clothing requirements, the rigid political system had its demands too. Whatever was considered remotely fashionable in western countries was deemed corruptible and an attack on local morality. So no bellbottoms were allowed for men and for women no miniskirts or trousers. Both for Kathy and many expatriate women, whole wardrobes had to be discarded and a rapid resort to either made-to-measure or make their own.

Insider knowledge of the expatriate life

After signing details were completed, the main information books arrived. They definitely had a style with a distinctly 1950s look. All were rather bulky and even the covers were type written with such titles as *The Preservation of Health in Warm Climates* or simply *Living in Malawi*. They were no nonsense, practical guides to the serious business of not only survival, but also how to live and adjust to life on a day-to-day basis, in a remote and sometimes inaccessible territory. The authors were serious in their intentions of what practical life for the expatriate was going to be. It's always necessary to remember just how remote the world was in the 1970s and these handbooks are a testimony to that world. In no way did they attempt to glamorize or encourage the new recruit, or even less add to the mystery of a country located in the heart of Africa, or anywhere else where the home flag either flew or had recently been quietly folded up.

As in any career move, especially in what were once crown territories, organizations existed to support expatriates in adjusting to a new environment. Membership of the London based Overseas Development Service Association, was available to anyone embarking on a government contract. With a club and advice centre it was able to supply contacts and letters of introduction to any of its territories.

In the 64-page booklet *Living in Malawi*, pages were devoted to coming to terms with the strangeness of the new environment and the sources of help the new arrival could draw upon. The detail and range of facilities available were extraordinary to the newcomer in an expatriate world. It demonstrated how a support system had been honed to practical efficiency by sheer necessity. In future years I assumed the whole system would slowly be dismantled as far-flung countries matured, distances became shorter and the old experts in conditions 'up country' simply faded away.

There existed the Women's Corona Society with offices in London and a large overseas network, devoted entirely to expatriate women and issues relating to children. Little things like the importance of bringing mementos from home to ease the initial newness, were included. There was information on the ladies' groups who would loan kitchen essentials. There were tips on shopping in the local market and how to manage a kitchen staff. It was pointed out that the hiring of servants was expected and their management would need to be a delicate blend of careful instruction while still being allowed to demonstrate their own ability. Being a house servant of a *bwana* and *dona* was a position of status. Reading the section on servants emphasized their importance. It was considered very unwise not to employ one or even two just to save money. It was not just because of the heat, but presumably as it was the done thing. It gave someone a job and enabled the newcomer to blend in that much more easily into the expatriate community. The importance of how to buy headloads of firewood was revealed and the places mosquitoes would hide at night. It was certainly not the stuff of tourist leaflets.

A book for saving lives

The most intriguing of all literature was a red covered book entitled *Preservation of Personal Health in Warm Climates*. This was a down to earth, formidable information pack for serious survival in the most isolated of bush environments. Its 92 pages of advice from the London School of Hygiene and Tropical Medicine was a textbook for man (and woman) against sun and insect. Descriptions were given of practically every insect land-borne or aerial, which would seek revenge on the human intruder to its domain. The documentation on the use of drugs to combat these intrusions was lengthy and pulled no punches as to the dangers one would face should any of the precautions be neglected.

Persons of a nervous disposition were surely to be appalled by some of the possibilities of clinical dangers to be faced. It could raise memories in the minds of readers of the historical accounts from early settlers, many of whom suffered an early death due to these very diseases. All the well-known diseases were present: typhoid, cholera, yellow fever, sleeping sickness, sand-fly fever, kala azar, plague, such an overwhelming compilation that one wondered how anyone ever survived in the early days. The truth is many did not; at least half of the early Europeans who came to seek their fortune never returned, having succumbed to one (or more) of these deadly diseases.

The readers of the publication were without doubt relieved at the modern armoury of defences now available. Of course the prevention of heat stroke and sunburn came early on in the list. The more 'exotic' conditions caused by insects were something of a lurid fascination with descriptions of fungal infections, dysenteries, flies (of which seven major groups were listed), mosquitoes, fleas, ticks, mites, lice, midges, bugs, snake bites, scorpions, centipedes, spiders, leeches and (naturally) cockroaches. Perhaps it was the worms, practically unknown in the UK, which could be considered the bench-mark by which all tropical diseases could be ranked. They seemed to come in all shapes and sizes. The varieties of intestinal worms and their cures perhaps more than anything, emphasized the tropical nature of the environment and its dangers. The hookworm and roundworm varieties occupied several pages of description; where they are found, how one will pick up the infection and how to treat it. All the necessary drugs were mentioned right down to the actual dosages necessary to get the blighters out of the system.

Hookworm Infections: In many parts of the tropics 70%-90% of the local inhabitants harbour hookworms. . . . larvae hatch out of the eggs and after 7-10 days development are ready to penetrate the skin of barefooted passers-by. From the feet they are carried by the blood stream to the lungs and thence via the windpipe, the gullet and the stomach to the bowel where the cycle starts once more.

It appeared danger lurked from every quarter.

Stand the legs of food safes in dishes of antiseptic to keep ants out . . . protection against rodents, flies and cockroaches is necessary . . . servants may convey infection to food and plates, and typhoid carriers are a special danger in this respect.

A lengthy survey followed on as to how all these dangers could be minimized. The numerous pages on personal hygiene examined everything from washing daily to the importance of ironing clothes (not for appearances but to eliminate insect eggs, which could hatch out on warm skin). Lack of such attention could well bring on a case of the infamous 'dhobhi's itch' (a ringworm infection), something which must have been every bit as disconcerting as its name suggests. From all of this it might be construed there was an element of scare tactics to ram home how dangerous it all could be. This was definitely not the intention. It was advice both to the city dweller and to those who could be stationed in really remote and inaccessible territory. Life saving it really could be!

The 92-page book was a fascinating source of information and must now be regarded as a primary reference of defence by the expatriate against tropical diseases. It was first published in 1951, a time when the prospect that the sun would at sometime set on the empire was never contemplated. Even though the British had left India by this time, the prospect of African nationalism appeared non-existent. The idea of long-term occupation was very much alive. Considering what must appear to be a formidable range of diseases, it is remarkable that so many individuals, often with families and young children, decided to take the risk. It was pointed out:

The responsibility for guarding his and his family's health, therefore, rests on the individual himself.

The allure of Africa as a place of mystery, of adventure with a remoteness on a scale inconceivable in western countries did hold some element of fascination. Many countries of the continent were little heard of except when a disaster occurred or a political insurgency surfaced. Whatever the inspiration for the journey to such a potentially remote destination, the practical necessities for day-to-day life was the stuff of this essential publication.

The author's experience is shown in a section devoted to mental health. It makes reference to the numbers of Europeans invalided out of the tropics, of which half were due to mental ill-health. There are some guidelines given of which a selection are worth reviewing:

. . . most (mental) ill-health arises from a temperamental incompatibility - an inability to adjust outlook and habits to the strange people, customs, social life and climate of a tropical environment. Inflexible people and those with definite racial or cultural prejudices find this adjustment most difficult, and those to whom the glamour of tropical life seems an escape from the competition 'at home' are sure to be disillusioned. . . . the heat and humidity tend to magnify the petty irritations that would pass unnoticed in more temperate regions.

It is only when I look back over the years I spent in such an environment that the importance of this advice becomes understandable. I saw many who tried to take on this continent and fashion it after their own thinking. They had tried to get their own way of thinking and working installed in a culture, which was in many ways incomparably different to their own and expect it to work. It was for the most part attempted sincerely, but often an impossible task. One has to work within a culture, not impose one's own. Change is a gradual thing. I also had some misplaced ideals, but before they became insurmountable burdens, I had the pragmatism to modify them into something workable. Those who failed to see the outcome became the victim. The Rudyard Kipling saga of *Here lies the man who tried to hurry the east* was pertinent on more than one continent. But for some it was as the *Preservation of Health* book predicted - the environment, perhaps the escape that had not worked out, which took its toll. Many did stay despite everything - to go back to a life in their home country for many was also too problematic. Here their standard of living was high, at least many of the simple practical things of day-to-day life were available. But the price was often a gradual and irrevocable marital breakdown and for many a slide into drinking problems. As the text referred: *. . . in the tropics mental stability is no less important than physical fitness.*

The health hurdle

It was always going to be conditional for my acceptance to be confirmed by a series of health examinations. To get an expatriate established in a territory after weeks of processing, only to find he or she could not take the heat or succumbed to every tropical ailment would have been disastrous. It was a balancing of procedures for the recruiting authorities - a minimum pile of information had to be sent out, to enable the candidate to size up the job and situation. This took time, especially as a spouse and children were often involved. But before the process had gone too far, a health assessment was always going to be top priority.

I had never been for a health check, either before or since, where the examiner demanded a stark naked specimen for scrutiny. But as he walked around me with the scrutiny of a fossil collector, comments ensued on what he saw:

"Those are funny feet."

It was a bizarre medical comment, as I indeed did have bunions, but my feet could see most off when it came to putting them to good use. I was not about to question the comment as I was in dire need of a clean medical record. Could a contract in the heart of Africa really be jeopardized because of bunions? Maybe this doctor was just over zealous or considered only super athletes could survive the rigours of the tropics. Even the eye test caused me some anxiety as it was conducted with the letter board pinned up at the end of a dark corridor with door lights behind. My problem was identifying the board, irrespective of what was on it. A final discussion followed.

"So you want to go to the Dark Continent?"

Whether this was part of a psychological test to establish whether I had suspicious motives for my career move, I couldn't establish. He may have been just curious. Perhaps it was simply just light conversation. But no advice was given or suggestions made about maintaining a healthy life amidst an onslaught of parasites the literature suggested I should guard against. Eventually the x-ray results confirmed I was in good shape and I was declared fit for duty. Like a successful A-level student having just received good grades, I was as good as being on my way.

As I became adjusted to the conditions and entitlements, returned all the necessary documents and found my health was in good shape, there was yet another preparation for the new life of a first-time expatriate. This was a two-day seminar, expenses paid, at a country retreat somewhere in the south of England. It was here that experienced and recently returned expatriates would give talks and advise about the practicalities of life in developing countries. I actually missed out on what must have been a grand affair. I cannot think what could have been more important at the time than what must have been a splendid couple of days soaking up advice somewhere in the Sussex countryside.

When you return the O.S.R.B. will be there

Apart from the documents and advice that were given to all departing personnel, I was to discover there was another entire department of the

Overseas Development Administration. This was devoted to assisting those who were returning home from missions in those same far flung corners of the world. Although I only discovered this some years later and while still in Zambia, the services of the 'Overseas Services Resettlement Bureau' were another influential advice centre.

It was in some ways similar to a centralized 'job club', but with staff knowledgeable about the specific problems encountered by personnel returning to the UK, after what may have been a career based entirely in overseas territories. Their job involved not just de-fusing the culture shock of returning to western life, but practical help on relocating, work placements, retraining, even returning overseas. As the bureau realistically pointed out:

The UK to which you will be returning will be different from the one you left. . . . There has also been considerable progress in localizing posts and also more independent countries are using their own recruitment agencies.

There were considerable comments about the difficulty of finding placements due to the gap between skills necessary in developing countries and the ones required upon returning home:

Many officers . . . sometimes appear to get out of touch with their own professions and particular skills, and when they return to the UK find it difficult to get back into their normal occupations. It is therefore important when working overseas to keep in touch with the 'nuts and bolts' of your profession.

The bureau was well-off enough to give bursaries not only to enable easier retraining to settle in the UK, but also to enable serving personnel to return to developing countries. The numbers of personnel declined over the years and government budgets trimmed as dependent territories became not only self-governing, but employed greater numbers of their own staff. The Bureau was finally wound-up in December 1980. But it still managed to produce a 70 page manual and advice brochures to the dwindling numbers of returning expatriates. Once again this too resembles a historical document, a testimony of the way things were.

It was not the Resettlement Bureau who came looking, but what can be loosely described as a 'head-hunter', from Kenya.

It was about a year after my contract with the Zambian Government finished, I discovered my legacy of overseas experience was still intact. In 1983 I was working as a lecturer in what was Kitson College in Leeds and had given up all ideas about working as an expatriate. It was not the Resettlement Bureau who came looking, but what can be loosely described as a 'head-hunter', from Kenya. A college in Nairobi required a lecturer and word through the grapevine discovered my location.

It was not only appropriate qualifications, but the quality of being a survivor was an essential requirement in recruitment policy. Not everyone can survive in a strange culture far from home, as I was to discover during my years in Africa. Someone who has demonstrated this durability can become a valuable asset. It was always a risk, an expensive risk, to engage a raw recruit and find he or she could not adapt. This 'head-hunter' had not travelled from Kenya only to see me; he was on leave, but one of his duties was to sign me up for a contract. The job was mine; all I had to do was sign the document. It was an opportunity I had to think long and hard about.

My job was going well and the college was investing in new Apple Macintosh computer equipment. For the first time, I was enrolled in a serious pension scheme! As far as I could tell, the college in Nairobi was years behind in modern technology. This was not a career progression and I would have little chance of catching up. Returning from Africa with dated experience would not have worked out well. I eventually declined this invitation, for what I thought were very good reasons. Also my son Lloyd had just started school and needed a change of environment.

I state this because it is typical of the special circumstances expatriates can find themselves facing. Had I accepted this offer, perhaps the rest of my working life would have been spent as a seasoned expatriate, forever roaming far-flung exotic lands. This too could be a good life and many still prefer this option. Life choices are not always easy.

A time to reflect

All the documents were now signed and advice booklets absorbed. But it's during the crating up of possessions that the whirlwind of activity ceases and you suddenly focus on the reality of the changes, which are about to take place. As the paraphernalia of recommended living items were sent to be crated, I realized they would not be seen again until several months had passed and the crates had travelled thousands of miles across sea and land. That is, I trusted they really would be seen again. Not knowing what to do with my old car, a faithful Morris Minor Traveller - later to become a sought-after classic, I looked around for storage. While asking around the area for such a place, I came upon a family who had also resided on contract overseas for some years. More advice was forthcoming.

"Haven't enough space in our barn I'm afraid, but why bother with that car? By the time you return you'll be buying a Mercedes".

Perhaps there was an element of truth about the fortunes of an expatriate and perhaps they were right, but I actually did lay the car up for something over two and a half years. It was later to make its own extraordinary journey to Africa, upon my return for a second contract.

With the persistent onslaught of information coming through every few days, it was possible to get detached from what the end of the process was all about. It was more than a change of job; it was about a complete change of life-style contained in a departure to a destination unheard of a few weeks earlier. At some point a gradual understanding starts and I found the jargon of documents became legible, the country and feeling about the life-style became understandable and an awareness started to grow – a feeling you get to know about making the right decision. I had to admit at being rather proud of doing something drastically different. But being without a job at the time dilutes the risk involved in embarking on such an adventure. It had an air of expectancy and anticipation. Getting away from the grey skies of seventies Britain and the approaching years of austerity had attractions.

The system appeared cleverly, perhaps purposely, engineered to dispel any indecision a potential recruit may have had about such a destination and life-style to a far-flung corner of the world, in a culture so different to anything experienced before. To be fair, there was no hard sell. The information met head-on the questions any new recruit would need to be answered.

The weeks went by and the machinery of the Overseas Development Administration slowly and systematically discharged the information. Perhaps it's something to do with the practical emphasis of their literature, which proved to be factual and with an emphasis extracted from expert experience. Looking back at it now convinces me it was a genuine desire to be as truthful and up-to-date about local conditions as possible.

Nothing about it suggested anything to do with armchair officials handing out propaganda made-up either from conjecture or dubious sources, on the chance some of it might be useful. In the early days especially, it was essential to get as much information about local conditions as accurately as possible. Individuals were often involved in administering territories in remote areas, or on survey expeditions, where they could easily find themselves having to rely upon their own initiative. When initiative is backed up by solid intelligence, it can be a lifesaver.

Maybe this thoroughness had much to do with the success of the colonial campaign. Although there is much in this legacy history would prefer to forget. There were many who gained enormous wealth from those early campaigns, but equally much valuable infrastructure was given to the host country. This legacy of empire was present in Malawi and Zambia and a certain respect for what it stood for still remains. It did come as some surprise to find this and that some good came out of the whole colonial experience.

CHAPTER 3

Final departure and a new arrival

WITHIN THE next month I had my flight date. It was an early October day and from the Boeing 707's tiny windows, splashed with rain, the puddles on the loading area dimly reflected the airport's glaring lights. For Kathy and myself, it was to be the last rain we would see for several months. The departure had an almost nostalgic sensation; from the gloom of an early evening into a destination of which there had been so much preparation - changing now to a heightened anticipation. This was before the age of organized tourism to this part of the world and the majority of passengers had business of some kind or were visiting friends and relatives.

Lake Malawi from Salima

The flight to Malawi was interrupted by various stopovers for refuelling. Details about the flight remain more vivid than perhaps any other I have made. Yet nothing particularly exciting took place, but here I was getting my first look at an African landscape.

The flight path gave beautiful views through a cloudless sky of Lake Malawi, a 450-mile expanse of fresh water. It was a sight most travellers on board wanted to see no matter how many times they had witnessed one of southern Africa's most impressive aerial vistas. This was October, one of the hottest months and almost at the end of the dry season in this area of the continent. The flat arid landscape of red-brown earth was swirling in dust bowls whipped up by the early morning hot air currents. Vegetation was sparse with bushes interspersed with long scorched grass. I did not expect it to look so dry. The exacting contrasts between the dry and wet seasons I had no appreciation of. Within two months the swirling dust clouds would give way to a blanket of luscious green with elephant grass eight feet tall and dormant trees bursting into life. But now this was a landscape fashioned by six months without rain.

Touchdown was at Chileka Airport about ten miles outside the commercial capital, Blantyre. The exit from the plane was via an open-air stairway. The light was startlingly brilliant and the hot air was being jostled by the thrust of the morning thermals. Just a hundred metres or so away was the terminal building crowded with sightseers and visitors on the open roof area within shouting distance of the passengers. The scene had reflections of those 1940s movies. The arrival of the weekly UK flight was something of an occasion, and no one needed to be informed which it was. On this day of the week it was the only international arrival. The flight had the aura normally reserved for the majestic appearance of a transatlantic ocean liner. Most aircraft were turbo-prop and it was only a few years previous that the now historic DC3 aircraft was in normal service. The appearance of a massive 707 jetliner was an occasion and coupled with being within almost touching distance from the viewing area of the terminal building, made the arrival that much more momentous.

Customs in developing countries can be a fractious affair especially in Malawi, which had tedious conditions on what could be imported – dress included. Perhaps our impeccable dress impressed the officials, as customs waved their usual search for subversive literature, a finding that could result in a rapid departure, usually within twenty-four hours. Kathy held her wide white sun hat against the gentle breeze, her colourful long skirt, swirling around her ankles. My tropical suit and recently trimmed hair were just what the customs ordered. Formalities were brief and courteous. Customs here demanded a certain 'respectable' appearance together with entry papers that did not arouse suspicions.

An expatriate and his wife from the Government Printing Department, which I was contracted to, collected us, plus baggage, for the forty miles or so journey to Zomba, the administrative capital where the department is located. This must surely be one of the most important roads in the country and for me, where Africa really began.

Colours and light

No amount of reading about what to expect can ever substitute or do very much to diminish the impact of instant cultural change. The association with western life had begun to fade even as we exited the airport gates and after five minutes drive it seemed like a memory, filtered out by the sights, sounds and aromas of a strange culture. It is difficult to organize one's memory of this particular moment in time, of which images were the most striking. It was like walking into a newly decorated room for the first time. There was a heightened sense of intense light and colour, all in close proximity, an artist's palette where the paints have all mixed together. The differences of everything extended from the brilliant blue sky to the rust brown earth, the tall dazzling yellow grass, dark people with loads on their heads, people walking everywhere, some on bicycles, some just sitting by the roadside, mud huts with dried grass roofs, mangoes and bananas in piles on make-shift tables, and all disappearing into a swirling heat haze.

Village near Zomba Plateau

The black tarmac strip of road stood vividly out from the dusty red earth, which came right up to its very edge. After the British tradition, vehicles drove on the left-hand side, but whatever the danger, would often use the left side to overtake. Those with the most nerve dictated road etiquette. Constant successions of overtaking vehicles had worn the earth sides down and produced a steep camber. Not surprisingly this resulted in the road often projecting a few centimetres higher than the sides, giving it an added carpet-like prominence. Vehicles that overtook on the left-hand side lurched onto the earth sides amidst much horn blasting and clouds of dust with an occasional volley of roadside stones. This explained the numerous cracked windscreens.

It was the number of people who were physically on the road, which really attracted my attention - either walking, running, cycling or occasionally just sitting on its edge. Their numbers far outweighed the number of vehicles, and drivers had to apply a special form of highway code by weaving around people who seemed oblivious to traffic. The vehicle horn was such an essential item of road safety that when traffic police occasionally (perhaps often) inspected one's vehicle, it was the most frequently tested appliance. The use of the car horn was obligatory and the shriller the better. But while an auditory blast did encourage some to get off the road, many gave only a slight turn of the head just to ascertain whether the vehicle was a potential enough danger to demand a change of course. Buses had the quality of emptying the road of all before them - nobody messed with buses.

CHAPTER 4

A town called Zomba

IT TOOK something over an hour to reach Zomba, the administrative capital. Built by the first settlers to the area in the 1870s, it has been described as the setting of one of the most beautiful towns in southern Africa. It does not take long to see why. The town nestles at the base of a plateau, which rises steeply to over 1,000 metres. Its slopes are covered with tropical vegetation through which granite rock protrudes to reveal the occasional wisps of cascading mountain streams. The high rainfall produces streams that in some instances exist all the way through the long dry season. These crystal clear plumes of water eventually combine with the Mulunguzi River far below.

On the flatter, lower slopes the shapes of houses could be seen jutting through the forest clearings. Many of these were impressive substantial personal dwellings dating from the early years of the 19th century, with incredibly thick whitewashed walls and towering rooms. From their wide

khondi (veranda) there were breathtaking views of the green plateau slopes, which blended into the scorched haze of the flat distant plains. These houses with their solid structure were built only a few years after the country first became a colonial protectorate and must have represented the permanence this territory meant to its colonial builders.

Old government house, Zomba

Only some eighty years later they were to be inherited by the new government with a different category of occupants.

The edge of town displayed a sprawling assembly of the essential services such an urban population would need. A whitewashed catholic mission sparkled in the brilliant light, with its attendant church and school just beyond. A kilometre further on, the granite stonewalls of the local prison appeared, with its every-ready labour force of prisoners. Its entrance was resplendent with a gigantic flame tree covered in crimson flowers every year before the rains started. Next, on the opposite side of the road was the local hospital, its spacious grounds always busy with waiting relatives and friends. All spiritual and physical necessities of the human condition neatly placed within walking distance. And finally, the road straightened and entered the town, lined on both sides by jacaranda trees, at this time of the year their blue flowers billowed into the sky. As their blooms fell, the brown earth was coated with a purple carpet. Put in by the town's founders, they transformed the main street into a causeway, which could have led to a king's palace. It nearly did, as just off this road laid the presidential residence.

Zomba commercial area

The road into Zomba cut right through the centre of the town. On the northbound route the view to the left gave a stunning vista of the plateau, with its granite out-crops, jungle foliage and white whiffs of tumbling streams. Snaking through the lower slopes and largely invisible from the road was a network of government offices. To the right laid the commercial centre with its collection of one-storey shops clustering around the market area.

Mr Chisale can make any suit within a day!

It was a melting pot of occupations; the people who populated this area were both Indians and Africans; they were old and young, men and women, some rich and others barely scraping a living from selling everything from fruit to scrap metal. This was the area of town centred around the market where everyone would come - or at least their servants would - at some time, whether to sell or buy, to meet friends and gossip, maybe to trade something when money was short or to seek out something the authorities turned a blind eye to. This was likely to be 'pot' or some other low-grade drug, to while away the evening hours. It was a vibrant, colourful place, of exotic smells, moving with people, a balance to the staid offices of government, which silently and with shades of grey plied their own business on the upper slopes.

A single mile will effectively leave the town behind. A road sign in the centre of town simply stating 'Zomba 0' confirms there is no doubt where one was. The road heads north towards Lilongwe, later to eclipse Zomba and become the capital. This road was named the 'M1', possibly from its English namesake, as both were the central transport link heading north. This one having the only long distance tarred surface at the time.

Where everyone comes to shop

The whitewashed general stores surrounding the market area, all had a large concrete *khondi* occupied by a trade's person of some kind, but almost always with one or more treadle sewing machinists. These nimble fingered operators could put anything together from suits to shirts either on the spot or probably the next day. It was nearly always men who plied this business - perhaps the women of the family were either in the fields doing the heavy work or at home minding the children. These people were experts with repairs and could save almost anything from destruction. Shirts with intricate patterns of patches and apparently thousands of stitches were a standard product. A garment that was discarded would be the source of possibly twenty patches on another that was nearing extinction. The machinists had an eye for shape and size and with a minimum of actual measurements, finished articles could appear at speed.

With the ability on their doorstep to manufacture the whole clothing article, it was not surprising to find an amazing selection of fabric stores. With the extreme weather and physical abuse most clothes had to put up with, fabrics were always in demand. In between the fabric shops were the general stores, an Aladdin's cave of articles and oddities, with nails, paints, tools, oil lamps, car parts and bits to mend almost anything which had fallen apart. In the little space there was for a window display was a selection of the most extreme range of products stocked.

Tins of screws vied for attention with handtool kits, with the widest selection of oil lamp wicks thrust behind cure-all cough medicine and an array of hair cream jars; insect repellent and drain cleaners were centre stage with faded advertisements of the latest Indian imports of bicycles.

A force for business

Indians from the sub-continent owned almost all the stores, with most of the family usually involved somewhere within the business. Ask for something and it would either appear or be known to exist at an adjacent store, or failing that, the article would be sourced from who knows where amongst the network of traders. The Indians were a formidable force of business entrepreneurs, owning not only small businesses in the most remote of locations but they were also the mind and muscle behind most of the larger private sector organizations in the major commercial centres.

They kept almost exclusively to themselves, in their own areas, attending their own social organizations, religious customs and tight family networks. In the centre of the trading district, their mosque dominated the area with its spires equipped with loud hailers, giving the call to prayer. The call would infiltrate the whole area and be a constant reminder of the importance of their place in the community. The Indians only contact with the wider social world was in the later 1970s, when the younger and more liberal (but only the males) joined the expatriate sporting clubs. They not surprisingly dominated the cricket teams. This community kept out of any contact with politics, despite their considerable economic influence. Their strangle hold on businesses of any sort was such that in 1974 President Kamuzu Banda ordered all Asian businesses in the rural areas to be re-located to the towns. The pretence was cooked up to relate their activities with corruption, but it was a plain move to give Malawian businesses a chance to survive.

A seat of historical power

We stayed temporarily at what is known as the Government Hostel. An incongruous name for what was once the governor's residence. The main part was essentially unchanged since those early years and its colonial elegance had been maintained by making no alterations except decorating. Known as 'the hostel', it served as short stay accommodation for expatriates before being housed, and for MPs and ministers during the periods when parliament met. The hostel, like the town, represented the permanence of the late 19th century. Nothing had changed much since those days.

In the humid nights on the trimmed grass lawns of the hostel you could if you looked closely, imagine faint reflections of the governor's staff in military uniform and helmets in this same spot. Yet, while the town and its whitewashed general stores and shady market stalls looked on, history had overtaken with a completely new regime and different thinking. The new regime was about using power, not only for the benefits it could bring the country, but for the prestige and influence power could bring to its holder. Perhaps that's not so different from anywhere else. But to keep power in Malawi, any opposition had better know its place.

Power in the market place

The hand-over from a colonial power to a local politician did not alter this colourful and confusing local shopping area. In the traders' shops and in the market, life continued at its leisurely pace, almost without concern as to who was running things out there in a world that for many was so remote.

Zomba Government Hostel. Used as initial accommodation for expatriates and government ministers on business

The shops and market changed little over the years and were not affected by political personalities or by changes in the regimes that came and went. It was here that local people bought their oil lamps and traded tomatoes. To them, this was the place where they felt at home and where the real world belonged. But like everyone else, party officials also came here, not always to shop, but to give political speeches. It was here the foot soldiers of the party would appear to scoop up truckloads of market idlers to cheer the president as he left for parliament. Party officials had little interest in changing everyday shopping habits - their agenda was higher and on a grander scale. The people would listen but words would not mean much unless promises were made to build a new school or borehole. They wanted a better standard of living and more jobs. Where many of the market traders lived, out in the countryside, within a few miles of the town and into the rural areas, life had more to do with firmly entrenched local customs. Tribal rituals handed down through the generations were trusted more than newly arrived politicians.

A new regime

The late 1970s and early 1980s would see the last lingering vestiges of the colonial era disappear. It would come with speed as is common with political change in Africa. Newly appointed black officials, many the party faithful, would rise rapidly up the ranks and replace a white colonial regime. It was government policy to replace the expatriate civil service under the localisation programme. As this policy gathered momentum during the 1970s, a style of life and a social atmosphere, which had existed almost without change for sixty years, became eroded and soon would be gone forever.

The change would be hastened by the construction of a new capital city site in Lilongwe about 200 miles to the north of Zomba in the Central Region. This 'new city' project was financed almost exclusively by the apartheid regime in South Africa, who saw political gain from such a venture in an attempt to avoid an increasingly isolated future. As the new city grew, the ministries in Zomba packed their typewriters and filing cabinets and travelled north. Many of the 'permanent and pensionable' expatriates, nearing retirement age after a life-time in the country decided to move on, either to retire or relocate, to jobs in neighbouring countries, often to the then 'white' regimes of Rhodesia (Zimbabwe) or South Africa. Many, reluctantly returned to their home country. Temporary replacements, when necessary were always short-term contracts of around two years and often more associated with technical skills. These newcomers, like myself, were often taking up a first appointment overseas and together with newly appointed local personnel introduced a different atmosphere into the final phase of the colonial experience.

Moving in

The pleasant environment of 'the hostel' was our base for the first two weeks in Malawi, after which we were allocated a ground floor apartment in a block of four. 'Apartment' was a rather inappropriate term for an extremely spacious two bedrooms, separate bathroom and toilet, two living rooms and kitchen, including *khondi* and garage. Attractive tropical gardens surrounded all sides. Each change of occupant appeared to demand a complete interior renovation and our accommodation was no exception. Immediately prior to moving in, a team of decorators from the maintenance section of the Ministry of Works arrived in force to paint the interior. As just about every house interior in the government sector was white, but with obligatory red concrete floors, ours inevitably became likewise.

I was never sure how many workers actually occupied each room at the same time, but with an average of two painters to a wall, progress although slow, proceeded steadily. Huge drums of emulsion occupied all the rooms, all the time. The painters sang, talked, laughed and generally operated as a social unit as they spread themselves throughout the apartment. They arrived each day in the back of a pick-up truck and this small army of painters and cleaners in well-used blue overalls attacked the barrels of emulsion. Attack was not an excessive description, for every room was awash in ladders, scaffolding, planks, paint rollers, brushes and covering cloths. Whenever I arrived to check progress, the sound of *spangee mangee* music (the local popular bar/dance sound) could be heard a good fifty metres away, occasionally challenged by several voices in unison and uncontrolled laughter.

To complete furnishing our new home we visited the government furniture store. The furniture was all made locally in dark hardwood, heavily polished by years of constant use, which gave it a seasoned and slightly rustic appearance. All was constructed to the same utility manufactured style, with traditional dovetailed jointing - and weight to match! The furniture was strong enough to withstand years of heavy use and constant movement to new quarters, yet still retained its dignity. As decorating finished, our selection duly arrived. All the pieces arrived in the back of a pick-up truck, together with a considerable labour force who manhandled everything from the truck to the allotted rooms.

Cockroaches move in too

Whenever you took over a residence there were always smaller occupants who were already there. In the tropics many creatures will invade your living space, coming and going more or less at their convenience. Cockroaches seem to have a permanent residence. Inevitably the all invasive smell of white emulsion and red floor polish does have a mitigating effect on their numbers, together with the clean sweep the place undergoes before the new (human) occupants arrive. But this is purely a stopgap measure. Numbers of cockroaches appear to reach establishment levels within a few weeks - the nearer to the rains and heat the quicker this number is reached. Their arrival is routed through drains, sinks, toilets and the smallest of invisible crevices, all of which provide a route of easy retreat. This creature seems able to survive any onslaught its human neighbour may wage against it with an arsenal of chemical washes, sprays and ingredients with seemingly enough power to strip paint.

After all this warfare it's a fallacy to imagine the battle is won as numbers are generally quickly brought up to the establishment level once again. Cockroaches arrive in many sizes from perhaps five millimetres in length to those that resemble field mice, some forty millimetres long, all with a speed and ability to manoeuvre belying their size. Their shiny dark brown bodies appear as a veritable armour plating with a head sprouting an incredibly long pair of antennae.

Sudden detection does not appear to panic the cockroach; there is a stand off as the human and the army of cockroaches examine each other

I have stayed or temporarily lived in houses and apartments (apartments are generally worse as there are more connections) that appear to be extremely clean, yet switching on a light at night would reveal a small force scattered across the floor. Tapping cupboards before opening the doors could produce a sound like folding newspapers as the shiny army moved in behind pipes and into escape routes.

Sudden detection does not appear to panic the cockroach; there is a stand off as the human and the army of cockroaches examine each other to determine who is the intruder. The only movement is the twitching of antennae - each side now finalising tactics. Perhaps it's a footstep or an unintentional signal from one side, but the scurrying inhabitants move as one, but in all different directions. It's as though outlets had been preplanned to prevent congestion. In seconds they have gone and both human and cockroach have their own territory under control again.

The ritual of becoming an employer

It was inevitable we were to become employers. Even before we moved into our apartment word spread there was a new expatriate in town. Expatriates were greatly sought after by jobseekers as they paid better than the well-off local people, were lenient in their work expectations and their employees were much better treated. From early morning, would-be house servants and garden boys would linger at a discreet distance from our room at the hostel usually clutching an envelope giving various references. The job-seekers came from all over the country to seek work in towns such as Zomba and stayed with either friends or relatives in the 'locations' - low cost housing on the outside of town - while the daily search was carried out. All would be very persistent and wait for hours if necessary for either of us to turn up. Competition was fierce and dealing with all who arrived was a time-consuming experience. There were applications from every age group including teenagers to quite elderly men. And the vast majority were men. Women would usually only appear if young children were in the family and a nanny was needed. The letters accompanying each application not only contained references from previous employers, but usually a lengthy preamble from the applicant himself detailing his employment history and why it was a necessity to be selected for this job.

The employer was expected to provide accommodation free of charge and consequently all houses for those in more senior posts had servants' quarters. Work clothes also were expected to be provided plus a weekly food allowance or *porcha*. It was therefore possible for servants to save the greater part of their salaries. Having servants was not considered to be a sign of affluence or social hierarchy, rather not having one, was considered odd and in the pre-service literature was advised against.

Servants as employers

Virtually everyone in work employed someone on occasions, irrespective of their position or how much they were paid. Even servants often employed one or more people back in their village, to tend crops or look after cattle. One person then, even at the bottom of the salary scale could provide casual work for several others. There were no social benefits of any kind, let alone pension or insurance – only employees of large companies or the government had this luxury. Any benefits were at the discretion of the employer. But anyone fortunate enough to secure a paying job instantly became not only self-supporting, but also a benefactor in the form of a possible casual employer and certainly a family supporter to a host of relatives.

It was not surprising the effort that was made in job seeking. Those in work would be expected to support other members of their family with hospital fees and school expenses and goodness knows whatever debts they had accumulated. It was the natural order of the extended family as it had been for generations past. Any working family member was expected to assist those in trouble, usually with a financial problem. Even if this meant sacrificing his or her own wellbeing, it had to be done, it was the custom.

Money and work

The use to which money was put was as diverse as the salary structure from which it was paid. It was quite common within one factory or office for the full-time salary of the highest paid to be forty times that of the lowest. Apart from the expected family commitments the next priority for many was to own a status symbol of some kind. For most, status combined with practicality emerged in the form of acquiring one's own transport. The really well-paid required a car, the ultimate status symbol. Even if the vehicle had actually expired some years ago but was now held together only by the resurrecting ingenuity of the local garage, it was still a *car*. Motorcycles were the most affordable form of transport for the better-paid skilled workers, but bicycles were the best that could be afforded for the average factory worker or office clerk.

Appearance in the form of a suit was also a desirable social asset - following the president's example who always appeared impeccably dressed. But whatever the wage was spent on, money was to many people a novelty. For many they were the first member of the family to have ever had a regular income and they quite possibly came from a village environment where few others had either. For many ordinary village people money was not used as something to be saved for a long-term purpose, rather it was something, it was hoped, which would last until the next payday.

The abundance of cheap labour revealed itself in every sector of employment activity, especially within government service. This availability of labour and its cheapness made its impression on almost every aspect of life. The low wages were not a reflection on corrupt employment práctice. With so many unemployed, it was simply economically viable to spread the budget by employing more people to do the work even if their productivity was absurdly low, rather than use fewer but higher paid staff using specialised machinery. This was especially important as most machinery would generally be imported and require expensive maintenance, including specialised personnel.

Of course the argument could be applied that the same cheap labour with higher productivity would bring more people into employment with a beneficial effect on the economy. But this was Africa and things were never quite that simple. Malawi was not an industrial economy where a low wage or no job is a social and financial disaster. In western society one's work places a status on who you are. In Malawi this did not apply or at least only to the elite who were a tiny part of the work force. Paid work was still a rarity. Anyone who had a job was considered fortunate, whatever that job may be. It was an attractive alternative to which many aspired but few achieved. For the vast majority subsistence farming and a rural life often distant from the attraction of towns was the reality. This was not something to fall back on in case a job never materialised, but the established life style for all born in the vast countryside. It was an honourable existence and one, which provided a livelihood to the majority of the population as it had for centuries past.

The servant's pecking order

Our first employee was a 'houseboy' or cook to work inside the house doing cleaning, washing, and often preparing all or some of the meals. In fact, over a period of weeks we employed at least two on a trial basis. For various reasons they did not last, whether it was not arriving for work or problems with drink. With employment opportunities relatively rare, it was extraordinary how landing of a job could be regarded so frivolously. Finally James arrived. He was a small, older man with a slightly wonky eye and a serious expression. He was a devout Muslim and no doubt it was his strict religious principles that resulted in his abstinence of drink and scrupulous honesty.

Humphrey, (left) garden boy and James, houseboy

He wore his Muslim head cap at all times and spent an hour every night in his quarters reciting the Koran. His melodious chant drifted on to the night air and mingled with the thousands of crickets chirping in the surrounding trees. Although he spoke reasonable English, he could not write it. His entire note taking for shopping lists and the like were written in Arabic, the language he had learnt in the Muslim school he had attended.

It was the custom to employ someone to work outside and so a 'garden boy' was employed to look after our flowerbeds and small vegetable plots. Again, after several trials we employed Humphrey, a likeable young man who had once worked in my department. The houseboy or cook was paid more and was socially higher than the garden boy, to whom he would often give instructions regarding the choice of vegetables for the next meal.

The shades of status between the ranks in the servant hierarchy were jealously guarded and arguments would break out if one servant encroached on the other's turf. The position of cook was the highest in the pecking order and was usually employed only by larger households. His wage was considerably above all the other ranks. His skills in preparing 'European' dishes definitely set him on a level above all the other servants. He could indeed be a revered asset to a family, being in many cases able to organise and oversee everything from ordinary meals to dinner parties. He would not condescend to do any of the household cleaning tasks and held himself aloof from any of the other employees. Most small families however employed the combination cook/houseboy, who would probably just assist in food preparation; his main occupation was with cleaning and washing.

The lowest rank was the gardener. Larger households would often employ a *dhobi* to take charge of the extra washing and ironing. All these rigidly structured servant positions were a hangover from the days when a virtual army of servants ran the employer's household. The garden boy, for example, was not normally allowed in the house, but on occasions when the houseboy was absent, he would be allowed in and instructed in house procedures. These occasions were enthusiastically seized upon as it allowed new skills and experience to be gained and thus a step up the employment ladder to the status of a houseboy.

It was Kathy's job as the *dona* or mistress to instruct the 'boys' as they were known on what to do each day. Calling the servants 'boys' would no doubt be regarded as derogatory in today's politically correct climate, but then it was quite acceptable and was used almost exclusively in place of reference to 'servants', even amongst themselves. A pattern of work soon emerged, which 'the boys' accepted. It was never wise to change the pattern too often or introduce complexities, for although servants were generally adaptable and conscientious, a well-oiled routine meant both master and servants knew what was expected and to what standard.

Many of the older, 'permanent' expatriate staff who may well have spent the majority of their career in the country, employed three or four servants, who often took charge of running the entire household. Early photographs often show the European household surrounded by what appears to be a team of servants sufficient to run a small hotel. Such was the opulent home life up to perhaps only ten years earlier in the period leading up to independence in 1964, when a large household often employed six or seven servants. There would be a 'headboy' employed as a sort of butler, with his own distinctive uniform, who was in charge of all the servants. This must have been leisurely living indeed and reflected a Victorian heritage that was in decline as the twentieth century progressed. It had set the pattern that even in the 1970s was still more or less in place. This style of living slowly became dismantled as the established staff retired and newer recruits on short contracts arrived. For them a lifetime career in the colonial service or as a civil servant in the new territories was fast becoming part of history. This was not to say that the style of life was still anything less than leisurely and for those able to make the adjustment it presented a quality and prestige few had experienced in their home country.

**From our bungalow on Zomba Plateau,
looking south towards the Shire Highlands**

CHAPTER 5

A town in the sun

T HE ADMINISTRATIVE capital of Malawi was Zomba and the government ministries were the major employer. The town became host to both individuals and families from all over the country, attracted by the chance of a secure job and the security offered by government sector employment. It was a melting pot of all ages and ethnic tribal groups thrown together by a demand for that rare combination of a secure job and a pension at the end of it. Those who were indigenous to the area lived in their villages around the outside of town. For those from outside the area living was restricted to either cheap rented rooms on the edge of town or, if they were fortunate in getting a job in one of the ministry's, in basic government quarters, in the 'locations' as they were known.

A place to live - the 'locations'

Rented accommodation could be anything from traditional village houses built with mud blocks and grass roofs to small brick rooms with corrugated sheeting. The cheap government owned houses were painted white, all of identical size and arranged in symmetrical rows that followed the curve of the road as it weaved through the confusion of the locations. They were so prominent they could easily be identified a few miles distant from the plateau slopes. It was as if so many white blobs had been deposited by a giant's paintbrush. Their precision contrasted with just about everything else within the locations. The bars, shacks, shops, sellers' stalls and all manner of local businesses, had sprouted as if determined by the organic growth of nature itself. It blended well with the lives of so many of its inhabitants.

Living in the locations had all the problems of town life. It was overcrowded, prone to theft, attracted prostitutes, petty criminals and unscrupulous get rich quick dealers. There were grades of accommodation, but for the lowest, facilities were basic, with a communal water supply - sometimes one tap for up to 40 people - shared toilets and often no electricity. Kerosene provided fuel for both lights and cooking, with meals prepared on simple one-burner stoves or open fires outside the room. The whole family could reside in the one room, which usually meant much of the time was spent outside in a small garden. There was always a local bar nearby, which although controlled by official drinking hours, in effect kept open while there were still paying drinkers.

Leaving the controlled environment of the village many of the new arrivals were easy prey to the drinking dens, drugs, and the slick dealers of the townships. The new attractions and temptations of the town were the downfall of many a newcomer.

To a visitor, the locations represented a confusion of noise and activity. Laughter and conversation emerged from both within the houses, through their open windows, through their doors and from the groups relaxing in their tiny gardens. Children played in the street while taking care of their younger siblings. It was common practice for whole extended families to have descended on their working relative possibly to seek assistance with hospital care or entry to local schools.

These were families without closed doors. It was the closest of communities who lived side by side in little houses, had the same day-to-day lives and shared their communal problems. Something of the village had come to town. The sidewalks around the houses were plain earth, rutted with great channels from the torrential rainstorms. In the dry season the dust mingled with the smoke from numerous cooking fires and lay as a haze over the low clustered roofs.

The people were poor by western standards, but they had a dignity and it could be said were proud of where they lived . . .

The locations, although basic, provided respectable low cost housing for many government employees and were a step up from the notorious, lawless shantytowns common to so many developing countries. Just about all the larger cities in southern Africa have these townships either within or a few miles from the city. Even with their limited facilities, the locations were still an improvement on village life, where even the water supply could be an hour's walk away. These were not slum dwellings. The people were poor by western standards, but they had a dignity and it could be said were proud of where they lived and the position that they had attained. Every morning it would be a common sight to see the employees leaving their one-roomed home in a perfectly ironed shirt and tie. They emerged from their modest houses amidst the cooking fires and swirling wind evoked dust, through the rain gouged channels to the tar road and the two mile walk to work.

Whoever was left behind for the day would keep the place clean by incessant sweeping of the area around the house. This was a uniquely African tradition, enacted with a time-honoured bamboo or cane brush about sixty centimetres long. As it almost never had a handle, it required the user to bend almost double, but its stiff spines would seemingly shift anything except small boulders from its path. Incessant sweeping certainly must have contributed to the dust clouds of the dry season and the almost total lack of grass around these houses.

In the locations there was no vandalism and as far as I saw or heard, the only 'extravagant' behaviour was loud exchanges on the way home from the bars. There was some sort of self-policing and persistent troublemakers would face the wrath of their neighbours. In any case, obtaining rented rooms, especially the government owned ones, was a prize worth hanging on to.

Very often small maize plots had been established on the tiny enclosures attached to the houses, sometimes as little as a dozen plants. Some gesture perhaps to the village identity many had left behind. Very few white expatriates visited these areas and when they did, were a source of curiosity. As I worked with many of the younger local people I did get invited to their homes on several occasions and would always find the same curiosity, with an overwhelming number of smiling faces and a welcome that was genuine. After all, I was a visitor and tradition demands that visitors should be respected.

My job

It was a five-minute drive to the Government Printing and Stationery department from our now occupied apartment. It was a narrow and windy plateau road with barely room for meeting on-coming traffic, but it gave panoramic views of the plains below. To the east the shimmering blue of Lake Chilwa merged into the skyline. To the south-east, some sixty miles distant, the massive shape of Mlange, the highest mountain in south-east Africa, thrust into the sky, coloured by faint hues of mauve as it emerged above the early morning mists of the valley floor. With an almost absence of traffic and such beautiful scenery, this must have set a precedence to what could hardly be described as commuting.

The department employed around 200 who came from all over the country. As this was a government department with security of employment and a pension upon retirement, there was considerable competition to get in. One of my responsibilities was for trainee recruitment. There would frequently be 100-200 applications for each advertised vacancy that I had to whittle down to four or five for interview. It was quite probable an almost identical application was sent to just about every other government vacancy the applicant was qualified for. The government was a good employer. It was not likely to go bust or close down and once in, steady pay and good conditions were guaranteed.

There was a familiar pattern to many of the applications. After detailing a list of qualifications, there followed an additional enthusiastic commentary about what the job would mean to their life plans. It probably was also true. To qualify for consideration applicants must have obtained the minimum requirement of Junior Certificate - two years of secondary school, which applied perhaps to only 25% of the school-age population. The lucky ones would be invited to attend a public service interview board of which I was a member. This was a deadly serious occasion, which meant so much to the interviewees and their families.

Zomba Government Press – my trainees

I was responsible for constructing and delivering a training plan, which would serve the needs of the department. It was left to me to decide what went in, what didn't, how it was delivered, setting the questions to tests and marking the papers. There was no examining body to oversee how it was administered or conducted. To have all these roles under the control of one person could well result in an abuse of authority, but this was not unusual in Africa. The main criteria was that as long as the necessary results were achieved it provided the opportunity and responsibility, to put one's own ideas into practice. This freedom was common throughout most government and many commercial posts and presented opportunities and experience not to be found in the equivalent home post. It was the reason many gave for liking what they did. They were very much in control. They often had, as individuals, an entrenched power over large ministries and (relatively) large budgets.

The final say over decisions would increasingly be taken by the newly appointed Malawian head, but for much of the day-to-day decision-making, power was still held by the personnel employed in the colonial system. But for many of the members of this long established system, things were about to change. And for those higher up the government managerial command, the quicker the pace of change would become. These were the seats of power the new government was eager to take over.

For long-term personnel who had for years held considerable power and responsibility, returning home would undoubtedly lead to a loss of this responsibility and influence. Added to this was the realisation that the experience of presiding over large areas of territory populated by scattered villages or even being manager of a large organization did not necessarily mean much to a western company. It was a move many long-term expatriates did not want. Many had in fact become 'Africanised'. It was Africa that had become their adopted country. Many would complete their working lives here and opt for retirement in their home country - usually England. Perhaps a final resting place on the south coast in a bungalow with a name to remember their old territory by on a plaque attached to the porch. For others their experience was brought further south to the then Rhodesia or South Africa, which at the time had a viable white immigration policy.

Ministries in the countryside

My department was sited on the road leading to the plateau. It was one of the last office buildings before the road narrowed and started its steep and winding journey through the mixture of pine forest and tropical woodland, which lead to the summit. There was a commanding view of the town with the misty mauve mountains on the far horizon. Across the road was the Parliament Building, where MPs gathered, debated and generally followed the dictates of their president for around two weeks about four times a year. This building was constructed to house the new incoming government. Its outline was clean and simple and it contrasted abruptly with the government offices, which were sited immediately behind, but dated from the earliest colonial times. Zomba was a ministry town. Here were the administrations of finance, legal affairs, justice, and agriculture, together with housing and local government. Their total area occupied no more than a large town hall in England, yet here resided most of the senior administrators of the country. The ministries were by far the major employers apart from the university, newly located on a campus a few miles from the town centre.

The ministerial buildings were constructed around a rectangle, mostly single storey, with long green painted galvanised iron roofs, which extended over a wide walkway. All the walls were of castle-like construction, often 70 cm thick and painted mat white, their rough brick construction was smoothed by repeated applications of emulsion applied over many decades. Their concrete floors were all gleaming with similar applications of red polish. The windows were just above desk-top height and resembled those from an English country cottage, with small squares of glass. Each window could be opened with a brass handle to let the breeze in. The whole structure had a frontier feel to it, built of massive proportions with simple materials. Built to last like castles, there was an air of solidarity about it all, a permanence that the regime would be as indestructible as these buildings. As with all things made in this era it would remain as a monument to its builders. In the centre of the rectangle, bloom laden frangipani trees added a tropical garden feel to the country cottage.

The contrast of old and new was everywhere. The nineteenth century structure and atmosphere of the ministerial buildings now housed the new government putting its own stamp of approval on the country. The office-suited Malawian ministers and staff moved alongside colonial expatriates kitted out in traditional open-necked shirts, shorts and knee-high socks. It was a powerhouse of ministries and their secretariat staff who held (with the express say-so of the president) ultimate power, residing in offices with country cottage doorknobs. Offices that were some of the oldest in the country and more suited to a tourist itinerary.

Whenever I crossed the road into this authority, the contrast of the new Africa was always startling. Walkers with plastic sandals and patch-laden shirts would push their bicycles laden with market produce up the incline towards their settlements on the plateau slopes. They would be passed by women with headloads of firewood coming at a slow trot down the hill towards the distant locations. As the ministers in their chauffeur driven black Mercedes pulled into the road they would give way to the firewood vendors. Each inhabited a world so remote from the other, they could have been on different planets. Yet here they passed each other, so close, yet so distant. It was now black faces inside the shiny new cars.

The messengers not only conveyed a trail of every type of both verbal and written message, but also acted as postmen, sandwich buyers and back-up to the telephone

All the floors were of concrete, both in offices and in houses. This was to counteract the armies of termite ants, which would consume anything wooden. Not even wooden windows one or two metres above ground were immune, for trails of these incessantly moving tiny creatures were often seen winding up through cracks in the floor. The myriad of tunnels eaten out from the centre may not even be noticed until the whole structure suddenly disintegrated. Food dropped on the floor would be located, surrounded, divided and carried off before the diner's tea was served. It was an efficient, natural cleansing operation ideally suited to the climate.

There were ministerial offices in other areas of the town, all within reasonable walking distance from the parliamentary complex and all were built to the same general pattern and retained that distinctive early colonial rustic atmosphere. To aid communication between the offices, the civil service employed armies of messengers. Despite their low pay and low status on the establishment hierarchy, they were a communication lifeline and without their existence many functions would cease to operate.

Of all things inherited from the British, the obsession with paper documents had infiltrated throughout the civil service establishment. The recording of all manner of minutia together with umpteen quadruplicate receipt books for the most minor of items was only matched by the legions of filing cases to keep it all in. The messengers not only conveyed a trail of every type of both verbal and written message, but also acted as postmen, sandwich buyers and back-up to the telephone. In hot weather soft drinks distributor was added to their duties. In the local market they could often be seen buying household food for their bosses. Messengers were instantly recognisable by their uniform. A heavy-weight calico of a dull fawn shade; short trousers with a long sleeved jacket studded with brass buttons and knee length socks disappearing into heavy black army boots. They sat on chairs or benches outside their superior's office door and it was quite common for them to be summoned by hand bell to receive their directions. They represented what was a perfect example of a plentiful supply of labour at a price that guaranteed much needed employment.

Original government buildings, close to State House

The line-up of messengers was a daily routine outside the office of my immediate boss, the Press Superintendent. He was an expatriate of years spent in similar posts throughout the old empire and used to deploying messengers on journeys not only throughout the department, but to ministerial destinations far and wide. It was a common occurrence to hear the continual clanging of the summoning bell, but with no messenger available to answer. At this point the bell would be dispatched across the adjacent clerical office with much swearing about the uselessness of the messenger staff, but to laughter from the twenty or so typists. I never did discover whether messengers actually hid to precipitate this comedy act, but if they did, it would have been a delightful display of humour, bringing a spark of life to a dull job.

There was a sleepy atmosphere in this government town of corrugated metal roofs. An unhurried movement of walkers and bicycles were a constant reminder of the importance of muscle power over the powered vehicle. They plied the narrow winding roads between shops, offices and home. And between them all, tall almost startlingly white limbs of the bluegum trees waved in the breeze dwarfing the giant elephant grass. This almost incandescent green seemed an impossible contrast to the red ochre soil, which darkened its shade as the rain penetrated. Even the white of the constantly re-painted buildings could not escape re-colouring, as the rain splattered the soil around their walls. There was no litter, except for the shredding of sugar cane stems, eaten by the carriers with teeth as strong as masonry chisels. There were very few government offices above a single floor height and on the streets there were no billboards proclaiming the merits of buying the latest product. Consumerism had not arrived. Here was the power centre of the country, hidden between bluegum trees and elephant grass.

CHAPTER 6

Different lifestyles

WITHIN THE local population, a vast gulf existed between the messengers and department heads. This was only surpassed by comparison to that of the expatriate community. In the late sixties and early seventies many of the intermediate ministerial posts in government and practically all managerial posts in the larger companies, were staffed by expatriates, usually British because of the colonial connection. Many had spent the greater part of their working lives here with memories of days in the 1930s, when a horse-drawn stagecoach would ply the 200 kilometres between Zomba and Lilongwe. With reminiscences of the westerns, a shotgun rider guarding against attacks by lions was used on the remoter parts of the journey.

Considering this was a mere forty years earlier, there had been enormous changes within the country. It is worth remembering it was only one hundred years previously that Dr. Livingstone had trekked through this interior - the first white man to chart the area. The first two decades of the 20th century had seen the first roads, railways and lake steamers. There was a special sense of history in personally talking to elderly administrators who had commenced careers just years after such basic infrastructure had been introduced.

Many of the expatriate government staff were on 'permanent and pensionable' conditions - a term applied to all civil servants seconded by the British government on virtual permanent loan to administer the far flung regions of the empire. These staff had considerable experience of colonial administration and had seen the country emerge from a colony through to its independence. They may have had personal responsibility over territory a quarter of the size of England and even had a working knowledge of the local language. Without their dedication territories such as Malawi would never have seen the change-over to independence proceed in such a smooth and peaceful transition as it did in 1964.

The early days

In these early days, expeditions into the bush to administer the far flung regions of the territory were commonplace and were often quite lengthy affairs, as travel on the precarious roads was exhausting and protracted.

The amount of kit provided was so extensive that an army of porters would be necessary whenever journeys going 'up-country' or into 'the interior' were necessary. It was not only the elaborate tents, but included on the itinerary was an impressive array of table refinements including starched tablecloths, silver cutlery and a collection of decoration more fitting to the Victorian dining room. It was standard routine on these expeditions for the ritual of dressing up for dinner to be commonplace and fine table laying was often used as an established mode of behaviour against the harshness of the environment. It was seen as a preserve of civilised society. The expression of 'going bush' was applied to those who succumbed to the isolation of their surroundings by a drop in standards of anything from dress to personal habits and a disintegration of so-called 'civilised' living. Once again, the pre-service literature had references and accounts of how the environment could manipulate an individual's personality.

It must have been a bizarre sight indeed to see a solitary figure in evening dress at such a table illuminated by lantern glow, with a backdrop of arcadia trees amidst clouds of night-time insects.

It was quite probable these early surveyors never questioned the reasons for their behaviour; it was the nature of the society that had dedicated them to this style of life. But such was the climate of the times, where appearance and respectability were essential for the protection of standards, even in glorious isolation. These customs were already part of history during my stay and I was never to see such refined table manners in the wild. This was indeed a harsh environment and could change an individual's outlook and for many their adopted life began to be accepted as 'home'.

CHAPTER 7

The expatriates

THERE WERE no more than a few hundred expatriates within Zomba township. Their life style had many of the associations common to the colonial era, yet for an increasing majority their expected stay could be no more than three or four years. They were assigned large houses often located on the lower slopes of Zomba Plateau with lush gardens breaking into stunning views of the surrounding countryside. With basic household duties taken care of by their servants and maintenance by the housing department, there was time to spare, but with few opportunities to spend it outside of sport and socialising.

Back at the office even in the 1970s, the long-term expatriate would have had working clothes, which were the closest one would ever see to that of the early settlers, but without the ubiquitous sun hat. Short sleeved open-necked white cotton shirts; shorts with knee length socks and black shoes completed the standard attire for the office. Often given the name of 'safari suit', it was never regarded as casual, but suitable for the climate and took the equivalent place of the traditional western office suit. By contrast, their Malawian colleagues would be dressed in the smartest western style suit they could afford.

It was possible, probably inevitable, to know almost everyone both within the town and its greater environment. Apart from sporting activities there was a distinct absence of things to do. Things to do had to be invented, which is essentially what happened.

In western society, many people's lives are broken up by the endless necessities of life, which despite the washing machine era, take up an intolerable amount of time. Simply organizing a daily routine of running the house, preparing meals and the other numerous and mundane everyday tasks seem to most, an endless campaign. But here, with servants and housing maintained for you, an enormous amount of free time is opened up. It was a new life, freed from the boring necessities of fixing-up the kid's room or trimming the lawn, but for some there was a problem of what to do with this new found freedom.

A new life in a new country

This was a small community in relative isolation and it was not a place where you could hide away. Just by being white made you stand out. But it was the unique combination of circumstances that made possible the social life of this community. Indeed, the pre-service books had warned about this, but it was quite different reading about it and then living it. But like the dream of a desert island, the reality can be something less than the anticipated paradise.

This was an age before satellite communication, electronic mail and mobile phones, with many houses not connected to landlines. Apart from the government sponsored radio only a few short-wave broadcasts of mainly news material could be received. Listening to the 'Voice of America' or the 'BBC World Service' were one of the few authoritative means of knowing what was going on elsewhere in the world. Imported newspapers, flown in, did help, but they could be up to a week old and censored for critical comments of the government. It made the sense of isolation more apparent.

Expatriate life – mingling with Malawians was commonplace

In Zomba a twice-weekly film was shown at the Gymkhana Club with premier league soccer films several weeks old, highlighting the weekends. Theatre was essentially home grown. A very occasional professional music quartet did make its appearance.

Outside of work, taking up a new hobby could be difficult. The social round was fine, but for those who wanted more, the options were limited. One generally had to be a self-starter and determined. Correspondence courses were one outlet that thrived. Perhaps it was a paradox, living in a newly emerging African country and obtaining a qualification in ancient European history by correspondence from London. It was even possible to take the examination, organised through a local school.

However, a philanthropic outlet was always possible. Wives with professional skills, who accompanied their husbands, could put their experience to work in many useful activities. Joining the Red Cross for charity work was only one such option; organizing immunization programmes; 'under-fives' clinics in the villages were staffed; teaching Malawian women essential baby care. Their contribution was often as valuable as the contract worker they accompanied. Kathy put her nursing skills to use in one of the 'under-fives' clinics that toured the local villages.

The new arrivals

A new arrival would be unlikely to know anyone within the expatriate community. With the constant changing of their population as contracts ended and new ones began, it produced something of a transient way of life. Most had to make some effort to fit in. The communal places where expatriates were able to meet were few and at first you would be unlikely to know whom you were sitting next to at the bar. It was little different to an English village with a solitary pub as the centre of life. Except here, in this isolated community, just about everyone was working at some sort of professional level, or at least they were in the country to do a job which required some form of expertise.

In a way, this 'being here for a legitimate purpose' applied to just about everyone, and anyway general gossip soon got around about who you were. In Zomba, this meant in the vast majority of cases, that you either worked for some part of the government, the newly established university, or as manager on one of the surrounding farms. There was no need for questions about where you came from, it was possibly more important to know what drink you preferred.

Expatriate wives were an especially endangered group. They appeared to either love the life or loathe it. Few in number and often left to their own initiatives, they formed their own small groups. The day could be a relaxed affair. After instructing the servants, priorities were divided between shopping and which coffee morning to attend. These were excellent opportunities for local gossip: who was doing what, especially scandals and emotional liaisons, new arrivals and what they were like, even the latest government policies. Without this grapevine of essential information, much about what was going on would have been lost.

Afternoons could be for sport, card games or lying around the pool. By five in the afternoon, invites to tea took precedence, with more socializing and possible arrangements for the next party. Taken together with their philanthropic activities, most wives considered themselves busy and wondered how they fitted it all in.

The new expatriates were like 'freshers' at university, they were all in the same boat and soon got to know the old hands. Under these conditions things became relaxed, people had to get to know one another. They relied on other expatriates for support and to know what was going on in the country. Perhaps the climate helped. All warmer countries seem to invoke an atmosphere of greater relaxation, it breaks down barriers and things often seem better in an outdoor life where the sun shines.

Zomba was like a desert island and for many desk-bound expatriates it represented the boundary of their existence. It can seem ironic that for many the opportunity, perhaps their only one, to explore the surrounding countryside was never considered important enough to do. Nothing much existed in the hinterland 'out there' and, unless ordered to, they did not venture far out.

A new culture

The change in their way of life was for many expatriates something of a culture shock. The literature and the courses available before departure did help to inform and prepare. But the gap between information and reality can be huge.

The obligation for (especially new) expatriates to conform to a life style expected of them in their new country had been explained in the pre-service documents. The government was explicit in the public appearance of all expatriates, spelling out what was expected in standards of dress, appearance and behaviour. This went as far as having legal statutes, which applied rigidly to expatriates. Rules regarding the length of ladies dresses, together with the length of men's hair were physically stipulated, with exact descriptions ensuring there was no room for error.

This was part of the president's campaign to stop the corrupting influences associated with 'exotic' western dress, which really meant any association towards the outward appearance of 'anti-establishment' values on the part of the wearer. Government surveillance ensured these standards were kept (more on this later). But whatever the expatriate community got up to amongst themselves was really their own business - provided it did not affect Malawians or was made public. This dual life seemed to keep both communities happy.

Because this was such a small country, and the expatriate community so relatively insignificant in number, the closeness of the government machine was always apparent. The president's entourage was a familiar sight as it sped to and fro from State House.

Amongst expatriates, the rules regarding public dress and behaviour caused only minor irritation. Any trauma suffered was from being incapable of adjusting to a new environment. Many newcomers were experiencing this life for the first-time, not like the seasoned life-timers who knew little else. Whatever the circumstances were, the effect of this exotic new country changed the outlook of the newcomers. Perhaps it was because of the isolation, or the freedom emulating from the mystical influence of the African effect, producing a changed attitude by exerting its own kind of confusion and magic.

For rules that were made so explicit for public observance, in private the expatriate was as free as practically anywhere on earth to do as he or she pleased. To fill off-duty hours, drinking and parties became a natural order and something of a way of life. For some the separation from family and familiar places, perhaps with children lodged in a foreign boarding school and surrounded by a different culture with different aspirations and customs, all had some effect.

For some this period of their lives was a wonderful opportunity to escape. For a few it destroyed their marriage and home life. The country became a scapegoat for all their inadequacies. There were still others for whom the change was permanent and changed forever their way of life. Returning to that previous 'normal' life was no longer possible. Many did stay on or went to Rhodesia where jobs for whites were available. Some returned 'home' and adjusted once more to the weather and the way of life. For others, the effect of the tropics was permanent, and after sampling a western style of life, they returned to Africa and once again fitted back into a society with which they had more in common.

Fun in the sunshine

It was against this background that the community lived. There was for many a unique opportunity for individuals of various backgrounds to mix and socialise. It did not seem to matter whether you were a doctor or farm manager, as long as you could enjoy a drink, tell a joke and even better, play a sport of some kind. It appeared to be a relief for many to be away from the social constraints of their home country. For those who came without their wives, it was even more so. It was often seen as a time to make the best use of what a lax social life could offer.

For those who came without their wives, relationships were often formed with the local African girls

There was an added mixture of fun and spice to the local social scene with the continual changing of the so-called 'sunshine girls'. These aptly named young European women were secretaries sent out, usually on similar contract terms, to look after the paperwork of the new ministers of government. Surrounded by people unknown to them only a few months earlier, with amply quantities of time and booze, this desert island was for some a joyous place of sex and good living. They wanted to live-it-up for as long as it lasted and the consequences, if they were to be any, could disappear into the sunset.

Many expatriates did become alcoholics. There were many marriages that came under strain, partly from the lack of any family support and partly from wives not being able to adjust to the new way of life and returning home. New relationships were easily formed in the easy-going lifestyle that was a major attraction of the community. The relationships were not just with other members of the expatriate set, but were formed with the local African girls as well. Although there was a gulf between the expatriates and the Malawians, there was a limited amount of socialising extending across the sexes.

It was almost always white men and black girls. But it was rare to see black girls being entertained or partying with white men at the expatriate clubs. This was just a step too far. Their affairs were kept behind closed doors or at the local bars further out of town. It was surprising how many of the local girls formed a steady relationship with expatriates. Only a few white women took up with black men, perhaps because white women were a relatively rare species in the expatriate world. There were several white women married to Malawians. In most cases however, they had met while their husband was studying overseas and had come back to live in Malawi. Almost always it was a return to a high-ranking job or political position.

Down to dinner

There was a formal social side and this took the form of dinner parties that were a regular feature of the expatriate calendar, but would often include Malawian friends, or those who had ascended the social ladder. The style of the evening's entertainment varied enormously, according to the host's position in the community. Some were indeed very formal affairs.

I well remember one such formal affair Kathy and I attended, given by a British army captain, a medical doctor to the small British army training unit. About ten expatriates were invited, all seated around a long table, which was prepared with all the splendour expected of a five-star hotel reception. The host was dressed in his official military splendour and some of the guests were dressed in formal black tie dinner suits and as far as I can remember, complete with campaign medals. Ladies, naturally, were dressed in evening gowns.

They may well have been upstaged by the five servants who stood silently and equally spaced around the room at a discreet distance behind each pair of guests. They were all dressed in white tunics, fastened with brass military-style buttons, dark trousers with stripes and a coloured waist-band held with a brass shackle. Headgear was a fez cap with tassels, a style worn by traditional Indian traders in the early colonial years.

The scene could have been lifted from a set of a Somerset Maughan novel. The waiters moved silently and efficiently around the candle-lit table, noticing without being asked, to fill a glass, bring on a next course, or to pounce on any breadcrumb that was neglected. I was experiencing just a glimpse of something that was increasingly out of place in the twentieth century, apart from perhaps a diplomatic banquet set up to impress a visiting dignitary. This was not a special occasion intended to leave a lasting impression, as might be expected for a farewell banquet. It was just a formal dinner party, and possibly one not so very much different from other formal occasions. There was some part of it that brought to mind the extravagance of bush expeditions thirty years before, with their silver cutlery and starched tablecloths.

Looking out of the window into the moon illuminated distance, all that could be seen was the plateau jungle with thatched mud dwellings barely a mile away. It all seemed so unreal, yet looking back into that room here was a reflection of a scene from the empire. I do not think anyone there that night thought anything special was taking place. And nothing was, except it could have been one of the last times a spectacle belonging to a period in the 1930s was displayed with such seriousness.

Expatriate clubs

A centre for social occasions amongst all expatriate staff were the clubs, which provided a focus for entertainment outside the house and where one was certain to find someone – another expatriate - to talk to at almost any hour of the day or late into the night. Wherever the British held colonial power, a club to serve their needs was always present, irrespective of the remoteness of the location.

They still exist today and many are still present throughout the old empire or where there was a former British presence. In India these centres of recreational power have today been taken over by the Indian elite and have retained their exclusiveness and customs almost intact. At the Bombay Gymkhana or the Wellington Club, the staff still dress in the British authorised style. They still serve sweet tea in the finest bone china and the best (so I am told) buttered toast to be found anywhere.

In the early years of the twentieth century soon after the first expatriate clubs' were formed in Malawi, they were essentially segregated places, with restricted entry to any of the local population. This changed over the years with fees high enough to keep undesirable elements out - the local population in lower grade posts. But after independence, as more of the indigenous population came into positions of influence, they became members in increasing numbers. It was, for the upwardly mobile local population a certain sign of status and an acquisition of that much sought after elitism. This coincided with the decline of the expatriate community.

The clubs main activities were essentially sports, but were a focus for any entertainment, either homemade or by visiting touring groups. All boasted grand looking sports boards with their year captains' names often dating back to the early years of the 1900s. A look at these names illustrated the changing membership over the years. Up to 1960 there was an almost exclusive European dominance, which increasingly gave way to names like Banda and Chinsulu. Asian names also started appearing, as the well-heeled business classes found the club to be less intimidating and a status place to join. They increasingly dominated the cricket boards but with golf remaining almost exclusively a European pass-time.

Two expatriate clubs existed in Zomba. The small and informal 'Turf Club', which originally boasted a horse racing course in its heyday. By the 1970s only bowls remained as an active sport, the facilities being used as a base for the local flying club. Its extensive grounds provided a landing strip for small aircraft. At this time only 100 members remained with equal numbers of expatriate and local people - this mix was exceptional and provided something approaching an atmosphere where expatriates and Malawians freely mixed.

The colonial charm of the Gymkhana Club

The largest and by far the most popular was the 'Gymkhana Club'. With several hundred members, many from out of town, it was the focal point for the expatriate community of Zomba. Its name originated from its earlier days when horse trials and related 'gymkhana' events predominated and officers were reported to have ridden their horses up the steps and on to the *khondi* during special occasions. Now such flamboyant occasions had gone with golf being the major occupation, closely followed by tennis, squash and - bridge.

The grandeur of the Zomba Gymkhana Club

The club reflected the austere glory of its earlier days. Built in 1923 with a splendid 70-metre frontage of massive white painted stonewalls, it stood in impressive grounds with a football field to the front, while across the road an immense 18-hole golf course stretched away into the distance with the rock face of the plateau as a backdrop. The Gymkhana Club was situated only 200 metres from State House, President Banda's official residence, where his guards maintained a twenty-four duty outside its steel-gated entrance.

The club was a single storey building reminiscent of the government buildings further around the slopes of the town. Its black cottage-style window frames held tiny glass panels, which pushed open allowing cool breezes to circulate its large rooms. Inside was a main bar and seating area, leading to a ballroom able to accommodate several hundred guests. An L-shaped bar near the entrance was referred to as the 'golf bar' or 'back bar', while towards the rear was a small, smart dress only exclusive dining-drinking area known as the 'Kudu Room'. The ballroom doubled as a theatre and cinema. Leading off from this centre-point of official entertainment, a huge *khondi* and 'front bar', overlooked the football field.

In the seated, recreational area, a focal point was the huge log fireplace, used perhaps for two months of the year in the cool, dry season. Over the fire was hung a large sepia-tinted print of Queen Victoria, in a heavy oak frame. No-one seemed to know just how long it had been there, or where it came from. But its presence in the heart of Africa reflected the historical connection of the club to its colonial heritage, now so rapidly becoming an element of history. The portrait stared across the room towards another, that of President Banda, a legal necessity in every public place throughout the country. Even on a return visit sixteen years later, with the club almost devoid of European members and showing signs of neglect, the sepia-tinted Victoria was still there, a timeless symbol in a now changing country. By 1992 the Banda portrait would be gone, as he was ousted from power in Malawi's first multi-party elections. As far as I know she is still there now glaring towards a new figure, filling the void on the far side of the room.

There was always much support from members to whatever activity the club was staging. This included stage plays and twice weekly film shows. Theatre was especially well supported, partly because of the total absence of such entertainment anywhere else, and because patrons knew almost everyone in the cast anyway. Besides it was an excuse to dress up to go somewhere and meet friends for a good evening out. Occasional visits from western musical groups occurred, usually in conjunction with the Blantyre Musical Society. Such events were glittery occasions, with dinner suits and evening dress and British Army officers in full regalia, including whatever medals they were entitled to wear.

New arrivals who joined the club were invited to a monthly 'new members' evening. It was an effective way of ensuring loyalty to the club by being introduced to other new arrivals who were also would-be members. Existing members' wives would help any new recruits with settling in problems to new and strange accommodation. They would arrange loans of household goods from ladies' groups and of course with the support from others in the same situation. For most it was the start of a liaison that would continue for the whole of their stay.

Sport and booze - a club routine

Evenings at the Zomba Gymkhana Club were as predictable as the weather. Darkness would fall rapidly and by around 6.30 pm, two hours after offices closed, the African night would be total. There was no more than an hour's variation at any time of the year. This almost equal division between night and day and the brief time between dusk and dark demonstrated the location of Malawi in the southern hemisphere only 16 degrees south of the equator.

Golfers would pay off their caddies and make their way to the golf bar. Caddies were local lads who hung around the teeing off area looking for casual work. Many were hired on a regular basis because of their knowledge of the game and became the nearest thing to a team with some of the club members. With no floodlighting, the tennis players would abandon the courts, pay-off their ball-boys, and all would make their way to the changing rooms and bars.

The bar areas would be crowded for around two hours after which numbers would dwindle as the evening progressed. But if anything the noise increased, at least from the hard-core of regular drinkers who now occupied the 'back bar' and the larger 'front bar'. Although most of the occupants knew each other, both occasional visitors and regulars were fully integrated into the atmosphere of the place. This was something different from most English pub gatherings where numerous small groups would dominate the proceedings.

An evening at the bar

The regular personalities were as varied as their occupations. One such was a pig farmer from an estate twenty miles or so from Zomba. He was a retired army officer and had somehow obtained the position of farm manager on one of the president's personal estates. He was a large fat man with a full red face who always arrived late in the evening. Without doubt, this was the high point of his day, after the isolation of his farm amidst the animal sheds and his work force. Perched on his bar stool, the only comments he made were interjections - usually inaudible - about events from his old campaign days. As the drinks progressed, I never discovered whether he really knew what was being discussed in the general bar conversations going on around him. His driver was another fixture to the scenario. He would wait outside for the late-night journey home.

Not far from him sat another regular, a long-serving expatriate from the Geological Survey office who would come in straight from golf every evening. A squat grey-haired man who would blurt out laconic sentences that would get briefer and more incomprehensible as the hours passed. Having little effect on the general raucous conversation going on around, he frequently dropped off to sleep, his head slumped on the bar top. When he was not perfectly balanced on his stool, he would topple over backwards and crash to the floor. The impact would appear to bring him round and he would stagger back to his seat and resume his former posture. The comedy of this accidental state of affairs approached a farce, because the rest of the company appeared to take little or no notice of the whole performance.

It would be possible to be in the bar and receive several rounds of drinks without really knowing who had ordered their delivery. A wave of the hand was enough instruction to the barman to supply yet another round. Drinks were cheap and plentiful. The costs of a night out were negligible and for many there was little to go home to. For some their family had remained in their home country either because their children were at boarding school, or their wives could not adjust to this far-flung community in such isolation. The bar would stay open until the last person left. Drinking and driving were never viewed with the same antagonism as is the case in all traffic congested western countries. For all the absence of traffic, the number of serious accidents was horrendous. This was partly due to faulty vehicles, but drinking was a serious contributor. Even in the commercial capital Blantyre, traffic jams were practically non-existent. In fact, it was not until the early 1970s that the first traffic lights were installed in the city.

Drinking and driving seemed inseparable; everyone knew the chaos it caused, but it was easier to simply ignore the consequences. It was normal for the remnants of the late night drinkers to head for their cars on what could well be a precarious journey home. The winding narrow roads along the plateau side with no lighting or safety barriers and perilous drops off the edge, had to be negotiated. For some just getting their car onto the road was to prove a hazardous operation. Surrounding much of the Gymkhana Club car park was an enormous storm-water drain, around a metre deep and almost as wide. Going by the club in the morning, it was a common sight to see cars nose-dived into this gully. The local Carlsberg brews had taken their toll and exacted revenge for the extravagances of the previous night.

CHAPTER 8

There is nothing like payday

IT WAS always at the end of the month when one was advised to stay off the roads. For this was payday - something longed for in all countries, but in Malawi it was revered like a monthly May Day holiday, or possibly like the week before Christmas, when so much preparation and organization must be achieved at all costs. It was also something akin to a carnival day; celebrating the return of a lost relative who has had a minor lottery win. It was a day when a part of someone's dream may become reality. Payday was a bit of all of these things. Suddenly, like the predictability of green shoots after the first rains, cars were seen back on the road. Money to fund repairs or simply to fill the tank was available on a window of opportunity, which may only last for a few days. It was a time when loans for the month (or indeed many previous months) had to be settled, a time to meet a younger cousin's school fees, or to buy maize to send across country to one's home village, or simply a chance to have a good time. A time in fact that demanded time. As pay packets were distributed, payday took its toll on the working routine. It could well have been designated a holiday, for all the disruption that it caused. From dawn on payday all government offices in the town would be besieged by a steadily growing crowd of hopefuls for a share of someone's monthly wage.

For the majority of the workers', salaries were paid in cash; only the senior supervisors and managers had bank accounts. The would-be claimants to this monthly handout came from the nearby locations or the employees' home village. They brought the family members who could not be left at home, including babies and children, together with all the provisions for the day. The scene was something reminiscent of the colourful confusion of a local market, with the inevitable produce sellers moving in on the monthly happening. The throng of people arrived by foot or bus and sat in quiet groups on the grass verges, in empty car park spaces, on the low flat walls surrounding the offices, but essentially near to the office exits. Some may have arrived on the overnight bus from Lilongwe, in desperate need of a youngster's school fees. The women who arrived came with their provisions parcelled in carefully balanced headloads, their bodies and necks in vertical symmetry with only an occasional touch of the hand to steady the load. A baby was inevitably present.

Payday was also a social occasion. Many of the employees' family members would congregate at the offices on a regular basis every month; greetings would be exchanged and stories told. As the day wore on and the climax hour of paytime was nigh, more and more visitors swelled the now anxious throng. As the paid employees emerged during the mid-day break, their respective family or friends to whom money was owed or promised, took their opportunity and seized their benefactor before escape was possible.

Amidst this colourful scene there were always a few serious and sombre figures who stood out amongst the crowd. These men were the official debt collectors who were instantly recognisable from their over-large suits and trilby hats. They were the closest possible to an African version of the American mob, but without the menace. They always carried a well-worn two-strap leather briefcase, looking as though it had experienced many campaigns of this nature. I never ascertained whether this was for effect or to collect the money owed. It was the Asian storekeepers in town who resorted to the employment of debt-collectors. They allowed credit to government employees as their job was secure and the chances of recovering their loan high.

As the mission of the debt collectors was of a more serious nature it demanded a single-minded approach and they always appeared to adopt a somewhat aloof relationship to the crowd and other on-lookers. They rarely spoke and waited like vultures until the time their victims would be at their most vulnerable. They were distinguished and patient, on a mission they intended to accomplish with professional integrity. What methods of money extraction they applied was a guarded secret, but they apparently acted alone. Without doubt the combination of their dress and general overall air of sophistication had a high success rate, for they were always present.

For some the prospect of meeting their debtors was too much. Avoidance procedures took on the antics of pop stars attempting to leave the theatre before the avalanche of fans descended. My own department, being host to a very large number of employees with a large graduation of pay scales, attracted some of the bigger crowds. Not only were side exit doors used as escape routes, but the rear perimeter fence proved no obstacle for those agile enough to scale it. This was made of chain-link around two metres high topped with barbed wire. I always saw a few who used this escape route to avoid the consequences of being broke before the next month had actually started. Although these activities comprised the on-going performance every month, it was all accepted as part of this special day.

For those that did make it to town with enough spending money, or for those higher paid salary earners, the social life of the town suddenly came alive. Cars appeared on the roads, owned by those who could not really afford them, but were the ultimate status symbol. The bars emerged from a twilight world of mid-month blues into a frenzied round of merry-making. The payday revellers abandoned any notion of tomorrow and with the support of friends and the always available bargirls, drank the night away.

**Typical township bar –
soon after payday**

Like the clubs, the bars stayed open until the last drinkers swayed out. Homeward journeys were hazardously made by the occasional car, often bicycle, but mostly on foot. It was a common sight at this time of the month to see people staggering in the middle of the road, singly or in groups. This day would claim its share of winners and losers, but for everyone concerned the prospect of another month of moderation until the next payday, would bring a sobering reality.

The money go-round

Despite the anxiousness of many workers to escape to town and enjoy its pleasures, the persistent demands of their family were never far from their minds. The responsibility was either a source of pride in that they were perhaps the sole provider for so many; or they saw their family as a crowd of vultures waiting to descend. But for the majority of employees, although fortunate to have a job, they still had relatively little and were prepared to give this away to those whose needs were greater. His village family saw anyone who worked as being well-off. The culture demanded the needs of today to be satisfied: the future was, like the rains, an unpredictable time, beyond their control, a time out of sight and over the horizon.

But for those able to sport a suit and tie and ride home on a gleaming Suzuki motorcycle, wealth had truly arrived. With his extended family owning nothing more than old cooking pots and a patched up bicycle, why shouldn't their wealthy member attend to their needs? His Suzuki could easily carry three or four of the children to school. And if he was granted a government house in one of the locations, they would have a place to stay during term time. As his position improved, his responsibilities to all others in the family expanded proportionately; he would become a benefactor in their time of need, a lender of the last resort.

The houses loaned to employees were not only places where children were boarded during term times. Location houses truly formed a social function; they became refuges for the needy from the occupants' home village. There would always be in residence a baby (or more) to be cared for whilst the mother was in hospital, or an aging relative and a brother temporarily staying while looking for work. For those seeking this refuge, it was seen as their right, a sharing of the communal wealth of the family - they had relatively nothing and their relative had so much. It was traditional law that this should be shared.

But for those who were fortunate enough to enter even the starting ranks of the wealthy or at least be relatively well-off, attitudes often changed. They had acquired status symbols and on the horizon even more desirable acquisitions were coming within reach. The possibility of a small car and better house furnishings were possible. There was a dilemma now between acquiring these things or paying endless hospital bills and schools' fees. It was not that the upwardly mobile would refuse to help, but that they would often find excuses to reduce their assistance to yet more needy applicants. It was for them a balance between being seen to fulfil their obligations yet still retaining enough of their salary to enjoy themselves and to obtain the good things of life.

The burden of helping less fortunate family members did not rest with just the wealthier members of the extended family network. There was a sort of hierarchy with the wealthiest at the top contributing the most, with those at the bottom of the wage pile, with barely enough to live on, still expected to give assistance and support to their own (usually large) family. It was a tricky business knowing quite how much to give, depending on what it was for (was it really a life or death case?), how convincing their argument was and whether there was any chance of the sum being paid back. Or, if they really did not have the money, and the working relative was sincerely broke, whom to borrow it from. It was truly a money go-round.

For the moderately well-off, the path ahead was often a conscious decision on acquiring the trappings of luxuries now, while they were so much nearer their grasp. They had entered a sort of never-never land, like soccer stars plucked from obscurity, to find themselves with money they had never seen before. But these were ordinary people who had the extraordinary good fortune to have a job. Handling money for many was a skill yet to be acquired.

There were others who did not aspire to live the dream. When they left their office sanctuary for an evening at their government-owned house they sat with everyone else in the garden around the fire-burning cooking pot. They had only temporarily left the village, they had never forgotten or could forget its importance and its effect upon their mentality. When they returned to the village it was as though they had returned to their true home.

The search for a loan

For probably the majority of employees, those whose wage did not last until next payday, the process of getting a loan could be a lengthy and exhausting course of action. There could well exist outstanding debts, which required renegotiating repayment terms. Dodging these creditors with their debt collectors on the loose required quick wits and a fast pair of heels. The business of loans was an essential part of an alternative economy. Loans were often sought from others within the place where the individual worked. Expatriates came high up on the request list, not just because they were paid more, but white expatriates were considered more sympathetic to persuasive arguments. The well-off indigenous employees were notoriously difficult to extract loans from. Those who invariably did give loan money - with no guarantee of being paid back - or were helpful in some manner, were given the affectionate term of 'uncle'. This was a loose term, not associated as in a relative, but referring to someone who could be relied upon in the hour of need.

It was not long before I too became an 'uncle'. During the latter stages of the month, as money disappeared and demands mounted up, requests increased. Even on pay day itself quite genuine desperation surfaced. Joseph Mtonga was such a person. He was a labourer and had debts that exceeded his complete salary for the month. One would wonder why he even bothered to work at all. He appeared to be constantly in debt with what little money he earned, was loaned (given) to a family member who had practically nothing.

But this was the difference, he did earn something, possibly the only member of his family to have a job. Quite possibly he could fund his children to reach Junior Certificate level (the minimum secondary school certificate demanded by most offices and government departments). They would then be on a path to possible employment and a secure future. Even if he was a labourer, when he came home to his village for the holidays he was someone who was to be respected. Children would rush along the path to carry his bags and he would tell them stories of life in the town. With his help, maybe the village would even have a well. The elders would be proud.

There were many like Joseph this month. The rains were late and existing stocks of maize at home were almost exhausted. He would loiter around the door of my office for some minutes, getting courage to present his case, but also to ensure no one else was there and my attention could not be diverted. He would give a polite greeting only, no explanation as to the nature of his visit and present a document letter in a 'both hands' gesture. With a slight bow Joseph would withdraw to a discreet distance while I examined the document. It obviously took some time to put together and was approaching two sides of A4 in length. One could not dismiss its importance and how much depended upon its acceptance.

African villages have a young population

There was a preamble about the problems facing his family with a detailed account of how an even bigger financial crisis was looming. He had to spend money on his parents' house after a wall had collapsed. All had turned to him because of a demand for his younger sister's school fees. There was a reference to his older sister who had to buy some expensive medicine for an elderly relative. She had approached him for some last minute assistance. Then a younger brother was in financial trouble as he was starting school in Lilongwe and needed a bus fare in order to meet the start of the term. The strategy of the letter was directed to ensure whichever demand on his resources I was to question, an even greater urgency further down the document would reveal itself and be impossible to overlook. I was cornered into having to except something; it must be beyond question I would turn down so *many* requests.

The final few lines came with directness that betrayed the previously extensive explanations on how the money would be spent; this revealed the true amount of the loan. In Joseph's rugged style, the letter reflected the pleasantries all so common in traditional greetings, namely, the long preliminaries before one could move on to the business of the day. As with greetings in the market place, there would always be room (and time) for a negotiation agreeable to both parties. This also was part of the procedure. No one settled immediately. We agreed a figure, the cash was handed over and Joseph (with at least one of his relatives) was a happy man.

CHAPTER 9

Bars and the meaning of life

I N SOUTHERN Africa bars exist everywhere, they rival market places in the popularity given to them by the working people in towns and the rural poor in the remote savanna heartland. Outside of the relatively rare international hotels, only found in the capital cities and tourist resorts, the twilight world of the truly African bar begins.

They are found on the side streets of towns often close to the busy market areas, in the 'locations' on the outside of towns and in the vast world of the interior. In the larger towns they boast electric lighting and refrigerated bottled beers. They will be almost indistinguishable from the shops alongside and in their dim interiors maybe some new decorations

can be made out. Their clients will be from the workers in town and quite possibly the premises will be used as a hang-out for the criminal fraternity. The further out you travel from the larger towns, the greater the embrace of the countryside becomes.

Only bars situated close to a large village or roadside stop will have corrugated metal roofs. Maybe these places will even be painted with white emulsion or be decorated. But the African bars belong to the small towns and villages, close to their roots where the rural population is found; close to the cheaper rest houses on roadsides, but all within walking distance of nearby habitation, however remote. Some seem to be in total isolation with no visible indication of life for miles. It is as though a community or factory once used their facilities, but it closed or was re-located and the bar simply carried on.

Built from the soil

In this vast interior the bars blend into the savanna lands of the countryside as if they had an organic growth. Their walls are typically mud blocks, which have been hewn from the earth itself and their roofs made from bales of the same grasses growing nearby and dried to yellow sticks. Their timbers are rarely sawn, but are branches hacked from local trees with the builders' machete. It is as if they are a natural camouflage, a place the same colour and texture as the landscape from which they are built; a place of retreat for all who seek refuge from the outside.

Most of the occupants to be found in these bars are subsistence farmers and local business owners. They earn their living from the same materials that made the bar. There is a particular atmosphere to these places, a confusion of noise, smells of old grass, of wood burning fires and packed mud floors. But above it all there is a particular blend of chaos and relaxation that has a distinctly African nature. There are no clocks or ways of determining the time. There is only daylight or night. And for many even this is an irrelevance. This is a place of escape, yet with its mud walls and grass roof, it resembles the land they are working and a way of life most are destined to follow. A storm could wash away the whole place and it would return to the source from which it had been built. The bar is as natural as the countryside.

Just the essentials

There is usually no electricity, with lighting supplied by paraffin lamps and just possibly a fridge, it too running on paraffin. They are no frills places, but with all essentials necessary to keep the punters happy - cheap drinks, good time girls, and perhaps some impromptu music, but always happy places with flexible opening hours. The clients do not frequent their local for a posh night out; the bar is a seamless progression from their place of work to a place of escape. For the majority their whole lives are located just a walk away through a trail, to a tiny town, a nearby village or a factory with accommodation for its employees.

For the majority there is nowhere else to go and nothing else is expected, except the hope that the rains will arrive on time. It is in the bar that one's status does not count and everyone can have a good time without having to keep up appearances. The dim interiors in no way represent the mood of the patrons. On most occasions, especially near to payday, (at least near to towns) it seems as though almost everyone is in party mood. There is always loud talking and laughter. Whispers suggest seriousness and these are not serious places; talking to your companion is an invitation to talk to all. It is generally impossible to sit with your own thoughts; these are public places, you belong, just for a few hours, to the people there. It is as though all present wish to know one's identity and origin - and always with the possibility that a new round of drinks may appear.

Even though the people have few possessions and little money, it in no way inhibits the spontaneous good humour of the patrons in these places. The people anyway are generally happy, always open and direct and welcoming to strangers. Perhaps this is a reaction to the stark reality of their lives, over which they have little control.

Although there is little the owners do in the way of smartening their premises up, some of the larger bars boast original advertising art work, covering either an entire wall or even the complete side of a boundary wall, if one existed. Without doubt, a local artist executes the paintings. They are usually in full dazzling colour, striking in their contrast to the mud blocks of surrounding walls and rough-hewn wooden doorways. The subject often depicts some kind of hangover medicine being conveyed by river or road towards anxious patients who are smiling with joy at the prospect of being released from the trauma of the previous night's heavy merry-making. They are painted in a truly locally inspired 'naïve' style in a size approaching that of murals. The work brightens up walls in towns, but the arresting colours appear strangely out of place in a countryside burnt into red earth and yellow grass by six months of waterless heat.

A limited range of poison

All southern African countries have a limited range of bottled beers, but these become increasingly hard to find as you travel further from the towns. In Malawi they consist of just two kinds: 'green' the local lager and 'brown' a type of ale. Both are products from the Danish Carlsberg brewery. But a so-called 'international brew' can be found in all these countries, which is why it earned so presumptuous a title. This is a much cheaper and more popular alternative, supplied in cartons similar to western supermarket milk containers. This is known as 'shake-shake' and can be found practically everywhere, except in the smarter and expensive city establishments where the average man in the street doesn't go. This is indeed the people's drink. It is found in the smaller town bars, in the remote countryside and in every village bar throughout the entire southern continent. It is brewed from maize and is quite nutritious, but with a fairly low alcohol content. Its name is derived from the vigorous shaking necessary to distribute the maize particles prior to drinking.

There are many other alcoholic drinks produced: rum, whisky, vodka and gin, all of surprisingly good quality, especially the well-liked Malawi Gin. Although sold in the smart town bars, spirit drinks are rarely seen outside towns, as these are just too expensive. An affordable alternative is an illegal and potentially dangerous brew produced in the villages, known as *kachasu*. It is distilled from rice and concocted using home-made stills. These contraptions are likely to be pieced together from anything, including scrap materials; the most popular distillation process is apparently through bicycle tubes. It is officially banned by the government because of its lethal reputation, but is widely available, very cheap and continues to wreak havoc on many who imbibe. This firebomb concoction is sold in discarded spirit bottles. It has a pale cloudy appearance with an odour rivalling a combination of methylated spirits and antiseptic solution. When I had the opportunity to try some, just a sip exploded in my mouth like a combination of chillies mixed with white spirit. It would be difficult to find a more terrifying beverage.

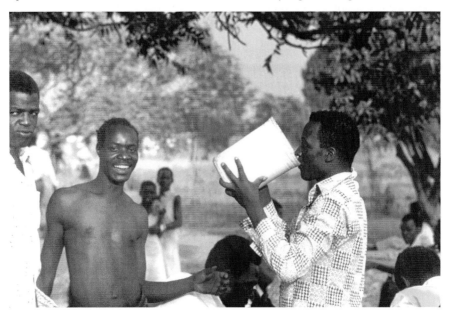

'Chibuku' drinking party

Bar life

Although the bars have no official hours and remain open while any customers are around, the evenings are the busiest periods. Live groups appear from nowhere to provide music, usually for dancing to the local pop known throughout southern Africa as *spangee-mangee*. There are no amplifiers or electric add-ons; even battery power is beyond the means of these musicians. But their ingenuity at improvisation in the construction of their instruments make up for any gadgetry they lack. Not only are they self-taught, but these groups assemble the most imaginative collection of musical instruments, all home-made.

Guitars consist of metal oil containers with a hole cut in one side for the sound box plus a wooden fret arm to hold the strings. The strings are of various thicknesses from either discarded baling wire or the windings from magneto coils. Drums are made in the age-old tradition of goatskin over hollowed logs. The bass is made with a string line attached to a short pole, which is then attached to a plywood crate for sound control. Tambourines are assembled by wire through shells and whatever else is needed by an equally home produced ingenuity. And so to the home-made sound of *spangee-mangee*, the drinkers and dancers laugh and tell their stories until either drinks or money dries up.

The bars seamlessly fit into village life. Outside of the larger towns they are the only places where a few hours can be loitered away. Restaurants, when they can be found, are rather like the stores, places to eat or buy and then leave. But in the bars, women and children roam in and out, often acting as helpers, bringing the local brew to the tables or to patrons sitting on the ground outside.

Looking in from outside through the glassless windows one can see the silhouettes of people talking and dancing against the yellow gleam of paraffin lamps. The sounds of the tin guitars and bamboo flutes mingle with the shouts and laughter and compete with the crickets and distant animal calls as the surrounding bush takes on its night attire.

Bar girls

All bars have a selection of prostitutes or 'bar girls' who either dance with or provide sexual services for the customers. They are not necessarily particularly young or scantily dressed and can easily be mistaken for someone's wife. However, not many wives are generally found in bars. They are usually at home looking after children or helping in the extended family. This is essentially a man's reserve. Malawi is one of the poorest sub-saharan countries with a traditional rural population that is really quite conservative. Even in bars, these girls cover up and will look essentially no different from any other girl in the street, doing her shopping. The girls are seen to be as much a part of bar life as drink itself.

No bar can be deemed really open for business without them, but no-one really pays much notice to their presence, unless their services are needed. For much of the time they simply chat to customers and ease themselves into conversations as much for the occasional offered drink as to be hired out. They appear to be part of the general merry-making in the bar. For many patrons the girls' presence is like a range of drinks, one would expect them to be there but would not pay much notice unless the drink (or girls) suddenly dries up.

Bar girls are not restricted to the countryside drinking houses with their flickering lanterns and grass roofs, or the shady outskirts of town. They are a popular addition to life in the smart town centre establishments, including top hotels where many of the visiting business travellers stay. Always flush with expense accounts, they are homed in on by the cruising girls, who do battle for such a find. Here the girls dress for the location with revealing attire from the best shops in the city. They fit in with the city high-life, can speak English well and have honed both their etiquette and ways to pick up clients. Every evening (and probably during the day) when the offices turn out and the bars fill up, they cruise the corridors and lounges engaging customers with small talk and compliments.

The visiting business types are easy game. Away from the restrictions of their home turf and encouraged by the easy life of their present surroundings, the girls are a welcome distraction from tedious business meetings. Amid the infectious atmosphere and constant drinks, the noise and laughing increases, until late in to the evening. It is not unusual to see the well-dressed client swaying along the corridor, a girl on each arm and a bottle in each hand trying not to spill his drink. Maybe they will be heading out towards more seedy destinations or the quiet of a hotel room on the next floor. To the bar girls it is just another routine evening. Apart from the décor and prices of drinks, perhaps the scene is not so different from any bar on the other side of town.

The bars demonstrate another example of the uniquely African way of doing things. In this refuge from the starkness of the outside world the bar girls laugh with their customers; children quietly play or look after their siblings while the drinkers sing and down *shake-shake* at the bar or sit in groups outside. There is little tension, except for an occasional over-stressed drinker; everything has a natural feeling to it all.

The bars in towns still capture the atmosphere of their savanna equivalents. But the rowdy drinkers have more money and sometimes wear suits. Music blasts from radios or tape and CD players with electric amplifiers and the lights do not go out when the wind blows in. The walls are made of concrete and the roofs do not leak. The city equivalent to their country cousins are to be found either in the 'locations' around the outside of town, or in the townships near to large cities.

My first introduction to the township bars was when I was stationed in Lusaka, the capital of Zambia for three years from 1977. The country was a so-called 'front-line state' in the war to liberate Rhodesia. The city was a nightmare of crime, corruption, of illegal trade in smuggled goods and a free market in guns - many from the equally corrupt resistance fighters, many of whom were disillusioned with the conflict and deserted. And the melting pot for them all was in the townships, perhaps only five miles from the city centre.

It was here humanity took on another form and wore an identity that changed as they entered and the chaos of the place took hold. There were few police here, or at least honest ones, unless a special round-up was being planned. These were places where humanity was on the edge of the world; people were caught at the edges, against a wall, because on the other side there was nothing, just miles of flat nothingness. Further out on this flat featureless plain there were isolated farms, but the township people knew only of the city; it was here they had made their lives. At least here, people with no other home and few other choices had an existence, although it meant an uneasy life with a criminal underclass. It was insecure but outside of its perimeters, outside of the chaos, there was not an easy choice.

The drinking elite

The city hotels all have their own bustling version of bar life. With their better décor and alert doormen, keeping out those who would not fit-in, these are the more up-market places that the white and black population could be on something approaching neutral territory. But it is still only the upwardly mobile blacks who can afford the prices. Expensive or not, they are still noisy, friendly places, with possibly some live music entertainment.

There is little chance of going in for a quiet pint; these are places for social interaction – talking amidst a constant consumption of drinks. And certainly part of the décor is a selection of good-time girls, more flashily dressed than their country counterparts, but who still cruise the clients for drinks and services.

The language of choice is essentially English, not only as these are watering-holes where the business community meet and this is the communities' language, but it demonstrates an educational attainment, all can appreciate. In local countryside bars, it will be the local language raising its voice above the home-made music. These places are after all, where the ordinary people come to relax.

In the city bars, mingling amongst the locals, there will often be a selection of white business types, western-suited, maybe staying only a day or two, representing some foreign company or interest, a typical candidate for frequent-flyer status. Many are used to these places and fit in amongst the local elite, seeking some relaxation and conversation, or just a good time before their next destination.

The bars are bigger in the townships; the crowded ramshackle dwellings support a larger population. These places too are a refuge from a hostile world, except the hostile world came in and criminals fought over goods or turf or something else. I used to go there with some of the inhabitants, perhaps one of the few whites who ever did. On my own it would have been unthinkable, but with others who lived there, it was a security, as though protected by a private militia. I was welcomed perhaps just because I had gone, not as an official, but just to drink with friends like so many others.

I saw the violence, but it was somebody else's war and one didn't question it or get involved. Outside a bar sitting on oil-drums, I sat in on the communal drinking parties as they passed around a broken plastic bowl with something to raise the spirits brewing inside. There were cheers and handclapping when I took my swig. It was possible to live here and even to find a little escape, but when you left the bar the night-time sounds of the savanna could not be heard. The noise of the township had taken its place and the air was thick with the smell of open cooking fires.

The townships are isolated and crowded; they come to the world's attention in the fleeting glimpses of video news; they are places immersed in decay; rubbish and the debris of their inhabitants pervades every corner. But at the same time there is a constant renewal, like the villages, an organic growth of re-built squatters' houses and someone's tiny repair shop. It is a growth borne of desperation or self-reliance. People grow up in these places and move on but many rarely leave; the township provides everything they need.

There are still whites living around these places. Zambia has a long colonial history from the days when it was Northern Rhodesia and an influx of Europeans came to make their fortune in setting up farms or opening mineral mines. It was a new world of opportunity. Many stayed and made a fortune, or at least a good life and adjusted to the new order after independence. They often became fluent in the local language and their ability to fit in ensured their presence was accepted. There was some inter-marrying with local girls and thereby they became even more assimilated in the local population. Other settlers became almost forgotten, getting by on the small plots they owned, or continued running little businesses, selling the necessities of township life.

As the city expanded they were engulfed within its perimeters. I met some of these people in the township bars. They had been there as long as the indigenous population. In many cases having grown up side-by-side with the local Africans, even taking out Zambian citizenship; yet they did not belong to their society. But they were equally distant from the new breed of expatriates who were transients in the country, people with skills to sell who came to work for their contract time and then left.

Now middle-aged, with leather-skins and a drink-hardened determination, they lived in a limbo-land between them all, in a place that few knew about. Perhaps they resembled the last remaining residents of the old industrial lands in England. But this was their home too and they also had no intention of leaving; there was little choice for them on the other side of the city. Where you least expect it, you find people living in extraordinary places and this brings surprises and a kind of optimism. The bars displayed it all.

CHAPTER 10

Markets - where Africa shops

THE MARKET is the hub not only of the village but of the city as well. A market flourishes wherever it is easy for both the buyers and sellers to get to. And where better than a place almost everyone uses - the terminus for both around town and inter-city buses? Sellers can bring their goods from the villages and shoppers load up before heading home. It is the same in just about any African city. Where you find the buses, the market will not be far away.

It is to the market that just about everyone, from manager to  messenger comes at some time to browse, buy or sell and hopes to find something either not found in the shops or at least possibly at a cheaper price.

Market in Lilongwe

City workers come here to get the bus home or travellers to wait for a long distance bus to visit family across the country. While waiting for their transport, they stock up on supplies for the journey. The market is most likely to be the first sight a visitor has of the new village or town he or she has come to visit. Somewhere hidden behind the piles of herbs and spices you could find the drug and dope traders and possibly illicit booze from the villages.

It is here that the focus of ordinary life can be seen without embellishment or ceremony; a place which levels all comers irrespective of position or purpose, to that of buyer or seller. The food sellers from the local villages arrive by bus or bicycle to spread their produce on the ground before they sit bartering with their customers. The larger businesses have tables and possibly employ someone, even local children to manage the stall. Anything, especially if it is cheap, is likely to be found here. For it is in the market that many of the shopkeepers will find their supplies. It is a cascade of colour and smells, like a car boot sale without cars, like a village jumble sale after closing time. Similar products are loosely grouped together, so all the clothing whether new or second-hand are at least in the same area.

Bargaining is for everyone

The main focus of any African market is its food produce. Even in the 1970s, a centre like Lusaka was a step ahead of its rural neighbours and sold its produce by weight, on balance scales with weights or a spring balance suspended from a rafter or on a pole. The price was a matter for bargaining. Throughout all rural areas the sophistication of scales was never considered necessary, or was just too expensive. The business of selling produce had the traditional African solution. All the smaller fruit and vegetables were sold in delicately balanced piles. The piles were all arranged in neat lines and sold at the same price. The buyer must decide which pile presented the best value.

Bargaining is the only way to buy anything; it establishes what could be the 'right' price for the customer. It is pretty well recognized that the poorer rural customer will get a cheaper price than an office worker in a suit. Such people can afford to pay more and it was only right that they did. But bargaining also produces a rapport between seller and buyer; they get to know each other, exchange jokes and possibly gossip and if they get on, a better price can be extracted. It is the African way of doing things. Before the serious business of fixing a price, a time for pleasantries must be allowed for; time is not an important commodity but getting to know someone is. The next time they meet, they could greet each other and start something of a relationship; it would enhance each other's day.

After a few purchases the buyer would not just be another purchaser but become a 'customer'. This meant a special relationship had been formed and a loose bond established; in fact you would most probably buy from the same trader rather than from somewhere else - the seller would secure more business and the buyer a better deal. The 'special relationship' and the time spent in establishing it was perhaps just good business sense after all.

For the spirit and the body

A walk through the market shows not just what is for sale but gives a snapshot of the lives of the people who make their living there or of the local population who pass through. The barbers have their salons on wooden school chairs in the shade of jacaranda trees; the traditional medicine man spreads his bizarre array of cures for the inspection of the faithful. In some markets wooden shacks bearing a sign such as 'Dr Wanza, Witch Doctor' on the door, are places where consultations are made. Cures are claimed for anything from impotency to ensuring a healthy birth. But mysterious potions are also dispensed for the application or dispersal of spells.

All people have a strong spiritual basis to their lives, which is animistic, the cult of the spirits of the dead. There are both evil and good spirits and witchcraft is generally strongly believed in. In the villages, special occasions are designated when offerings of food and beer are made to the spirits, accompanied by traditional dancing with ancestral songs and loud drumming. But for specific conditions the traditional soothsayer is often consulted.

An African witch doctor markets his potions

There was greater practical trading, for instance, higher value goods and second-hand car parts, in city markets where an upwardly mobile local population existed. There could be mountains of scrap with every conceivable part of a car likely to be found somewhere in its midst. Come back in an hour and the scrap lads would quite possibly find the part, or get something close enough that with ingenuity would meet the requirement.

The market is also a place where illicit drugs are traded and black market money is transacted. Police patrols in the markets are regular and are meant to assure some kind of order. A blind eye is generally turned to background trading in drugs or money unless things are getting out of hand and a clean-up is demanded. As long as things looked peaceful they were not going to interfere. Second-hand clothes are a staple item in any market. Fabrics disintegrate rapidly under the fierce sun and working conditions in the fields. Donated clothes or *salaula* as they are locally known, from western aid agencies often find their way to the markets and though the donors expect them to be given away, middlemen see an opportunity to buy them up and make a profit on their stalls. Cheap and many of good quality, they are a fast-selling item. But they are often responsible for destroying much of the local clothing industry. Profits to some can be destruction to others.

In this pile there just could be a part for any car

A place for the people

Ordinary people regard the market place as their territory. They can bring or buy virtually anything, meet friends or while away the day. Whenever political problems surface and a clamp-down on public assembly is deemed necessary, it is often the market to be closed first. Whenever a ready-made crowd is needed to cheer a visiting dignitary, it is the market, or the local schools, which provide the necessary people power. In western countries, markets may be popular, but are generally regarded as the secondary source of supply after high street shops and the supermarkets. They are often transitory or located on the edge of towns. The African market is the centre of village or town, and it is the place that opens daily, where goods not found in the shops are sourced, and conveniently located next to the bus station. It is a place for the village entrepreneur to become established, to make his window frames or assemble bicycles.

In between the market stalls, the drug dealers and a variety of illegal traders, there would inevitably be some thieves or pickpockets fleecing the unwary or naive shoppers. Anyone caught in the act would need to have a quick escape route planned. Instant justice mobs emerge from the onlookers as if by a pre-arranged signal. The escapee would have to be fleet of foot and know his escape route well, for an equally agile group would be close on his heels. Amidst shouting and gesticulating at what his fate would be once caught, the pursuing mob would spill out into the nearby streets.

I have witnessed several such incidents around Lusaka market where a desperately faced thief shot passed me, just metres in front of such a mob. Whether he had discarded the goods or not, he would scatter crowds and brave traffic in an attempt to escape. As he ran, the crowd invariably increased in size and if caught something just short of a summary execution would be enacted. To have the police arrive before the mob caught up was the best escape a culprit could expect.

Observing market life

It's in markets where life can be observed and where the onlooker is least likely to attract attention. People have things to do, perhaps in a hurry with friends and family to meet. The market is the ideal place to see Africa and her ordinary everyday ways of doing things. To visit a village where people actually live would be a far better way to observe life. Everyone will be here with meals to prepare, the elders to consult, disputes to settle, houses to build or repair, children to mind and endless gossip to give. But a stranger would have to be made welcome and would be the centre of attraction with curious children peering through windows and around doors to see what was going on. It would take time to integrate and become less conspicuous.

In the market an onlooker will be anonymous. The everyday ordinary life can slip away as families set up shop, come to buy or just linger around the stalls. The young population is noticeable and there are usually several children to a family. It is quite rare to see a woman without a child being either carried, or with one or more trailing behind, sharing in carrying either a younger child or a headload.

The baby will be strapped to the mother's back with a brightly coloured length of fabric, lulled asleep by the rhythmic walking routine and oblivious to the noise and confusion going on all around. The responsibility for this child will soon pass to a younger sibling when the arrival of another baby will demand the mother's attention. Children soon became responsible minders. However large the family, everyone from the time they can walk has a pre-destined responsibility to share the workload. Everyone within the family group will be expected to take on some responsibility. From an early age children are weaned into this interdependence. Whether it is looking after siblings or minding the family's livestock, children are depended on and in being so, are integrated into the family.

Ironing in Lilongwe market

I sometimes supposed that some element of childhood was lost, the gain being the knowledge of being truly needed and of becoming an essential part of this family structure. The breakdown in western families with the problematic teenagers and isolation of its elderly members will be avoided in this traditional family pattern. As pebbles rounded and smoothed on a beach, the physical nearness of African families also rounds their temperaments and promotes an essential interdependence.

The importance of greetings

Meeting family and friends in the market is commonplace and as elsewhere, rules of etiquette must be applied. The traditional rules by which a family lives has its similarities in the respect shown during greetings. This could extend to an almost ceremonial exchange. On meeting friends and family members, the familiar traditional greeting procedures are always enacted. It always appears as if the meeting is truly memorable and a true source of pleasure. There is always much laughter from both sides and the handshakes are firm and long. The initial greeting will inevitably be:

"*Moni, muli-bwanji?*" (Greetings, how are you?)
"*Ndili bwino, zikomo.*" (I'm well, thank you.)

Repeated exchanges of "*chabwino*" (good, fine) and "*zikomo*" will go back and forth several times while the handshake continues. The arm will often be almost fully extended and if one person is in a lower social position, a slight, almost bowing pose will be adopted. This could, in very traditional circumstances, be accompanied by a couple of silent, almost gestured handclaps before grasping the other's hand in greeting. Women from the villages often give a slight curtsy during the handshake. To give greater emphasis, the left-hand may also grasp the wrist of the right-hand and give a so-called greeting with two hands. This is the highest respect that can be paid. Receiving a gift with two hands indicates the esteem to which the gift is accepted. It is only after a minute or two that the greeting can move on to some other exchanges, and always accompanied by smiles and laughter. This is not because of the quality of jokes, but merely the procedure of demonstrating an agreeable meeting. These rituals in the greeting process are the essence of politeness. It is a procedural process before any other business can be conducted.

The centuries of physical nearness demanded by the close-knit village community and the large family networks still exists to this day. African communities are close. There does not seem to be the necessity for the western idea of demanding 'one's own space'. The village huts are close; groups of people often sit near to one another, usually sharing a communal feeding bowl into which each member dips his or her hand. Women carry their babies. Men can often be seen walking hand-in-hand while they exchange gossip. It is part of the closeness of life.

CHAPTER 11

Profile of a president

The abrasive style of Malawi's President Banda

POLITICS IS very much about power and its acquisition; in Africa the seizing of power has brought out the best - and worst - features of those who sought it. The continent is a rich source of stories about the scramble for power, the manipulation of opponents - sometimes even their elimination - of wars fought and cunning applied in ways representative of the most bizarre fictional mystery stories. It seemed as if only presidential candidates with the trophy so nearly within their grasp could display the highest and lowest levels of manipulation, which would finally out-pace their opponents. Such displays of tenacity were very often displayed during the lead up to the change-over of power from the colonial administration to the new sovereign state.

Once the goal was won, the same ruthlessness was often brought into effect in order to hang on to everything they had fought for so long to control. For those with a fighting chance (perhaps an appropriate term) of the top job, it could literally mean a rocket launch from either years of fighting in the bush, or from obscurity into an international celebrity. The former typified the example of Rhodesia as it ran its tortuous course towards the new Zimbabwe. Although the latter represented the relatively peaceful transition of power from Nyasaland into the new territory of Malawi, it is never an easy assumption to know who is destined to get the top job. There was no meteoritic rise to power and certainly no military intervention. But the country was to become governed by a well-educated and shrewd politician with considerable experience of western life. But his term in power was to prove controversial.

The process was to take several years, but although no wars ensued it was an arduous path. The victor became the first president of Malawi, although in a convention in the northern town of Mzuzu in 1971, this was famously upgraded to Life President. Thence was established Life President Ngwazi Dr. Hastings Kamuzu Banda, to give his full title. *Ngwazi* literally means 'the fearless one'. He was from an ordinary background, born in 1902 of *Achewa* parents. He was named Hastings after one of the Livingstonia missionaries (an early settlement in the north of the country). His second name *Kamuzu* came from the word *Kamunkhwala* meaning 'small root'. His mother was given a traditional medicine in the form of a small root to assist her to become pregnant. African names are full of meaning.

Banda was one of the relatively few youngsters in those times to have gained an early education. He was taught to read and write while employed as a domestic by Dr. Prentice. The quality of this teaching was fundamental in his rapid progress through secondary education, which resulted in him being selected for training as a teacher.

He worked in Southern Rhodesia where further fortune came his way when he was sponsored by American missionaries for study at a high school in Ohio, USA. He went on to gain his doctorate in philosophy in 1931 and qualified as a medical doctor in 1937. He came to Britain and studied in Edinburgh to obtain a qualification for working in Nyasaland. But instead of returning he became vocal in his support for the Nyasaland African Congress formed in 1944. The colonial administration brought into being the Federation of Rhodesia and Nyasaland in 1953, with Banda yet to return to his home country. The Federation had many opponents, none greater than Banda who maintained strong criticism of the organization through his growing band of followers in Nyasaland. During this time he continued practising medicine in London and later in Ghana.

By 1958 a group of Nyasaland nationalists led by Chiume Chipembere judged the time ripe to strike for independence and invited Dr. Banda to return to his home country. Initially, this was to practice medicine in Blantyre, but ultimately to lead the newly formed Malawi Congress Party - the successor of the Nyasaland African Congress. His revolutionary speeches upset the colonial regime and in 1959, in what was known as 'Operation Sunrise', Banda was arrested and sent to Gwern Prison in Rhodesia. His release after a year ensured an instant martyrdom status.

This was to prove the real beginning of political power for the charismatic doctor, who soon took over leadership of the Malawi Congress Party. Independence was high on the agenda and Banda extracted a new constitution from the colonial office at Lancaster House in London. In 1964 independence was granted with Dr. Banda firmly in control as the first prime minister. With his opponents in exile, the new prime minister, later to become the new president, took decisive political control of the new country.

Banda takes control

President Banda started his reign of power with clarity over the direction the future course of the country would be steered. He was the ultimate authority and no one was to be in any doubt of the fact. His early association with and education by the country's missionaries influenced his attitude to life and he practised a relatively austere lifestyle (compared to others swept to power) and as far as is known, with little sign of extravagance. He apparently knew what was right for Malawi with an almost pre-ordained belief, which he would without faltering put into effect - and there was to be no opposition to his views. His very vocal proclamations on all aspects of life, especially relating to morality were frequent and lengthy and all deemed suitable for the country. It had to be, for any opposition was not only intolerable, but had dire consequences for those who challenged or even questioned his views.

From the start, his stamp of approval and long arm of control pervaded everything and led to a thirty-year autocratic reign by the Life President. No aspect of life or the economy was left out of his influence. The country became a reflection of his ideals. There could be no Malawi without Dr. Banda. Whatever institution, organization, business or statute, allowed to operate within its borders, did so only with his approval.

So complete was his dominance of the country it was difficult to distinguish whether the grass roots support displayed by the ordinary villager was due to a genuine respect for their leader, or a fear of the consequences of not displaying loyalty. Whether fear or loyalty, everyone could see there was a black face in power, who was going to improve their lives. Their first president had originated from a background similar to their own, and could therefore understand their plight. He had not been catapulted from an impoverished obscurity of a distant village. Through his own efforts he became an educated man. He had the experience of life in both the western world and in African countries many had barely heard of.

It was a relatively rare combination and it was conditioned with an understanding of what this new child he had inherited was going to need. In a way he was like a father to the nation, a village elder lesser mortals would seek wisdom from. But his power did not seem to be a corrupting force. The way it was brought into effect however, elicited a range of observations from muted approval to criticism from countries within the continent and beyond.

There was certainly much that the country could be proud of during these early years. The emphasis on an agrarian economy when there were little other natural resources, allowed the country not only to feed itself, but also be a considerable exporter of cash crops. Clean towns with shops displaying plenty of locally made basic merchandise and even a selection of imported luxury goods, contrasted sharply with several neighbouring countries. The largest cities, Blantyre and Lilongwe, did not have the urban squalor of 'shantytown' districts surrounding them. Townships were simply not allowed to descend into criminal ghettos. In Zambia, for example, the capital Lusaka had such notorious districts, which were virtually no-go areas for anyone but their inhabitants; a refuge for criminals and where crime was part of everyday life.

Banda's democracy

President Banda ordered all vagrants, those out of work, especially the young, and anyone with no apparent means of support, to be regularly rounded-up. They were taken back to their home villages to be put to work on the land. Frequent police raids ensured few potential troublemakers lingered around the townships. It was a major initiative in crime prevention and no doubt assisted in reviving the rural economy.

Whereas in Zambia the bribing of officials and indeed anyone with access to a scarce commodity was commonplace, it was virtually unknown in Malawi. There were no shortages of any staple product and a 'black market' economy was consequently absent.

Without an unchallenged authority it would have been virtually impossible to put the Banda seal of approval on the mechanism of government. The price of all this power was a vocal round of international criticism on the lack of democracy for an 'enslaved' work force. The country was indeed one of the poorest in Africa, but Banda maintained that western ideals of democracy were not appropriate to 'his' Malawi. However, as an autocrat with a sense of justice he was not alone. An example from more recent times (2003) shows how Africa can still produce leaders who are autocrats, yet their policies have proved to be substantial success stories.

A network of spies and informers was established, composed of loyal party members

Yoweri Museveni who has led Uganda for seventeen years, has developed what he calls a 'no-party democracy', had similar views. Within his period of presidency he took the country from a virtual ruin and turned the economy around. He argued that Uganda was not ready for multi-party politics, because parties would ultimately represent tribal groups rather than ideas or social policies. In his opinion, a western-style democracy would lead to ethnic strife.

Even though Banda could argue that his policies were what Malawi needed, he was not one to trust that his system would run without opposition. He had viewed other countries' power politics from personal experience and was too wily a campaigner to take chances. He had to devise a mechanism of support for a power system centred on his own personal supreme authority; a structure that would touch all aspects of public life and become influential in many minute facets of private life as well.

The system he installed was dynamic and self-policing by followers who believed fanatically in his vision for the country. A network of spies and informers was established, composed of loyal party members, which infiltrated every corner of the country, reporting back to their local headquarters on any suspicious activity.

Speeches to the people

It was to the ordinary people, many of whom were illiterate that the president directed many of his messages; how he was the leader who came to save them from colonial rule and establish a true and just life where hard work and loyalty would be rewarded. Little by little life did improve for the rural poor but it was not the end of the rainbow dream many had expected. They wanted wells, schools and better hospital clinics and these take time. His speeches were straightforward and direct, with arguments so well structured they would produce the adulation required time and time again.

Most importantly of all, the declarations and speeches were always delivered in a language the villager could understand. They were always peppered with examples of village life with assurances that as long as they followed his direction, prosperity would surely follow. With the vast majority of the people living a subsistence peasant farming life, it was essential to gain their hearts and minds. With such persuasive political rhetoric and with no other experience of a black leader, especially one drawn from a background similar to their own and educated in the white man's world, it was little surprise he enjoyed a largely popular support. His charismatic personal style and singular authority appeared untarnished by corruption. Here was the man they had been waiting for.

A new style in dress and literature

The president depicted the quintessential appearance of a somewhat old-fashioned aristocratic English gentleman, always impeccably dressed, sporting a black homburg and dark glasses. His small stature appeared quaint among the throngs of people surrounding him on his walk-about tours. He was a man they could see and hear; not someone who dictated policy from a marble lined palace who sent his henchmen to deliver his messages. There was even a movement to replicate his dress code. For the ordinary man, to be smartly dressed was regarded not only as a symbol of status, but reflected the president's style.

I can remember being in a quite remote part of the country, with the nearest small town many miles away, seeing an elderly man riding on an equally elderly bicycle, emerging from a pot-holed trail lined with the season's maize crop, in a smart pin-stripe suit and a homburg hat. He would not have been out of place on a London commuter train in the 1950s, but the spectacle of him in this situation focused for a moment on some of the quaintness and endearing qualities of the country.

83

The president's strict moral code went to extraordinary lengths, with even parliamentary declarations ensuring there was a legal framework for quite extraordinary intrusions into what western democracies would perceive to be personal affairs. Much of this was directed at the white, or as they were usually known, the 'European' expatriate population. This was the term historically reserved for the original colonialists as it was from Europe that the invaders essentially originated. But the term loosely applied to all whites, irrespective of their country of origin.

They were deemed to be the portrayers of a 'hippy' culture, so much a flavour of the 1960s with everything this represented, namely an infusion of sex, drugs and rock'n roll. But this was highly unlikely to be part of the moral baggage brought in by the average expatriate who was either a middle-aged civil servant or a technician of some sort. However, no risks were to be taken and no opportunities were to be given for the import of supposedly western moral corruption. Although the absolute numbers of Europeans were small, their influence far outreached their numbers and their habits/lifestyles were always a subject of scrutiny.

Such detail even prescribed the length of ladies' dresses and prohibited ladies wearing trousers in public. Dresses had to cover the knee completely when walking and women could be asked to wrap a shawl around to comply. Men's hair had exacting measurements detailing precisely its length and the *bete noire* of men's fashion, bell-bottom trousers, was definitely banned.

The censorship years

As the years of independence went by the president became increasingly paranoid by any influence from either outside the country or from within, which could result in criticism regarding his regime. This tiny country surrounded on all sides by three huge nations and needing their co-operation for transport links, was sealed in isolation as thoroughly as if there existed a glass wall on all frontiers. This structure of isolation and repression had strangely dual effects. President Banda maintained good relationships with both black and white regimes, conducting a delicate balancing act between them all. There were no safe havens for the freedom fighters in their attacks against Rhodesia, yet at the same time he accepted large consignments of aid from South Africa, the ultimate target of the liberation movements.

There was increasingly strict censorship on all imported literature with an army of surveillance personnel to ensure compliance. In the few foreign journals that were permitted, marker pens were used to manually black out advertisements or photographs where any ladies' undergarments were being modelled. In the cinemas no film scenes showing personal contact between men and women were permitted, with kissing scenes being cut at absurd places. Almost as an act of rebellion, an audience cheer would often arise when the two lovers would lean towards each other and then immediately draw apart. This chopping up of film reels, where censored strips were often lost, resulted in distributors banning deliveries to the country. Even expatriates' wives were recruited to ensure that the subversive content of picture and literature was eliminated.

The published list of material not deemed suitable was extensive and the number of titled books on the banned list included many that were classics and on English certificate courses in their home country. Orwell's *Animal Farm* with its obvious references to a popular uprising and the establishment of a republic, was on this list. The two local newspapers were close to being government mouthpieces with a little real world news interspersed by lengthy pronouncements regarding the virtues of the president's doctrines.

Most foreign journalists were banned from the country, as their reports were often critical of his regime. Such was the power of the president's dictates, the civil servants and police went even further in their interpretations of the statutes, so as to avoid any possibility of appearing to be lenient. His dislike of journalists was demonstrated in an antagonistic interview with the BBC. Every question was answered with "No comment.", until the reporter referred to the futility of the interview which was becoming pointless. To which the abrasive Dr Banda simply answered "Yes." and walked out.

Even though I was working in Malawi, upon entering through an 'up-country' border crossing, I was stopped and questioned because my passport gave my profession as 'printing technician'. There followed a lengthy explanation of what my job really consisted of and for a time there was a very real possibility of my being barred entry, despite my valid work permit.

"Your permit states you are a printer. This is like a journalist and our president does not permit their entry."

"I assure you I am definitely not a journalist. I work for the government and assist in printing only what is legal."

After further questioning along the same lines, the border guard summoned his legal interpretation of the point in question and appeared unconvinced by any of my explanations.

"But you could print something our government does not approve of."

"This is impossible as you will see, my work is as a printing technician."

Several loops of questioning were ending up at the same conclusion.

The late afternoon breeze was fanning gentle swirling dust clouds and closing time must have been creeping ever closer. Perhaps this sealed the debate and I eventually had to make a vow of sincerity that in no way was I writing reports for newspapers or magazines. As I drove down the dusty track into Malawi, I reflected that once again, diplomacy with border guards could carry the day.

Dr. Banda frequently made references to this "parasitical profession" in his speeches. Although such control of the media is seen as closely resembling the excesses of totalitarian regimes, which it really is, the effect of this action on the majority of the population was almost non-existent. For the relative few who could read anyway, access to even local newspapers was limited, let alone to imported books and magazines. Despite these excesses, President Banda was wily and shrewd. He saw that control of the media and a ban on the 'corrupting' influences and questioning attitudes towards all things political would reduce a threat to his hold on power.

His political ideals were anti-communist, which went well with his capitalist zeal for the merits of hard work. This was enforced by his strong puritanical religious beliefs. These capitalist ideals contrasted sharply with the left-leaning regimes of the countries at his borders. He used his persuasive speeches to gain long-term support of the people to encourage them to strive for improvements in their living standards. Although his political rhetoric was to ensure his continuing survival, no-one could question his desire to improve the economic status of the country. He seemed to see himself hand-in-hand with his fledgling country, dismissive of all criticism and opponents, blazing a path towards a future he alone was capable of leading. In any developing country this was difficult enough, but in Malawi with no valuable natural resources except the variety of its agriculture, this demanded a compliant population.

Banda on tour

The president travelled widely throughout Malawi inspecting new industries and on his infamous crop inspection tours. His cavalcade of outrider motorcyclists and attendant vehicles made a spectacular impact on the normally quiet rural roads. When such a visit was due, schools, markets and businesses in the immediate area were closed and their pupils and personnel obliged to line the approach route. It was a scene reminiscent of the opening day of parliament. Local businesses were persuaded to 'donate' their vehicles for the bussing about of school children and villagers for the day. A visit was a highly organised social occasion and would transform the community for several days before the event. Shops, markets and businesses on the approach road were cleaned and often repainted in the mandatory white emulsion. Gravel roads over which the cavalcade was to pass had mechanical graders working to smooth their surfaces. The appearance of a local squad of Young Pioneers and the Women's League (see *An alternative army*) left no doubt as to the importance of the visit.

As with all presidential visits, the high-pitched wailing of the outriders gave warning of their approach as they ignored any speed restrictions and embraced the whole width of the road. It was a parliamentary regulation for all to clear the road as they approached. Anyone not displaying a fast enough response or hindering the cavalcade's progress would be in serious trouble. I knew of an expatriate who accidentally turned from a Blantyre side street and somehow became entangled in the middle of the entourage. He received a prohibited immigrant classification with twenty-four hours to leave the country. This entourage of motorcyclists, ministerial limousines, security vehicles and of course the president's personal conveyance was assembled for whatever occasion necessitated his presence outside State House.

Speeches in the maize fields

All experts agreed that the salvation of Malawi was through its natural resources, its agriculture. The president was often seen in rural areas during the planting season, prior to the rains, encouraging villagers to maximise their efforts to ensure a good harvest. He was never seen in public except in his impeccable three-piece suit and homburg. It was the same on his agricultural tours, which took him to all areas of the country. It was an extraordinary sight to see this small statured figure standing in a field of maize surrounded by villagers and his bodyguards, enthusing about the necessity of crop cultivation.

His speeches were always mixed with ample assurances of how their lives had improved and would continue to do so if they followed his directives. Indeed, this emphasis on agrarian reform was exactly what was needed in a country at this stage of development. The audience of ordinary village people to whom he projected his arguments appeared to believe what they were told.

Long before his arrival at a pre-selected maize field, the party faithful would round up the village elders who transformed the surrounding fields into a venue capable of filling a mini stadium. The elders with their whitening hair and crooked yellow teeth, leant on their crafted walking sticks and held the front row, often sitting while conferring with party officials. The villagers spread out behind them, young and old still in their earth-stained clothes and carrying their farming hoes. It was mandatory to attend such gatherings. And the local party officials ensured a good turnout.

All essential preparations would have been put into place: the gravel road leading from the high-way smoothed by a grading machine; all party members ensured the media were in place to record the event for national radio and the next morning's newspapers; the local market, shops and schools closed; truck loads of women and children delivered early to wave flags and cheer on the road in. Many of the women were in the colourful local dress displaying the president's picture and children were in their blue and white school uniforms. The colours were a paint-box against the red earth as the assembled crowd waited anxiously for the motorcade to speed into view.

Its sirens could be heard minutes away and on cue accelerated the throng into waves and cheers. The president always used these attendances as a political platform. He would give lengthy advice on the importance of farming methods and how his vision of agrarian reform would lead the rural people to a better future.

The villagers were no doubt in awe of this entourage of power and prestige, which had arrived like a fairy-tale to their humble surroundings

"I had appealed to the ordinary people in the villages all over the country to work hard in the fields, I also appealed to those of our people, my people, who were a little better off, who could, to enter commerce or business. . . . What has been the results of all this? The results have been, to say the least, most encouraging. . . . To begin with, the people, my people, all over the country responded to my appeal to them to work hard in the fields."

Before departure, the president was sure to make considerable reference to how he had saved Malawi.

". . . The result was that I was brought back home. . . . Seventeen months later, on July 6th, 1964, the country became independent."

There were always numerous appropriate pauses for cheers and clapping. The villagers were no doubt in awe of this entourage of power and prestige, which had arrived like a fairy-tale to their humble surroundings. The dark-suited officials with their shiny limousines and newspapermen sporting flashing cameras could well have been something many had never seen before.

The politics of power

Dictators are a dangerous breed and are prone to corruption. Throughout sub-saharan Africa, countries have been pushed into a zone of hopelessness by dictators with personal ambitions and an agenda at odds with their country's necessities. Perhaps Dr. Banda was that unusual species of dictator who appeared to have no visible suggestion of corruption and certainly knew what was necessary to develop a very poor country with virtually no marketable mineral wealth. It was also desirable to unite the rival ethnic groups within the country and provide a stable structure. What was questionable was the ruthlessness with which he sought to accomplish these aims.

Whatever methods were used, it met with enough international approval to enable considerable aid to flow in. This facilitated a national road construction programme and various development projects throughout the country. He was the only viable leader after colonisation, possibly because he crushed all opponents. There was also his jail term, which ensured a degree of martyrdom. People generally had no reason to suspect he was involved in corruption. But it is true he held a majority holding in trading estates including the powerful PHC - Press Holding Company. This concern controlled agricultural businesses including the lucrative tobacco farms. However, when compared to other African leaders he led an almost austere life in keeping with his religious background with no outward show of affluence.

The presidential seat in Zomba was a palatial former governor's residence but not overly grand. His time was spent mainly here but also divided between another residence in Limbe - adjacent to the commercial capital Blantyre - and the admittedly rather splendid Neuru-ya-nawambe Lodge near the Kasungu Game Park in the Central Region. Although when he was eventually overthrown in forced elections during 1995, reports of foreign bank accounts surfaced, this was never satisfactorily established.

Although the rural poor led simple lives and could easily be manipulated, they were also open to influence from other sources. During the period prior to President Banda coming to power, there were other challengers vying for the seat at the top. After the transition to an independent state, which saw Banda victorious in the power struggle, they escaped to Tanzania and Zambia where they lived in exile. To return meant certain detention or even death as they were considered enemies of the state. It was the fear of the influence of these exiled dissidents and the questioning of presidential authority from within the country, which resulted in the extraordinary and often brutal measures used to ensure his personal brand of power.

The president knows best

The unique combination of President Banda's own personal moral crusade was inextricably linked with a shrewd political awareness. Even though this combination was exploited to an intolerable degree, there was much in his policies that was necessary for the country to present an outward prospect of peace to the world and to encourage the loans and foreign investment that were so essential. The western industrial ideal of freedom for political parties to market their policies upon an educated population is suitable for a developed western-style society. This has resulted in parties based around ideas of social class, income, socio-economic groups etc. For Malawi, which had only been discovered by Livingstone less than one hundred years before, such a system could have been fatally flawed. 'Political' parties would not have been based around the concepts of an industrial society, but upon individuals representing traditional ethnic tribal groups. The dominance and power of the majority ethnic groups would certainly have resulted in exploitation of the minority with a disruptive effect upon the country's progress.

I experienced numerous examples of ethnic disruption during my time with the Printing and Stationery Department. This took many forms including supervisors promoting members of their own clan, or people using their authority to cause general disquiet amongst members of other groups. The disruption and chaos caused by ethnic rivalry has examples from the countries of Eastern Europe to tribal warfare still rampart in several African nations.

There was little place for democracy in Malawi during its early years and all contenders for the post eventually fled the country. But if a nation is not ready for western-style democracy, because of ethnic rivalries, then perhaps autocracy has a role. However, recent history suggests autocratic regimes are linked to despots who are corrupt and bankrupt the country. But it is democracy that will ultimately unite a nation. This will not necessarily prevent ethnic rivalry; in emerging nations, strong leadership is necessary. But if a leader is to emerge and unite a country or its people on a course of freedom and hopefully, prosperity, an honest and pragmatic person is called for. President Banda was possibly as near to such requirements in a leader even with his autocratic style.

The funds given by South Africa to the project gave the apartheid regime a much needed black ally and benefited Malawi financially

Despite the president's appalling human rights record, his strong moral principles ensured corruption in Malawi was virtually absent from both within the public service and the small but growing private sector. His emphasis on agriculture for a poor country not only allowed people to feed themselves, but also encouraged large scale farming of cash crops. Numerous expatriate experts were brought in to manage these concerns, which were extremely successful. The early years of independence brought in several important foreign co-operative investments. There was even governmental contact with South Africa, at the time completely isolated from the majority of its black neighbours to the north because of its apartheid regime. Funds were generated from these contacts to build a new showcase capital in Lilongwe to house all government offices. There was much criticism from foreign donors of the questionable economic advantages of such a bold move and it was generally thought of as appeasing the president's power base in this his home region.

The funds given by South Africa to the project gave the apartheid regime a much needed black ally and benefited Malawi financially. These contacts infuriated not only the Organization for African Unity, but Malawi's neighbours who were also harbouring its most outspoken dissidents, outlawed at independence. But Banda ignored the criticism, even jokingly referring to himself as "the black sheep in the family". Lilongwe was to become a symbol of a new nation.

National surveillance

The president's intolerance of criticism became almost paranoid during the 1970s and rigorous censorship not only stifled dissent, but also ensured he was surrounded by a network of 'yes' men who could (would) not contribute any constructive ideas to his policies. The risk to their livelihoods would have been too great, for they too relied upon the patronage of the *Kamuzu*. He thus became increasingly isolated. It resulted in a network of surveillance methods that could bear comparison to Soviet cold war practices. Loyal members of the ruling Malawi Congress Party were distributed in a network of positions throughout the country to watch and report back to party headquarters on anything or anyone who was suspected of 'corrupt' practices.

This in effect meant anything from organizing a coup to a minor questioning or criticism of a presidential statement. Such informers were to be found everywhere. They did not wear any form of uniform, only the party badge, which almost anyone would wear, whether or not they were party members. As far as I knew, these individuals did not openly campaign on behalf of the president's policies, they kept quiet, but their ears and eyes were always open. Although their colleagues knew many as informers, the majority were known only to their party bosses. They were to be found in bars, public offices, factories, schools, in fact anywhere people gathered or met for business or public recreation. Moving seamlessly throughout the society they had been born into or using their employment as a front, the eyes and ears of the party were invisible.

It was just about impossible to know who belonged to this clandestine organization. It is quite possible one informant had little knowledge of others doing similar reporting. It produced an uneasy and eerie society, like being in a constantly bugged room, yet leaving it would still not bring about any sense of security. There were few, if any public places safe from detection. Information picked up may have been in all honesty quite innocent of corruption. But there were no questions asked, no risks taken and the culprits were beyond the reach of a protecting law.

'P.I.'ed and out

The penalty for expatriates who ran foul of the political system, for whatever reason, was to be designated a 'Prohibited Immigrant'. The bold stamp 'P.I.' on a passport was the standard treatment for accidental actions and even mild politically sensitive blunders. Even minor misdemeanours were dealt with harshly. For Malawian citizens, this would mean jail sentences, detention without trial or some instant justice dealt out by the president's personal militia. For expatriates it would often mean an instant deportation. There was no argument and it was usually a twenty-four hour forced departure. During the later years of presidential rule, when Banda became increasingly suspicious of even the slightest indication of dissidence, being 'P.I.'ed as it was called, became an increasingly common method of exiting the country.

I knew personally an expatriate hospital matron, who had been in the country for many years and was well respected. She made the error of telling a student nurse during an inspection, that her party badge was not part of her uniform. Within twenty-four hours she was on a flight home. On even the most private of occasions, surveillance was ever present. At an Asian wedding celebration, the radio was turned off during one of the president's addresses, while a guest made a presentation. A political party member reported this and within hours, the family was on a flight out.

However, one expatriate employee of my department deliberately incurred such wrath in order to make a premature exit; that is before his contract expired, on a paid departure ticket. Departing before a contract terminated was deemed to have broken its terms and the penalty would normally involve loss of gratuity benefits including the airfare home. P.I. status did not result in the errant being dumped on the other side of a border post in the bush, for the expatriate it had one advantage, a fully paid home air passage.

Only one-way out

John was a Scotsman employed on contract in the Printing Department, arriving about halfway through my time there. A large powerful man in his early forties, he soon established a reputation for heavy drinking with an aftermath of rowdy behaviour that did not go down well with the expatriate club population. Their opinion of him was of no consequence, as he had little to do with the mainstream expatriate community and took up residence with a local girl from a nearby village. This was not unknown but amongst the government employees at the time was frowned upon. His frequenting of the local bars on nightly binges had disastrous results on his performance the next day and did little to please his two expatriate superiors.

Also it came to light he had falsified his family details on his original application in order to obtain enhanced benefits. How he convinced a selection panel in the first place, shows how manipulation is always possible. Things came to a head after about six months at a time when he claimed an 'emergency' situation required him to return to the UK to sort out his affairs. It was without doubt a relief to the department that he was going - at any cost. But his chosen method of exit was as bizarre and dangerous as anyone could imagine. At such an early point in a contract he would not be able to return on a paid ticket, and unwilling to finance it himself, he deliberately set out to get himself 'P.I.'ed. A risky thing to do and most thought anyone would be crazy to try.

Whether the whole exit strategy was staged or it just evolved, I never did find out, but events progressed during an opening of parliament session. MPs and ministers took over the Government Hostel for their accommodation during this period. John was still drinking in the bar when the dignitaries arrived and as the evening progressed his behaviour became increasingly disruptive as his alcohol intake took effect. His references to the president resulted in the head barman, who was a party informer, taking John outside and asking him to leave. This had no effect and the police were called. The police must have been in a state of shock, for to see an out of control white person in proximity to MPs, was a unique situation for them to control.

Upon their arrival, John, who was by this time just about out of control, insisted they all had a drink before his departure to the notorious Zomba Jail. This rather bizarre situation did apparently take place, presumably because no-one wanted to tackle a drunken Scotsman and invite a brawl in front of the assembled MPs. He was kept in jail for about a week and even allowed home under police escort for meals. This equally exceptional concession can only surely have been allowed in an attempt to defuse the situation while deportation was proceeding. A possible reason was that it later transpired the jail contained political detainees whose whereabouts were being investigated by organizations like Amnesty International.

I did in fact drive John to the airport for his departure and saw for the first time what a prohibited immigrant stamp looked like on a passport. John wrote to me from the UK and told me about the detainees he had met, some even being quite young children. He had given Amnesty International detailed information about the jail and who was there and this was the first accurate and detailed information they had received. I never knew whether the antics of a drunken Scotsman did in fact finally benefit the cause of political detainees, but this was one P.I. case the system really was glad to be rid of.

Secrets and loyalty

This atmosphere of secrecy and intimidation, which permeated just about every situation where Malawian citizens were present, could have made for an uneasy relationship between the local people themselves and the expatriates. But this quite scary situation, forever a looming cloud like a distant thunderstorm, somehow never assumed the frightening aura it could have and seemed to be surprisingly quickly adjusted to. But you rarely let your guard down and unless you personally knew a Malawian on very good terms, it was not wise to say anything about politics or presidential policies.

One of my trainees was a party informer who reported to the local HQ on the political situation within the department. His loyalties were known to everyone, but as far as I could tell did not affect his relationship with the rest of the staff. There was no way in which he could be dismissed or even transferred. His contacts with the party bosses and through them to the policymakers, could well have meant he knew more about developments within the department than the management did. He even informed me of all details about my second contract renewal long before any official documents arrived. With such potential power and influence, it was always surprising to me he did not use his position for personal gain, or at least to further the interests of others within his own clan. I was never aware of any corruption on his part and his relationship with both his superiors and other workers, seemed completely normal. I always thought of 'spies' as clandestine, but in this topsy-turvy world of local politics, things were not as they seemed.

An alternative army

Although the army was loyal to the president, experience in other developing countries has shown how this could change should an opportunity arise in a power struggle. Disgruntled army chiefs with enough backing from loyal troops had all the necessary arms and equipment to take control within days. Banda realized how important it was to have grass roots support from the average villager, but however useful this may have been, it would be no defence in an emergency.

The Young Pioneers became a sort of presidential militia who could be relied upon to heed the president's directions and most importantly as an ally

He needed another force he could rely upon who genuinely owed allegiance to himself personally and to the party. One way in which this was cleverly achieved was by giving special privileges and status to the two groups of citizens most disadvantaged in society: young people with little or no educational qualifications and therefore with the least chance of job prospects and women who in traditional society are at the bottom of the hierarchy.

The 'Young Pioneers' were created, modelled on similar regimes in Russia and Ghana and were typical of the foresight Banda could exercise in case he ever had urgent need for support. They became a sort of presidential militia who could be relied upon to heed the president's directions and most importantly as an ally, if ever the army decided they could run things better. This 'alternative army' of young men and women were recruited throughout the country, given a military style uniform and answered only to the president or party. The criteria for selection seemed to consist of having displayed some sign of allegiance to the party machine. Although not armed they were trained in military style operations. They had no official power, but welded considerable influence both in the countryside and towns. Their distinctive uniform of green shirts, fawn shorts and a sort of Australian army hat with one side pinned up was always prominent at political functions or rallies. They became a force outside the control of either the police or military. There were numerous excesses of their power and they became a feared organization no one wished to argue with.

I was frequently stopped by members of this young persons' army for lifts into town. It would not be wise to ignore such a request. The Young Pioneers were publicised as a 'rural reconstruction' force, a role they did engage in, but they were more a presidential army of aides who saw their power backed by the unassailable authority of their leader.

There were numerous presidential initiatives, which enlisted minority or disadvantaged sections of the population to their leader's cause, and these included the 'Youth League', 'Spearhead' and the 'Women's League'. The Women's League with possibly the majority of members, was not a militia, but had considerable political influence. He referred to women as his 'mbumba', appropriating gender concerns for national development and his political goals. They were generally recruited from the villages, where they could easily keep an eye on things political and spread the president's message. Most of the force were made up of mature or the older political faithful. These women became a sort of cheerleader group. Dressed in a colourful uniform depicting the president's picture, they were always present at rallies and political gatherings dancing and singing to the accompaniment of traditional drummers.

President Banda opens parliament. Rare pictures from the balcony of Government Press across the road

A serious show

At the opening of parliament, which occurred three or four times a year, the Young Pioneers and Women's League were out in force. I had a bird's eye view of these proceedings from the balcony of my department just across the road from the parliament building. There was always an air of apprehension on these days; the headloads of firewood were no longer taking this direct route to the locations. The day began early with bussed in groups of villagers. Schools were closed and local school children arrived to line the route from State House to the parliament buildings. They arrived early in the day, their blue and white uniforms looking like a patchwork quilt stretching down the hill past the old government offices and into the shade of the giant jacaranda trees. As they sat and played little games amongst themselves, they nibbled on their picnic packs, their shrill voices echoing around the usually staid government offices.

The market was closed for the occasion with truck loads of vendors together with the idlers who used the place like a meeting lounge, brought up to reinforce the children. The Young Pioneers were positioned every twenty metres or so all along the presidential route, their uniforms conspicuous as they stood in front of the crowds. Either the police or the pioneers immediately stopped any cars that had inadvertently strayed on to the presidential route. All occupants were 'asked' to stand by the car and clap the entourage when it passed. As the time of arrival approached a detachment of the Malawi Rifles regiment lined up on the forecourt.

All personnel from the adjacent offices were obliged to join the assembled crowds; all work and activities ceased. The enormously rotund ladies of the Women's League danced and shrilled and blew whistles to the accompaniment of traditional drummers. As the heat of the late morning took effect, suddenly the distant wailing of the presidential cavalcade's sirens whispered from the direction of the now empty road. As the entourage approached, the wailing could be heard above the mixture of noise and colour, now reaching a crescendo from the drummers and the cheering onlookers.

Like a pop star taking centre stage the president was suddenly in full view, preceded by a speeding Land Rover with his two white uniformed bodyguards standing on the outside rear platform. The bodyguards were trained in their techniques by a European who was I suppose, expert in this business. I never did find out, but it always intrigued me as to how one acquired such a position.

The president himself was seated in the rear of a red open top Rolls Royce, dressed in a morning suit with a large grey topper and customary dark glasses. His immaculate, if somewhat bizarre appearance, was almost surreal when one remembers this is an African state and that most of the onlookers were a mixture of school children, general office workers and subsistence farming villagers. He waved a flywhisk of streaming white sisal hair, held aloft and when he descended from the car, his short stature disappeared among the bustling throng of the ladies of the Women's League. All that could be seen of his passage was the thrusting wave of the flywhisk. He suddenly appeared again as he climbed onto a podium as the military troop filed past for inspection. After a sombre silence for the playing of the national anthem he entered the parliament building to address the assembled MPs and ministers.

Both Kathy and I once had the opportunity of attending one of these parliamentary opening ceremonies, having applied personally to the Clerk of Parliament. All the assembled MPs and ministers were immaculately dressed and on their best behaviour. As was common practice, the president gave a speech which lasted something over two hours, all in English with a translator for the local language of *Chichewa*. Occasionally he would correct the translator to cheers from his audience, who obviously approved of his local dialect knowledge. Speeches took on a format that was characteristically predictable, with numerous references to his role of the leader who led the country from colonial domination to proud independence.

Cheering and clapping on all appropriate occasions would occasionally break the attentive silence of the audience. After the opening the president would return to his Rolls amidst the throng of the Women's League and the pounding of traditional drums. As the presidential vehicles sped past with their sirens wailing for their return to State House, the roadside crowds clapped and the blue and white uniforms waved their flags. After its departure the Young Pioneers returned to base, the office workers returned to their desks and the quiet of a late African afternoon established itself again.

A serious show-Zambia style

It was several years later, during my contract with the Zambian Government, I obtained an invitation for Kathy and I to attend the opening of parliament by President Kaunda. It was a different affair to the austere assembly controlled by President Banda, resplendent in his immaculate morning suit. Kaunda was dressed in traditional robes and carried his characteristic white handkerchief, a symbol of nationalist-socialist ideology, known as Zambian Humanism. Although dressed smartly, MPs and ministers slouched over their chairs and appeared anxious to get out and on to the reception party waiting nearby. And what a reception it was. For a country beset with shortages, this could have convinced a newcomer that Zambia was the land of plenty. The tables could barely cope with the accumulation of bottles of booze not only from local sources, but expensive imported varieties.

Arriving slightly late, I saw the assembly had already tucked in, with some already taking on a swaying motion with loud, raucous laughing to match. As I stood with Kathy at a side entrance deciding which table to descend upon, none other than President Kaunda and his Prime Minister

Mr Chomba entered and stood beside us taking in the scene. So there we were, a strange quartet, one expatriate and his wife, with two of the most powerful men in the nation, standing next to each other. No one in the drinking frenzy a few metres away seemed aware of the dignitaries who had just entered; no one came to pay respects and there was not a photographer in sight. I was rather embarrassed to be just standing next to Zambia's two leading figures, but as I was about to offer an introduction, they rapidly turned into the exit. Kaunda had a rather disgusted look and did not appear up for a day of heavy drinking.

Education for the elite

President Banda was not only western educated, but during his years practicing as a GP in London he absorbed much of the elitist English culture. Part of the baggage he returned with was a respect of the exclusive traditions of the British hierarchy. This probably explains how during the negotiations for a new constitution, Banda enjoyed hobnobbing with diplomats, fellow premiers and even royalty. It was not long after he became the Life President that Banda established his ideals in the formation of an exclusive school, in a remote area distant from the corrupting influences of nearby towns.

This was an establishment where only the brightest of the country's young gained entrance. It established his preferences not only for the best in formal education, but emphasized his desire for formal school attire in an environment that mimicked the best in English public school tradition. No expense was spared to make this a truly exclusive establishment, with conditions comparable to similar institutions in much wealthier countries.

The school is known as the Kamuzu Academy, and still exists. It is located several miles outside the new capital of Lilongwe in remote but picturesque surroundings. Its red brick buildings and angular colonnades exude exclusiveness and emphasize the gulf between this and all ordinary schools. The teachers were mainly expatriate and subjects included lavish amounts of the classics. Whether the graduates gained skills appropriate for a developing country is questionable, but still more so is the disproportionate amount of the education budget allotted to its maintenance. Primary schools at the same time were using chalk and slate under a presidential decree for a back to basics ideology. Not that anyone seemed to mind any of this, for any criticism would have been a risky venture and would certainly not have come from those selected to attend. Graduation here was a certain passport either to university or the best jobs the country had to offer.

Just about everyone revered education, not necessarily for its own sake but for the advantage it gave in getting a job. This was without doubt a privilege for anyone and even the minimum of a secondary school education was able to transform a person's life and therefore their whole family network. In the 1970s even primary education had to be paid for, although this was eventually made free. Secondary education was, and still is, fee-based and the guaranteed route to a better life-style.

Parents would beg, steal or borrow for the money necessary to complete the Junior Certificate examination. This was two years of secondary education, the minimum level that was asked for in most offices and certainly in all government jobs. Knowing the sacrifice being made and the prize being sought, most pupils would give scarce attention to the inadequacies of their schools and were quiet, attentive and hard working. For many expatriate teachers this was a revelation and relief after the hurly-burly of many western state schools.

The Malawi Certificate of Education (MCE) was a further two years of study and comparable to the English General Certificate of Education. It was even assessed in the UK. My wife Kathy worked with other expatriates on the compilation of the examination papers and results. It was deemed too prone to corruption to have Malawians involved. This was the minimum necessary for university entrance, or the most coveted prize of all, a chance of an overseas education.

It was a status sign to speak English and showed one's standing and education. Along the streets and even in the bars it was common to hear English spoken amongst the local people in everyday conversation. Only in the countryside did this change and you would need a smattering of *Chichewa* to make yourself understood. But even if you were a lost traveller, it was always possible to find someone with enough English and armed with a language guidebook, find what you needed. In any case, your efforts would be rewarded with much laughter and probably a newfound friend.

The secret life of Kamuzu

Despite the austere Christian background of President Banda, his personal life has always been something of a controversy. He never married and his relationships have been something of a mystery, inspiring several commentators to investigate his hidden side. During his life such an investigation would have been dangerous and not likely to reveal much. Even now, there still appears little to be revealed on his personal life. Whilst practising as a GP in England he is reputed to have had a relationship with his secretary, Mrs French. Presumably because of this relationship, her husband divorced her. Soon afterwards Banda relocated to Ghana. When he eventually moved back to Malawi to lead the independence struggle, Mrs French expected Banda to invite her to become the first lady. It was not to be.

Another controversial relationship was about to be formed with Cecilia Kadzamira, a nurse who worked at his Limbe clinic. This proved to be a lifelong affair and lasted throughout the thirty-year reign of the president. Any relationship was always strenuously denied and Mama Kadzamira (mother of the nation) became the official government hostess of the president. As years passed, she acquired considerable power. Her maternal uncle John Tembo had long-term ambitions to the presidency and together they were not only feared throughout the country, but had increasing influence over the ageing president. Kadzamira was a powerful figure in the background, directing appointments and government policy together with jobs given out to her relatives. Kadzamira's sister, Mary Kadzamira, was Banda's secretary and her brother, Dr Zimani Kadzamira, was principal of Malawi University, Chancellor College.

Despite her power, she remained faithful to the Kamuzu, nursing him until his death in November 1997. Her relationship with the president is still a topic of controversy within the country.

The fall from power

Even with all his power and single-minded autocratic rule over what he regarded as his country, by 1992 the reign of President Banda was coming to an end. The country had an increasing debt problem and a severe drought throughout the whole region, brought huge numbers of refugees from Mozambique. For the first time since 1964, Malawi experienced anti-government strikes and demonstrations, with nearly forty people killed by police gunfire. A new party, the Alliance for Democracy (AFORD) was formed that campaigned for multi-party elections. In 1993 Banda was forced to hold a referendum to decide what the political future of the country should be. It was to prove the end of the Banda reign. Even with his iron grip over political institutions and network of informers, it was not enough anymore. His health was in decline and times were changing. The title of life president was abolished; the MCP Young Pioneers disbanded; a bill of rights established; detention without trial ended with the release of political prisoners and the most notorious jails closed.

In 1994 the country's first multi-party elections took place. A new constitution took effect in May 1995. It was the final blow to an ailing president. Hastings Kamuzu Banda died in November 1997. Despite being forced from power, his memory is preserved in a mausoleum constructed in the capitol Lilongwe. Many who lived through his regime will wonder at how the new politics will shape a country still impoverished and near the bottom of Africa's economic league. Banda ruled the country with extreme policies. It will take daring policies from the new politicians to avoid the errors of other emerging nations.

The following comments from Malawi residents demonstrate the variety of reactions to the Banda regime:

Kamuzu deserves more than whatever we can do because Malawi is where she is because of him - no tribal wars and peaceful.

Malawi is also one of the poorest countries in the world and facing yet another year of famine. I grew up under Banda's thumb. I remember being forced out of school by the police to stand on the road for hours to applaud his motorcade. I was always looking over my shoulder to see who might be spying on what I was saying. The man was a disgrace but still not as bad as the cronies that surrounded him and fed him the information they thought he wanted to know, cutting him off from the potholes and poverty that diseased my lovely country.

In the Banda year's crimes such as murder and theft were unheard of and his people were never starved. Banda did the best for Malawi and always had Malawi's interests at heart. Just look what democracy has done to Malawi. Murders and theft are common and nearly all the houses have burglar bars and electric fencing to keep intruders out. This was not the case in the Banda years. The currency has devalued from once being 2 kwacha to the pound to over 205 kwacha today. Democracy in Malawi has taken Malawi back 200 years. Banda without doubt did the best for Malawi and now you have politicians stealing public funds and abusing government funds. Banda will always be the number one leader for Malawi. He deserves a monument.

Banda is just as emphatically his own man on Africa-wide matters. Last week Diallo Telli, Guinea's leftist secretary-general of the Organization of African Unity, was in Malawi for Banda's inauguration when he suddenly found some of his pet schemes under scathing attack during a Banda press conference. "I didn't fight the British to exchange British imperialism for Eastern imperialism," Banda snapped. Then looking Telli straight in the eye, Banda shouted: "I mean that! I'm saying that because you are here. You can expel Malawi from the O.A.U." Banda sneered at African countries that claim Socialist countries are their friends: "Tell that to the marines, not to Kamuzu."
Time Magazine 15th July 1966

As these comments suggest, Banda appeared both loathed and loved by the people he ruled over. He was indeed a controversial figure and it will be up to history to judge his record. President Banda had his own vision for Malawi, and he exerted extreme and individual methods of putting his vision into practice. The debate as to whether his dictatorial policies were excessive, or what a fledgling country in Africa needed to survive at the time is still ongoing.

President Banda is possibly one of the least known of post-colonial leaders, considering the thirty-odd years of his iron-rule in the country. Perhaps this was because of purposely not becoming involved in any of Africa's power struggles in the 1970s. These were on Malawi's doorstep and were international stories, but he remained aloof from it all, maintaining that a tiny land-locked country had enough problems already - which indeed it had. But after a slow start following independence, the 1970s saw economic growth averaging 6-7%. As this was almost entirely due to agricultural production, it was applaudable that the country could not only feed itself, but also have excesses for export. But his dictatorial style of power and abuse of democracy gained him notoriety amongst world leaders and they appeared to ignore this, provided peace reigned. Whether the country's economic growth had little prosperity trickling down to the masses seemed irrelevant. But Banda compares almost favourably to some of Africa's corrupt politicians. He remains a contradictory figure but like his country, will never attract the attention awarded to his contemporaries.

CHAPTER 12

The rains arrive

THE CONSTANTLY changing weather patterns of northern Europe, are a complete contrast to the stable climate existing throughout southern Africa. Over vast swathes of countryside, the daily radio forecast is brief but accurate: "in the south of the region it will be hot, in the north, very hot". For weeks, even months, only one or two sentences need to be added to the description. The climate resembles the regions' politics, a smooth almost unnervingly quiet time, interrupted by a violence that will, without warning, transform both sky and land. This climate seems to possess a personality that subdues one with its ability to imbue a calmness borne of weeks, even months without change. And then, after one is convinced of its quiet sameness, it retaliates like a water and fire-spitting dragon.

After the hot rainy season ends in April, the next six months of the year produces one almost monotonous unchanging day after another. There are seemingly endless dry, quiet days with an unblemished sun rising at six in the morning and traversing the sky almost directly overhead, until nearly twelve hours later it disappears into a blazing red inferno over the horizon. The temperature varies according to the altitude - perhaps up to 45° C in the lowlands near to rivers, but in Zomba at 1,000 metres it is pleasantly warm during the day, at around 25-30° C.

So permanent is the sun's presence that villagers indicate by the angle of their hand what time of day it is. Not even the massive form of Zomba Plateau rising 1,500 metres behind the town can influence this continuity. Sunsets are tropically short; from full sun through dusk to dark within the hour. Looking over the plains below, dropping to the lowlands near to the lakes, the slowly rising red dust forms a translucent blanket sharply merging into the blue above it. As the sun sinks behind this barrier, a parade of colours changes as you look, merging from the palest red through deepening shades to an eventual dark mauve glow. The red earth of the landscape throws back the colours of sunset until finally changing to the darkest maroon. Then, quite suddenly everything succumbs to the penetrating blackness of night.

Even late afternoon showers, so much a feature of Far East jungle terrain, rarely occur. The middle of this 'dry season', around June, is the coldest time of the year with daytime temperatures falling to 15° C on the plateau slopes. Log fires at night became necessary and the insect noises became more subdued. The more you descend off the plateau, towards the lower plains and lakes, the heat persists despite it being the coldest time of the year.

Dry weather turns roads into sand

During this dry period, vegetation growth comes to a standstill; grass turns a brilliant yellow straw colour. Yet in this limbo period where nothing seems to grow, the flame trees explode into a mass of violent red plumage.

As the year progresses, the temperatures slowly recover. Leaves from flowering deciduous trees fall and immense jacaranda trees burst into deep blue blossom for a month before carpeting the ground in swathes of fallen blooms.

All of nature's processes have to be completed on time before the November rains start. This applies equally to time honoured processes in the villages. Around September the villagers start grass fires to kill off last season's old growth and to encourage new shoots to be ready for the fast approaching rains. During my second contract we had a house on the side of the plateau, quite high up with clear views over the surrounding hills and plains. From this vantage point the night-time vista of these fire trails appeared as snakes of light crawling in waving columns over the hillsides. Although discouraged by the government as dangerous and leading to soil erosion, they were like the seasons, an inevitable part of the cycle of life. The fires encourage new 'elephant grass' which is needed for new roofs in the villages. This grass can grow from three to four metres within a few months and age-old practices for its promotion are difficult to eradicate.

With the mixture of dust and bush fires the air takes on an unmistakable tang. It is something perfumed, like a distant garden fire on a still autumn day in England. The late afternoon sun appears to dim earlier and the pale pink light to last longer.

The deluge

In the south-east of Africa the rains start in November. The heat increases steadily over the preceding few weeks and the air becomes languid with increasing humidity. The sun becomes baking hot especially in the lower plains and the rising air currents produce spectacular cumulus clouds like mountains of cotton wool. As the first rainstorms approach, the base of these clouds becomes increasingly dark and threatening with sudden streaks of lightning and grumbles of thunder.

In the late afternoon the first of the season's rain heralds a climatic change, which is both sudden and awe-inspiring in its ferocity and the power of natural forces impacting on the landscape. From a viewpoint on the slopes of the plateau the clear-cut edge of the approaching rain and its grey-black carrier of cloud is like a curtain being slowly drawn over a window as dusk approaches. The plateau is a mass, which squeezes every ounce of energy and water from the storm system.

All the senses in turn are given a warning that something powerful is approaching. There is a wait that seems much longer than it actually is before the explosion of sky borne power reveals itself. First is a touch of a gentle breeze, almost without sound. Then comes the sight of a growing darkness that is all the more poignant as only thirty minutes earlier bright sunlight filled the sky. As the first raindrops hit the warm earth, a sweet fragrance like the aroma of dried sand fills the air. Finally, a distant sound like a rustling of a thousand flapping pages becomes louder and louder as raindrops batter the leaves of trees and vegetation. Now the wall of falling water is perhaps only several hundred metres away and the noise alone informs everyone of the power that is fast approaching.

The ferocity of the rain reaches a peak within just a couple of minutes, its impact being both frightening and inspiring at what the forces of nature can display. Even without the accompanying wind, the noise is intense and visibility can be reduced to less than one hundred metres. The cloud is now overhead and its blackness is as impenetrable as the thundering water that descends vertically. The raindrops are a size that the wind seems incapable of deflecting from their path to the ground. Within houses with their corrugated tin roofs, the pounding makes speech practically inaudible. The earthen roads cannot absorb such quantities and become rivers of mud practically within minutes. Paved roads in towns are usually sided by metre deep storm channels, which fill and become mini-aqueducts. They are soon obstructed with dislodged debris and shed their excess capacity across an already waterlogged road.

The rain continues in intensity for one or maybe two hours, with occasional slight lulls before returning to its full fury. On open land a micro formation of a Grand Canyon vista is formed by rain pounding away the soft soil, leaving stones perched precariously on a vertical pillar. Hundreds of these miniature creations cover flat land, perhaps reaching five centimetres high, all chiselled from the surrounding soil by the vertical methodical pounding of waterdrops.

The use of umbrellas is practically worthless. Their fine mesh produces a mist of waterdrops, which leaves one saturated after only a few minutes. Anyone walking on the open road, who cannot get to shelter before the deluge strikes, has to ignore any consequences the rain brings. After all once you are wet . . . There are always people walking and they walk on, irrespective of the torrents. In fact there is little to distinguish in their step and posture from that of a normal sun drenched day. They remain detached from it all.

Sound and light

Throughout the height of the storm, thunder crashes from practically overhead can produce an involuntary cringe in anyone, no matter how many explosions have been experienced. Instantaneous lightning flashes zigzag through the blackened clouds and strike home high up on the mountain somewhere.

In northern European countries, the effects of lighting strikes makes the headlines and maybe it is only the umbrella-holding caddy on a golf course who is at the greatest risk of being struck. Not so on the slopes of the Zomba Plateau, where the devastating effects of lightning strikes were often seen as the aftermath to a storm. But it was not just burnt out trees, singled out because they happened to stand proud of their surrounds. Houses were often targeted and the burnt out shells of such past hits could be seen on the road to the summit. It was not only because of their large expanse of metal roof, but often because of the faulty earthing of their wiring.

Our own house was perhaps a quarter-way up the plateau side and faced the on-coming weather fronts. This certainly made for spectacular storm viewing, but dangerous for lightning strikes. Although the place never actually caught fire, it must have been a close call on occasions. The strategy for our storm safety routine, was essentially to keep well away from where the power-cable entered the house and certainly a good distance from the fuse-box located in the hallway. During lightning flashes, this unit would regularly light up the house with an added crackling sound as an after-effect. It was too hazardous to put the lights on and our dog Hippy who slept under the bed, never emerged to investigate. As all repairs were the responsibility of the local power company, an enormous earthing cable coiled to a metre in circumference was buried in the ground next to the house. Even this did not stop the internal lighting displays.

After the storm

And then the storm vanishes, almost as suddenly as it starts. For a few minutes the rain lingers and the receding storm clouds and grumbles of thunder can be heard threatening the lowland plains out towards Lake Chilwa, shimmering in a brightening sky forty kilometres to the east. From the mountain slopes spectacular fireworks of lightning give an evening encore before the silence of the brief dusk sets in. The sandy soil soaks up the rain and by the next day only gullies with puddles give any clue to the previous day's soaking. But within hours the streams and rivers take up the burden of the inches of rain and become raging torrents. Sandy river-beds in the lowlands, which have been dry for several months are engulfed in flash floods from the force of water surging towards the main river outlets. The air, cleansed of its haze of dust and smoke becomes crystal clear and the sun shines with a renewed intensity and heat. Umbrellas, almost given up during the torrents are given a new purpose as sunshades, until the next deluge. At last the waiting for the rains is over and the planting of next season's crops can begin.

The climate in control

As in all sub-saharan countries, the extremes of weather dominate and control. Whether it is torrential rain, or lack of it, or whether it is the relentless burning sun, reducing rivers to pools and crops to fade, the climate dominates life. Torrential rain stops traffic and power supplies may fail when lines are brought down. The aftermath will continue as bridges are often washed away and roads subside. Humans can only stand aside and watch and wait; there is no intervention, as nature is now in control.

But these ravages have also a sympathetic face, for the water allows next season's crops to flourish and will provide everyone with this life-giving commodity for months in the soon to arrive dry season. This season too controls life, but in a much slower, more calculated way. As the sun arrives the crops mature, dried on the stalk maize will feed the villagers and the tobacco crop will provide export earnings. But if the sun out-stays its welcome and persists late into the year, its own form of control is harsh and brutal. When the dry season replaces the rain at the year's end, its heat is at its most furious. Its own effect is not instant like the washing away of bridges; it has a devastatingly slow, calculated effect, which as last season's food diminishes and water supplies dry up, succumbs the nation in a demoralising spiral. Nature's control is ultimate.

Provided the conditions are right, the valuable tobacco crop will keep the country in export earnings for the coming year. From the gently rolling hills of the farms, this crop is brought to the chaotic hustle of the selling floors in the commercial capital. Big buyers like Limbe Leaf descend on the season's crop and the world's cigarette companies' bid for the raw material of their products.

The 50-kilo sacks are arranged in vast rows over the floor of a building the size of an aircraft hanger.

Fast hand signs are essential for buyers at the Malawi tobacco auctions

The auctioneer or 'starter' is at the head of an anxious throng of buyers and assesses each sack in turn by picking up and feeling a sample, with an almost instantaneous shout to the buyers of a starting price. His voice can be compared to a sort of melody that fills the selling area, something like a song blaring out from a tape machine speeded up several times. The buyers indicate their intentions to purchase by a flurry of hand signals, giving a price they are prepared to pay. Someone with a note pad watches these sudden hand movements and assesses who will pay the most and at what price. All is happening at a slow walking pace.

This incredulous process is carried on along rows containing hundreds of sacks and millions of US dollars in revenue. I was told the life span of a buyer is only a matter of years. By their 30s sharpness and speed will have taken their toll. For the tobacco buyer, the year is not over, as the season ends in the southern hemisphere, another is about to open on the other side of the world further north.

The plateau streams, which have all but dried up in the previous six months of near drought become torrents, cascading over the rock sides on their way to the rivers below. The nearest river in Zomba is the Mulunguzi, which feeds into the mighty Shire River in the Shire Valley far to the south of the country. As the tributaries become torrents, the once rivers of sand become impassable, their outlets to the Shire produce its spectacular rapids. David Livingstone found these impassable on his search for an inland lake.

Fields of maize etched out of steep hillsides have little protection as soil is quickly eroded. There is little to compare to the far eastern rice fields, which in hilly areas are cut horizontally into the hillside to control deluges and preserve the precious topsoil. On the side of Zomba Mountain facing the prevailing winds, anything up to two and a half metres of rain can descend during the season, with possibly only half this amount on the opposite slopes. This torrent falls over no more than five months, the heaviest between November and December, with lighter more continuous rain from January to March. This is a type of rain called *chiperoni*, is so common Malawians even have this special word for it. Occasionally a gap of one week or more occurs between showers, but this only emphasises the intensity of the next deluge. By April crystal clear rain cleansed skies are back again.

CHAPTER 13

Creatures big and small

I T IS impossible to travel in Africa and not encounter a fair number of insects, of the most amazing varieties, either by size, shape or colour. It appeared to me, most will try to avoid you and can be fairly easily scared away by simple precautions. But mosquitoes are in a class all of their own. More pages in the pre-service manual *Preservation of Health* were devoted to malaria and its mosquito carrier than to any other disease. I learnt there were 1,600 species worldwide, which probably accounts for their remarkable variety of shapes, sizes and even colours.

Their techniques for attack I was to learn at firsthand. It is as though these tiny creatures have a system dedicated to guerrilla tactics. They only appear in low light and at night; they hide against dark surfaces where they can be less easily spotted - under the table for example, at mealtimes where stationary legs provide rich bites and where the air is calm. They can move with lightning speed and once they sense they are under threat, zigzag and take all manner of avoidance procedures to ensure escape. Their speed is such there is no chance of swatting one unless you wait until it settles on your body and prepares its biting stilette for entry into your skin. Only then will your tactics have the upper hand.

Mosquitoes are only a serious menace after the heat intensifies and the first rains transform the parched landscape into exotic vegetation with the stagnant water necessary for the breeding cycle to start once again. The heat seems to dull human speed but increases the manoeuvrability antics of the mosquito. There was recommended, both a daily and weekly consumption of prophylactics to hold the disease at bay. Malaria is considered the most lethal of all diseases, certainly to the local population and a major threat to the European. No wonder so much space was allocated to these insects.

During my stay in Africa I had several encounters with the local hospital services. None of the treatment was for serious illness, but I did require a deeply embedded sting in my finger, from an unknown airborne assailant, to be removed. I did not consider this to be anything but routine and the Queen Elizabeth General Hospital in Blantyre, the commercial capital, did not either. For some reason the extraction was to be done in an operating theatre. It must have been a slack period of the day although the numbers of relatives and friends waiting in the hospital grounds did not give this impression. An orderly was taking a nap on the operating table and after a request for his removal, was instructed to eradicate the flies that had invaded the theatre space through the open windows. Stifling clouds of spray were necessary before the flies departed and treatment began.

I jumped up and sat on the table before gritting my teeth ready for the local injection using the standard re-usable - and very blunt - needle. This was, I knew, standard procedure, but the cutting out went ahead before the numbing effect had commenced. As my tan seemed to fade with this onslaught, I was propped up from behind (rather than laid down) while the digging out progressed. Whatever was in there did not appear to come out, as I was back a couple of months later for a general anaesthetic and for some deeper investigation.

During my later time in Zambia, my routine dental treatment could not go ahead without scouring the local suppliers for sterilising fluids. It certainly did help to get the job done, but years later my dentist in England found that several of the fillings had started to rust. It was just possible I could have entered the dental procedures hall of fame with corroded filling material and stories of the frontier-style treatment.

Closer to insects

Insect activity, promoted by the slightly longer days and the sudden warming of the air, is audible and visible. Of course insects are synonymous with Africa. There are more of them, they are bigger, move faster and as all the films and books tell us, are far more dangerous. Although I found this to be essentially true, most insects try to avoid you and the simplest of precautions prevent most encounters. Walking barefoot is obviously dangerous, as mites can easily be picked up and bore into soft skin. Most of the Africans, especially in the rural areas never wear shoes and their feet develop a hide-like protection, practically impervious to attack from these assailants. Routines like ironing clothes has its own particular ritual, which if neglected has a nasty payback. Freshly washed clothes drying in the warm sun attract a potentially dangerous airborne assailant called the 'Putse Fly', which lays eggs on fabric. These hatch out upon contact with the skin and rise up like boils, with the larvae feeding away inside.

Ants everywhere

Ants are probably the most fearless of all the flightless insects and if threatened or if they imagine you could be a large meal, attack with zeal. There are innumerable varieties. Most common are small, pale coloured termites that invade virtually anything, except steel bars and concrete, by either eating their way through, or appearing out of the smallest cracks in buildings. They build enormous earth ant-hills or colonies, twice a person's height, with occasionally hundreds of these 'tower blocks' turning a flat plain into a bizarre sculpture park.

With so many varieties, they could well have been the inspiration for sci-fi material: terrifyingly huge dark brown predators fifteen mm. in length with large heads and pinchers, which wave aggressively at suspected trespassers; ones with short legs, long legs, with even a jet black variety which didn't attack, but warned predators off with a foul smelling odour. The pincher-welding gatherers arrive out of their underground colonies after the heat of the day but before dusk, to forage for the dried dropped leaves that the dry season has provided. On a quiet evening their millions of jaws dissecting leaves can be faintly discerned from the safety of a paved path. During times when eggs are being transported between colonies they are particularly ferocious and prone to attack, and on grass extremely hard to see.

It was on a hot day during a break in the rain when Kathy, myself and our dog arrived at our house on the plateau slopes. The ants had taken advantage of the temporary dry conditions to transport their eggs and had taken over the entire lawn surrounding the house. There was a six-metre barrier of these creatures, all moving at frightening speed and covering every blade of grass. They had no fear of any creature, of whatever size, as our dog soon discovered. The lawn was a no-go area as they quickly swarmed up her legs and she in turn did anguished acrobatics. Having cleared the ants from her paws we discovered there was no possibility of crossing this land until further rain or ant dispersant solution could clear a path.

The local Ministry of Works had a dedicated team experienced in ant clearance techniques. It was after a prolonged battle with ants verses the clearing team that a pathway was eventually made. But even these techniques were temporary measures only; it would be a matter of hours before the ants regained their ground. There is nothing these creatures fear or will avoid attacking if their security is threatened and their sheer numbers produce a formidable force.

Of all the insects and there are many, it is ants and cockroaches which make your home theirs. Cockroaches are night-time invaders and encroach upon their shared domain when a continued quietness envelopes the house. When disturbed they stop and seemingly eye you up before deciding the best time to make their move to escape. Ants are different, their activities are as active during the day or night and impervious to noise and activity. They never seem to stop moving and are always in such huge long columns, little can impede their onward march. Some sort of these indomitable survivors are always somewhere near you. Sitting in the garden they find your feet and as often as not bite into the first soft skin they find. Houses are built with concrete floors as any wood at ground level is eaten away by termites. Even roof supports, relatively far from the ground are not immune, once a column of ants discovers it as a suitable place of refuge. Food dropped on the floor, even tiny crumbs, are discovered in minutes and when located by an invading column, surround, separate into manageable pieces and drag it off with military precision.

Ants in the countryside

In towns and cities, ants compete with humans and their buildings for living space. There are fewer sources of natural prey and food sources, which together with less open ground, makes life difficult. But they are adaptable creatures. The almost total absence of wood and increasing amounts of steel building frames, are an alien combination. An uneasy alliance exists, as humans occupy territory above ground, while the ants largely tunnel deep below. But even here, through cracks and misplaced bricks, the columns ascend into the human world and climb to the tops of buildings to snatch trophies from whatever has been discarded that can sustain a night-time ambush. Permanent residences, made in gardens and parks, are their preferred territory, but in towns and cities it is a harder existence and even their enormous numbers cannot win against an incessant tide of concrete and steel.

Outside of the largest towns all insect life, including ants, becomes so close it seamlessly merges into the natural order of one's own life. It is in the vast savanna where ants display their dominance. Although they have predators, their highly organized colonies and capable learning abilities to locate food, give ants a credible defence. Their colonies dig deep into the earth and they scale the highest trees in search of food. Anything in their path is either bored through or traversed with the agility of miniature construction machines. Streams can be crossed by finding and bending long grass over to the adjacent bank. Anything not edible or destructible is either climbed over or an alternative route found in their onward drive.

Driving onwards

Throughout central and east Africa, the ant genus *Dorylus*, also known as 'saifu' ants are a formidable force. Their casual description as 'army', 'marching' or 'safari' ants is not given lightly. They do not form ant-hills, but reside in colonies containing anything from 20-50 million ants. In the dry season, when food is short, they emerge in enormous columns numbering into the millions. They are so densely packed, it is as if the whole army was a single entity.

A 'soldier' variety with huge pinchers, maintains security on the outside of the column, protecting smaller, worker ants on the inside. They prise their jaws upwards in a provocative display of defiance and attack anything that comes within threatening distance of the column. These columns are almost impossible to stop and will attack and consume any insect or animal unable to escape in time. It is as though a single purpose has enveloped each of those myriad creatures, yet the pincher-welding guardians display an individuality to search and investigate anything suspicious or threatening. As the column advances, the soldiers survey territory a metre or so either side of the swarm in a military-style manoeuvre. When eggs are being transported, the column's soldiers appear particularly sensitive to danger. Even the lightest of vibrations from the ground they are crossing produces visible concern, with the soldier outriders, twitching their feelers to pick up its source.

The spectacle of an army such as this marching relentlessly across open ground is to witness one of the wonders of the insect kingdom

In response to any perceived danger, reserves from the column appear almost instantly, as though summoned by telepathic communication. When surprised, most insects (or any other creature), will usually stop, or at least slow down, as they weigh up their next move. This may be just for a fraction of a second, but it displays a re-assessment of strategy. Marching ants however, do not need to stop or re-assess *their* strategy. They display a programmed ferocity as though each member believes it is part of an invincible force, with a pre-ordained destiny to crush all opposition in its onslaught to the destination.

Any insects caught within the swarm are overcome and consumed, with only the fleetest moving creatures able to escape. These species of ants are blind and communicate by the use of a chemical known as 'pheromone'. These chemical messengers trigger a natural response, which could be for alarm or warning of danger, for mating or sourcing food. The soldier ants will navigate the column and will make tunnels if necessary or direct the swarm around obstacles. Avoidance tactics are necessary for any human or animal, whatever its size. The spectacle of an army such as this marching relentlessly across open ground is to witness one of the wonders of the insect kingdom.

Avoiding ants – savanna survival

In the villages with dwellings made of mud blocks, thin wood and grass, ant invasions are a common threat. Maize supplies are stored in raised containers to escape rats, but are no deterrent to marching ants. Their organization and methodical reconnaissance together with the speed of the column's advance and sheer numbers involved, is an awesome spectacle of single-minded determination. Nothing can stop it and if the column chooses to invade a village home on its path, there is nothing its occupants can do but evacuate, until it passes. The only positive result of such an invasion, is that any scavengers to the maize supplies will quickly disappear.

When travelling into the surrounding bush on camping vacations, keeping food safe requires considerable ingenuity. Everything edible is an ant target and it appears as if the only truly safe location is suspended in mid-air. Food has to be wrapped in bags and a line erected that the bag can be suspended from. Make the line longer and increase the number of bags and there will be a better chance of having an ant-free container the following morning. People living in remote locations take unique precautions with any furniture holding food supplies. The furniture legs are stood in small containers of water, preventing any insect invasion. It is an application of siege conditions from these invaders. This is enough (perhaps) to stop an army in its tracks.

Heat, rain, animals and insects

The rain gives life and an awakening call to a myriad of insects. The life-giving effect of rain stirs every living thing, both plant and insect into a frenzy of growth. Pools of water heated by the relentless sun hatch the eggs of the dreaded malaria mosquitoes. They too seek shady places as a respite from the sun. Hiding under tables or dark corners, they only emerge when a victim comes within range. Their time comes as evening approaches and the usual heat breeze disappears. They use the ultimate in guerrilla warfare by attacking from camouflaged cover, striking the enemy and disappearing into the background darkness and obscurity.

The plateau terrain around our house on the Zomba Plateau slopes was home to many animals, as in the 1970s there was only the minimum of human dwelling. The encroachment of softwood planting for commercial purposes was still small enough to allow swathes of natural semi-tropical growth unrestricted access across its slopes. Typical savanna dwelling animals were frequently seen - even the occasional leopard, small troupes of baboon and naturally hordes of monkeys and a few antelope. All were hosts to ticks, which infested the long grass brought on by the season's rains.

Our housedog 'Hippy', a cross Alsatian with her long coat was a perfect home for these pests. She was very tolerant to the daily round of 'de-ticking' and seemed to acknowledge it was part of her daily routine. These creatures suck their victim's blood and in the process swell from being barely visible to a grey coloured oval the size of a peanut. Running one's hand along her coat felt the wart-like lumps that had to be picked off. It was something like plucking eyebrows. The blighters would find almost inaccessible attachments like the underside of eyelashes and the cavities of her ears. They were a deadly source of infection and an intolerable irritation. Hippy knew that their disposal was a reward for being patient. I can understand the bush animals' tolerance for the birds who straddle their backs and pluck off these parasites to eat, giving both cleansing to the host and nutriment to these airborne cleaning machines.

Hippy, possibly like all dogs, was a survivor. It was during a dry spell in the heat of the rains that the accident happened. She was at home in the garden, recuperating from an abdominal operation. Perhaps her stitches were removed too soon, or it was an erratic movement, but her wound burst and her intestines spilled out. For any animal, it was potentially life threatening.

Man and dog. The author with Hippy in our garden

Fortunately, Kathy was nearby and with characteristic coolness called to Humphrey our garden boy for assistance to keep the distressed dog quiet while she raced to the house for the first-aid bag. While Hippy attempted to lick her wounds, Kathy gathered dog and intestines into some towels and secured the whole package with medical bandages. Without this spontaneous intervention there would have been no chance of survival.

Hippy was lifted into the back of our car with Humphrey keeping her calm. There followed a speedy ride to the veterinary practice where Hippy was sedated, cleaned and stitched up again. After a massive dose of antibiotics she was back home. Whether this beautiful dog could survive such trauma no one knew. She lay on our cool concrete floor for around four to five days while Kathy gave regular antibiotic injections. She barely moved a muscle as we watched anxiously for tenuous signs of recovery, but there were little outward signs of a struggle for life. Then, suddenly she was standing, wanting food and apart from just a hint of weakness, seemed to wonder what all the fuss was about.

She was indeed a survivor. Had this situation occurred in England, it would have made headlines in a local paper. Kathy would have been hosted with an animal welfare award. This was a minor incident in a far away land where a struggle for survival is often part of everyday life.

In the open countryside, humans are almost as close as animals to the vulnerability of insect attack. It is not only ticks, but a host of many legged creatures have prospects of making you a part of their home. Ticks covered us after hacking our way through dense two metre high grass in a game park. A body inspection revealed myriads of the things to be picked from every part, from head, armpits, crotch, legs and feet. Our grooming lasted for a couple of hours and resembled the monkey groups who mirrored our behaviour high up in the trees. Our clothes either had to be discarded or soaked for hours before being fit for wearing again. Perhaps living out there, we would become closer to our ancestors and find it necessary to engage in this daily ritual. There was not so much difference between us after all. Looking back we would grin, but out there on the savanna, nature dictates and reminds us of who we really are.

**Surrounded by insects: top left: Bollworm Caterpillar;
top right: Elegant Grasshopper;
bottom left: African Mantis; bottom right: Armoured Corn Cricket**

Part of the animal kingdom

After several years of living in these surroundings, it was easy to adopt a certain affinity and closeness to all these creatures, a respect and appreciation that they all had a place and a part to play in the complex organization of life. This is not to say that all fear of whatever moved disappeared, but apprehension was replaced with fascination. Especially during the dry spells between the downpours, our garden on the slopes became a menagerie, as though it was a link route through which not only insects but also all manner of animal life must pass on its meandering route to find food or safety.

The house too became part of this animal kingdom. It was merely a concrete and wood block set randomly within this kingdom with open doors and windows to provide yet another way for various creatures to pass. Even though the house was cleaned daily, I found a scorpion on the bed mosquito netting and snakes curled up on the floor out of the hot sun. Four inch hunting spiders would make nightly incursions in a race across the floor, like scurrying mice and the termite ants would weave brown patterns across the white emulsion walls. In time they all became part of our world and were brushed outside even though they meant you no harm, they were merely travelling through a mutual territory.

A natural survivor

In the tropical world, rats are always close-by, even though they are rarely seen. They are both timid and will not provoke attention, but at the same time these creatures appear almost fearless in their search for food. Close encounters with these (usually nocturnal) visitors can with time and seeing each other often enough, result in a mutual respect. You keep your distance and they will keep theirs. In essence this attitude can well be applied to just about any of the creatures that live in your home, around it, or just pass through.

The more they visit and disappear when obviously not wanted, the more a familiarity with their presence starts to develop. But to drop your guard around the ones which could attack you can be disastrous, or at least remind you just to take that little bit more care and not be too familiar. To drop defences against mosquitoes could be disastrous; such as haphazard taking of anti-malarial tablets, or not bothering to use the cumbersome bed netting or repellant.

I have to acknowledge my familiarity with creatures also extended to rats, but it was a kind of mutual tolerance. They were not after you, they just wanted some of your luxuries and would occasionally venture inside to see what these luxuries were. There was no getting rid of them, so like many tropical creatures this tolerance was borne of seeing them so often, it was easy option to accept. The staff at my department would eat them if they could be caught. In Zambia they regularly raided the waste bin by the door and I got used to standing back when removing the lid, just to allow one of the furry intruders to jump out.

In Nairobi, during a cross-country journey, we stayed in a sort of overlander's rest house in the city suburbs. The rats had invaded the roof just above our bed, which was actually in the kitchen and proved to be an essential thoroughfare for all the lodgers. The rats must have been using the ceiling debris to make a nest and a constant trickle of straw was a night-time reminder of their endeavours to make a home. One of the residents was a French traveller hardened to cross country journeys. The rats nibbled through his bread each night, but undaunted, he trimmed off the remnants and consumed what was left, oblivious to the howls of disgust and laughter from the rest of us. In the Far East we have had rats who ate our soap and in Mumbai (Bombay) have stepped over them as they scurried along the pavement gutters. I have seen one jump over a cat in a restaurant as it made for an exit and watched one cleaning itself on the reception desk in a (admittedly seedy) hotel. These creatures are nature's survivors and I have no apprehension at their near presence. But we both instinctively keep our distance.

All creatures are a fascination

In Africa and the tropics generally it is not only insects that have adapted to the climate. They are bigger and more intrusive, but you become more tolerant of their presence. Perhaps it's just as well, for in a battle of who goes and stays, the insects will always win. It is we humans who must make an adjustment, a change of attitude. The climate enforces some of this change: the clothes you wear and how your house is built, for instance. Maybe the body's chemistry acts on an individual's personality to change attitudes to life.

The threshold barrier to tolerance is lowered; the heat and environment forces you to accept or adapt to a way of life, possibly alien to begin with, which would drive you to distraction in a cooler climate. Perhaps a brilliant blue sky, compared to grey days in the European north, brings a brighter, happier outlook, at least to some that is. Those who cannot, or will not adjust, must leave. An individual does not take on the climate and force it to conform. The heat carries with it an entourage of insects and their baggage of diseases that can have swift and dangerous retribution for those who let their guard (and defences) drop; they can establish themselves with a tropical vengeance. A balance must ultimately be struck, a harmony to be forced, between heat, rain, even diseases and those insects. It may even promote a force for enjoyment.

For a land drenched in sun even the indigenous creatures give way to its power and acknowledge it's a force not to be messed with. And it's when the sun goes down the creature domain comes into its own. Night-time in Africa and indeed anywhere in the tropics is when much of the wildlife comes out of hiding. In your home the ants are there day or night. But it's at night that the flying insects really emerge and with them their predators emerge too.

Sleeping behind pictures and curtains on house walls, behind shades on ceilings, gecko lizards with their translucent bodies are attracted by flying insects. Lights however dim are an attraction for these creatures. Held up by thousands of tiny suction pads all over their underside, these lizards wriggle out from their day-time hiding places and wait until a bedazzled winged visitor either settles or approaches within striking distance.

Especially during the rains, insects appear in quantity every night; moths appear with wings the size of saucers and colours like national flags, crawl along the light fittings. They move off after futile attempts by the geckos to make them a meal. These house lizards are cumbersome opportunists, their speed curtailed by a necessity to keep themselves anchored to the wall. When they get too anxious and speed up, their adhesion is often lost and they thud downwards onto whatever is below. There are many failed attempts to grab an airborne passer-by, but the night-life is so abundant it's not unusual to find several geckos patrolling a single living room wall.

Our garden, sheltered under the giant bluegum trees on the plateau slopes, was a menagerie of insects and creatures, which crawled, climbed or in some way found the territory a convenient traversing point to the forest beyond. Monkeys staged spectacular attacks on the vegetable plots. Usually at dusk, after the heat of the day had passed, their chattering army swung through the trees to attack and remove anything that took their fancy. They were adept at recognizing any new vegetables and tried anything that could be edible. These cheeky tree-dwellers became skilled at pulling up the choicest finds and then retiring back to the trees for a feast. The remnants were thrown back at our dog who barked and fretted below. These creatures resemble a genetic bridge between land-based creatures and birds, with their agility that seems acrobatic whether on the ground or in the trees.

Snakes could be detected by the way the grass quivered as their passage progressed. The tree snakes were my biggest surprise. I rescued a bird caught by one and was literally inches away before I realized what it was. The snake's camouflage was identical to the tree bark and only the movement with its prey gave anything away as to its identity. Land crabs would hesitantly dart in and out of the storm drains after deluges had disturbed their sanctuary.

The varieties of birds found on the plateau slopes were beautiful in the extreme and could only be surpassed in their exotic plumage by those residing around the lakeshore. Every day appeared to produce different varieties of snakes, lizards, chameleons and stick insects. It seemed as if the entire insect and animal kingdom was determined to transverse my territory. It was a botanist's dream. It was indeed a wonderful place to live and in all the years I resided there, familiarity never diluted its magnificence.

A big encounter

Travelling around Africa, it is extraordinarily rare to have close encounters with really big or dangerous animals. Even in this rugged domain the tragedy of over-exploitation has taken its toll, especially since the white man arrived. The local blacks, who discovered easy money could be made by selling rare souvenirs both to the legal and increasingly illegal overseas market, carried on the practice of extermination. It is a terrible indictment of what can happen over an entire continent within the course of less than a century. What magnificent animals still survive are in the game parks, which although not always secure, still provide the best means for their long-term survival.

Elephants enjoying a mud bath. Luangwa National Park

Our first visit to one of Africa's most remote parks was by road in 1971. This is the South Valley Luangwa Park in Zambia, which is reached by a (then) deteriorating dirt road through the crossing point from Malawi at Chipata. The Luangwa River forms a natural boundary to the park on its eastern side, by keeping the animals in and humans out. Kathy and I arrived at dusk and the rickety pontoon that carried cars across the

Luangwa River was closed. For late arrivals, there was a cleared patch of land close to the river and a nearby village, which could be used as a stopover until the pontoon opened the following day. We erected our small tent and were later joined by a solitary traveller who camped nearby. It never worried us that we were separated by a narrow stretch of river, from some of the most dangerous animals the continent could assemble.

During the early hours of a cloudless night, the moon rose and illuminated everything with an off-white glow, which dimmed the stars and silhouetted trees and bush against an off-black sky. The night stillness was disrupted when the tree some few metres from our tent began to shake and shed its dry season fruit sending it thudding to the ground. A sound of pounding and crunching interspersed between the shaking of the tree became more intense. Peeping from my tent at just above ground level I was face to face with a full size male tusker elephant who appeared oblivious to my presence in his eagerness to gather up the proceeds of his night-time assault on the tree fruit.

The size of the largest of the large land mammals viewed from close-range and from such a low spot represented something approaching dinosaur proportions. There was no rear escape for us in our tiny tent and I hesitated to clamber out front-ways towards this mountain of the jungle. My greatest fear was that he would simply walk through us, trampling down the tent and all it contained. Whether the elephant had scented us or not I had no idea; perhaps finding such a stash of food had diverted his attention.

In desperation I flashed the torch and clapped to let him know he was not alone on this side of the river. I suddenly realized that this was not a good idea, as he appeared to be startled and rearing his head high, bellowed loudly into the silent savanna night. It was at this point pandemonium erupted; the other traveller had been camped directly under the tree and had the disconcerting deluge of sticks and fruit descend on top of his tent. There was a frenzied shout and frantic scrambling.

"There's a whole herd coming through!"

I noticed a blurred shape as he scrambled out of his tent towards his vehicle. At which point Kathy trampled over me as she too made for our car. This was too much for our large interloper. Still watching from my low observation point at ground level, I saw him swing his head and flap his ears wildly as with loud trumpeting he made off through the nearby tall grass and thankfully away from the camping area. By now the small village was stirred and began lighting fires near to the entrance. The elephant could still be heard moving through the forest some distance away. I still spent the night in my tent, but the early red glow of dawn was a welcome sight.

The Luangwa Park has established walking safaris and is one of the most natural environments for wildlife on the continent. It has few roads, but a network of savanna trails. In a visit some years later, I joined a small group on a walking safari headed by a park ranger and guide. This was at the end of the dry season, a time with the best visibility as tall grass has been withered away by an intense sun and grazing by wildlife.

Our small group stayed in tents overnight near to waterholes and arose at dawn for a four to six hour hike through the trails. Without the noise and intrusion of a vehicle there was a sense of closeness to your surroundings and an awareness of nature. We remained hidden behind foliage while a herd of elephants passed by just yards away, apparently unaware of our presence.

The heat in the valley builds up during October, prior to the rains. By early afternoon, scorching temperatures are a warning to both man and animal to forget trekking and search out the shade. Everyone was thankful when the next camp was reached.

Hippo cooling off in Luangwa in National Park

The camps were basic bamboo and thatched roof constructions, brought to life not only by the groups pitching up after a hard day in the bush, but by their locations around waterholes. They often had their own surprises. My lodge was a roost for bats with upwards of fifty making a sudden dash for the newly opened door. A crocodile was resting in the shade as we approached one of our sites. He snapped angrily at the disturbance and slid reluctantly but gracefully over the bank into the cool of the waterhole. The hippos announced their displeasure at this intrusion into their space by a chorus of loud honking. As night-time approached other creatures encroached on the waterhole. From the viewpoint of our camp, it was a delight to experience the congregation of animal life seeking water after the day-time heat.

Showers were arranged from drums perforated to provide fine streams of cool water. The evening meals were illuminated by the light from pressure paraffin lamps and the myriad of sounds from night-time insects. Lavish amounts of food were somehow shipped in, with a substantial bar to match. The scene must have been reminiscent of what the early colonialists set-up on their up-country surveys decades before.

The only disturbance to our tranquil sleep came in the early hours one night. A pride of lions, possibly with young were in the vicinity and getting dangerously close. A whispered alarm quickly awoke all the camps occupants and loaded into two Land Rovers we made a quick evacuation. It was the kind of experience that emphasized the closeness these camps have to wildlife and make them such special places.

A preservation for wildlife

Zambia has some of the best wild life parks in Africa. And Africa has the best wild life parks in the world. Anyone who has been to these places of natural beauty and seen and experienced the primeval forces that are present, can only be moved. In these remote and often secluded areas, the emphasis is about nature and how it existed for the centuries before the encroachment of humans. Left to itself, with as few as possible contacts with the outside world, these places of beauty thrive. The more remote human contact is, the better.

Left alone these vast reserves will flourish. But they will only survive by a regular influx of visitors, who bring cash to the local economy and a trickle-down effect for the employment of people who keep facilities working. All this is the price for keeping national parks alive and encouraging tourists to continue coming.

National parks are a treasure house of species and fauna, very often not able to survive in a place subjected to human encroachment. But even national parks are not immune from the ravages of poachers. The local people who live around these sanctuaries are only beginning to understand the living treasure that has been there since the beginning of time.

Natural wildlife parks have an openness that is more than a physical reality of sky and terrain. Here the laws of survival are known and respected by all, even if they are loaded in favour of the strongest. Not all are places where the visitor must keep to the confines of safety in the lodge or car.

Such is the life in a little known national park in the south of Zambia called Lochinvar. The area extends for 33kms from the Kafue River in the north to low wooded hills in the south. The park is situated on the southern edge of the Kafue Flats, a wide floodplain of the Kafue River between the Itezhi tezhi dam in the west and the Kafue Gorge in the east. It is not known as a popular tourist destination, only appearing on official road maps of the country. With no dangerous animals, one can walk along its tracks and see panoramic vistas of the terrain. Without the inducement of seeing the 'big four', the number of visitors is small. There is a sense of peace in the place. A wide range of wildlife is there and the overwhelming sense of the primeval forces of nature is the most striking feature of the place.

A fragile environment for all

In this part of Africa there was and still is, a fragile balance of life between the animal kingdom and its human counterpart. I hope it can last forever. Perhaps the relentless surge of machines and population growth could be held back and somehow just pass by. But in the reality of today's world this is wishful thinking, and maybe a bit selfish. Local people living nearby deserve a better life too. These smallholder villagers tending their crops with a spoon of fertiliser for each plant of maize, must eventually give way to the already encroaching large-scale farming, for the benefit of all.

The needs of people and the natural environment must learn to coexist to the benefit of both. There has been enough destruction of the environment from decimated forests to destruction of the savanna. The best that can be hoped for is a balance between the needs of a growing population and the animal life already under threat. The national parks are a last resort.

In the headlong race for better returns and economic gains, short cuts are often taken especially where resources are tight. The disappearance of topsoil from cleared land in the deluges and risks of western-style pollution hazards such as run off from land over-doused with quick-gain chemicals, do not linger far behind. It is the price for hurried progress. When local conflicts occur, which has happened so often in Africa, with wars for independence and tribal rivalry, there are many losers and doubtful winners. The environment and wildlife have often been the losers. Once lost it is a difficult world to return to.

But some places still retain the ideal and the cascading streams are pure and clean and baboons still sit on the rocks along the dusty country roads. Perhaps progress will look back at its past mistakes and decide some places do not need its presence. With Africa on the threshold of industrialization, its environment will be under renewed threat. Perhaps the mistakes of the past will not be repeated. One must capture and enjoy the moment.

CHAPTER 14

Moving the masses: the enigma of public transport

TO TRAVEL outside the main centres of any post-colonial territory at this time required a positive outlook and a strong vehicle. Except for a major road link to the capitol city, most of the roads were in various stages of deconstruction. The vehicle traveller had to negotiate ridges, rocks, sand or mud and potholes, some of which would be close to swallowing the front of the vehicle. Many cross-country routes could be hazardous because of liberation wars or inter-ethnic fighting, with an assortment of freedom fighters, guerrillas, terrorists or just plain bandits. Picking the most suitable route, if there was a choice, was often a balancing act between choosing roads that were passable during the rainy season and a longer, less hazardous but better road surface. The distance between fuel stations and rest houses would be another factor. And in territories with local wars going on, finding reliable information about the conflict could make it questionable whether to go by road at all. For the majority of the population long distance travel demanded bus journeys, or occasionally rail. Shorter routes required either a pair of strong legs or an equally robust bicycle.

By popular choice - the bicycle

The casualty rate on the roads was high considering the low density of traffic. This was not only due to the reckless drivers and their unroadworthy vehicles - many which were way past their sell-by date - but to the throngs of walkers. Leaving work in the towns and getting to homes in surrounding villages or locations meant walking was the only option for many. The walkers or 'footers' as they were colloquially known, were fearless of traffic and stepped out without warning to flag down lifts. Drivers stopped oblivious to other road users, to load in paying customers or to shop at roadside vendors.

To this mix must be added the bicycle users who displayed an equally fearless contempt not only to the footers but also displayed insanity in their disregard of any danger to themselves or any other road user. Bicycles were ridden recklessly and many were in a desperate state of disrepair. Road travel was cheap but a hazardous affair.

Despite being much abused, there was a love affair with the bicycle and it pervaded throughout the whole of Malawi and Zambia. It was popular because it was the cheapest way of getting around, cost little to run and repairs were inexpensive. However, in remote villages even bicycles were essential status symbols that only few could afford. The bicycle was more than just a utility vehicle; it became a symbol of the country. It was the driving force of the working person. It carried their families, market goods, friends and anything else able to be strapped, balanced or laid across its frame from one village to the next, day after day. It was a friend and like all good friendships the owner kept the relationship intact by whatever repair was necessary.

Bicycles were either designed, or essentially resembled those of 1950s Britain. They were imported from either India or China and from their outward appearance had all the hallmarks of a robust form of transport. All refinements such as gears were absent - not only making a cheaper product but certainly less to go wrong. Brakes were rod operated and a carrying platform behind the rider was on all models. The abuse given to these machines was not intentional, it was just that a small truck would have best served the type of work they were expected to perform. It was the loads carried which tested the ultimate friendship between man and machine.

The life style of the bicycle started from day one on the rough tracks out to the villages. I have seen the village carpenter with a bed strapped across the rear carrier with an additional table and four chairs tied on top in an acrobatic balancing feat. The rider displayed all the nerve and heroism demanded in order to keep such a load on the road. And on the road it went, with the projections each side of the bicycle taking up  most of one side of the carriageway. As the assembly wobbled along, the traffic took this as just another obstacle to be weaved around.

Whole families would be transported by bicycle, with the mother side-saddled on the pillion seat with the baby on her back, while two children straddled the cross bar. Occasionally loads were so massive that they took over the whole machine with the owner reduced to pushing the bicycle while struggling to keep the whole assembly upright. Complete tree trunks were transported this way. I even saw a goat going home, sitting on the cross bar in front of the rider with its front hooves supported on the handlebars. In fact the bicycle is so integrated with the fabric of all southern African countries, it is so much a part of the everyday life of ordinary people, any discussion about transport would be incomplete without it.

The arduous working life of the bicycle took its toll and breakdowns were commonplace. Without the necessary appropriate tools some horrendous repairs were applied to keep it on the road. The bicycle generally survived such treatment and this seemed to validate the robustness of the machine. Buckled wheels were often forced into some form of roundness by bending the spokes, as proper spoke tightening tools were just not available. The not quite round wheel rendered the brakes just about useless as when they were applied, they either missed the rim completely or else jammed suddenly against an eccentric bulge and unless the brakes were quickly released, resulted in the rider being thrown over the handlebars. I once borrowed such a bicycle in what I thought would be a quick journey into town. The machine had undergone this wheel repair treatment and only my fast reactions prevented me from being just another of the road victim statistics. A whole new technique of bicycle control must be quickly mastered.

The frames too suffered from this severe maltreatment and frequently simply sheered off at the joints. Specialist welders were both expensive, fairly exclusive and were usually employed by garages and so out of reach of the ordinary villager. Even this disaster was not beyond the ingenuity of the local repair shop. The bicycle would be stripped of everything removable until only the frame remained and the whole thing placed on a furiously blown charcoal fire with the offending break as near to the hottest part as possible. The weld material was somehow applied to the red-hot frame and after cooling down and re-assembly was put straight back to full service. Suffice to say repeat breaks were frequent, with the whole process repeated. There was no such thing as the irreparable bicycle.

The indestructible mini-bus

For journeys within the larger cities with a correspondingly high working population and for many better pay packets, mini-buses were another addition to the transport maelstrom. The first traffic lights were installed in Malawi's capital Blantyre, in the early 1970s. Whether the addition of these poles with flashing coloured lights actually had a calming effect on the drivers is questionable. As mere pedestrians thronging the road did not impede drivers in their urgency to escape traffic chaos, blinking lights took some time to exert their influence. However, traffic lights are common in larger cities such as Lusaka. With seemingly hundreds of mini-buses plying the popular routes to the city centre, their presence at major intersections at least give the crazed drivers a brief respite.

I travelled on these buses for some time immediately prior to leaving Lusaka after my car had been sold. They had seats for around twenty passengers but frequently carried at least double that figure. As with all developing countries' bus systems, roof racks carried all goods larger than a suitcase. Although some form of licensing was in force, all the buses were privately owned with the drivers demonstrating an intense competition for custom. If the entrepreneurial spirit of enterprise displayed by the mini-bus drivers could have been applied in the rural areas it would have transformed life throughout the villages. The drivers were single-minded in their homing instinct for returning as fast as possible to the city centre. Their conductor held on to the side door, half in and half out, shouting their destination and being interrupted only by occasional forays into the interior for cash collection.

Whatever anxiety the passengers may have endured, it was seldom revealed

On the Lusaka urban routes fast turn-around times were essential. More money was to be made the faster the route could be run, with as many passengers packed in as possible. The driver had that fearless streak so essential to the mastery of urban traffic survival. He was the captain of a chariot of fire on a road to glory; he was impervious to other road users, especially pedestrians and bicycles. All larger vehicles were obstacles, which were simply weaved around; whatever else was encountered on the road was a lesser mortal who impeded his progress. Every journey was just another test of his skill in that invincible quest to make more bucks than the opposition.

On route the vehicle rarely completely stopped to drop off or pick up a passenger. The vital few seconds saved all added up. The constant rapid braking and screeching take-off, together with side-ways lurching played havoc with the vehicle's brakes and suspension and especially the passenger's nerves. Whatever anxiety the passengers may have endured, it was seldom revealed. As they sat or (usually) stood, their faces showed no emotion and one assumed they held a complete faith in the driver to get them to their destination in the shortest possible time. They were immune and insulated in their own world and appeared unconcerned with the road battle ensuing outside. They had grown accustomed to the danger. As the bus swayed and lurched they held on and swayed back in rhythm.

Roadside repairs

Although bicycles had an arduous life, the mini-bus had an equally violent existence as it was pushed to its limits around the city streets. It was a common sight to see running repairs being carried out along the routes and in the bus station itself. But repairs were only considered necessary if it was absolutely impossible to get the vehicle moving. No matter how lethal the vehicle may be on the road, as long as it was capable of moving and earning money, it was put to work. It was as if a return to the garage was to be avoided at all costs. Where the vehicle broke down it would be fixed - if at all possible. The 'have tools and will travel' repair specialists seemed able to virtually strip down and re-build a vehicle on the side of a road. Armed with only tools that could be carried in the back of a pick-up truck, they seemed capable of repairing anything but the most serious case of vehicle neglect.

By the side of the roadway even welding could be done and if the lifting jack was not high enough, piles of stones made-up the difference. The main mechanic always had several helpers whom he constantly shouted instructions to and if necessary all heaved together on the vehicle to get it a little higher off the ground. Amidst the constant chatter, the hammering of metal against metal, the replaced chassis parts and the array of tools, the vehicle would rise phoenix-like into a bus once more. In only a few feverish hours work, axles were replaced and engines coached back to life. The only signs left of the activity were pools of black vehicle oil.

The long distance bus

Many adventures started with the departure from the market of the inter-town bus. Although the generic term of 'bus' might describe their general features, their evolutionary history made them as adaptable to the African terrain as perfectly as a leopard is adapted for forest camouflage. They were robust single deckers, usually built on a lorry or truck chassis with a suspension, or sometimes lack of it, to match. What the buses lacked in speed they made up for in robustness. They were generally supplied by the Indian TATA company and across these two great continents this universal icon of cross-country travel clocked up thousands of miles.

The heavy diesel engine which was located alongside the driver was only semi-silenced and upon take-off the bus was obscured in a black-blue smoke cloud which belched from a street level exhaust. When accelerated hard the exhaust note had a high-speed crackle about it, something like a hot-rod street machine heard through earmuffs. The buses were inevitably battered with dents and heavily worn paintwork, often with missing windows. In fact, during my whole time in Africa, I cannot remember seeing a new bus. It was as if they rolled off some production line with 10,000 miles already clocked up.

The interiors were austere with tough plastic padded seating showing the effects of a hard life dished out by the travelling public. The space around the massive frame of the engine was often the reserve of passenger baggage; the only place passengers could store what would not fit on the roof. The roof area had a retaining frame to tie baggage to, with a rear ladder to gain access. The interior baggage space often extended the full length of the entrance and exit gangway between the seats from the door to the rear. In rural areas just about anything was taken on board. I am not sure what the actual limitations were, but I was convinced that anything that could not fit through the door or window after the roof was full, must have been discarded. However, any amount of time and ingenuity were taken by both passengers and crew to get the package on board.

Boarding through windows is allowed.
Long distance bus travel is often an adventure

I have been on rural buses with the aisle between the seats filled with scrap metal and bags of maize stacked halfway to the roof. Entry and exit was only possible by actually climbing up the side of the sacks, crouching over their tops and dropping off the other side. But it did mean there was a natural barrier to keep the small pigs and chickens in their place.

Travelling by public transport in developing countries is inevitably an adventure, which can be exhilarating or frustrating, but never boring. The experience really starts before departure and appears to blend seamlessly into the journey itself. It is as if all the confusion and chaos of the waiting time accompanies you on to the vehicle itself. It is a mechanism by which the western traveller can get the closest to local life without the insulation of tour buses and even taxis. It is a confrontation with the heat, jostling, noise, smells, delays and characteristics of the country. A ready-made package of culture, which you the traveller must interact with, adjust to, come to terms with and realise it is not a show. This is real life carried on by ordinary people, every day and in every town and city.

The market stalls come to the bus window

Long distance buses were notorious for their unpredictable departure times, often hours after the scheduled time. Passengers would start arriving with their *katundu* or baggage prepared for a wait, which they invariably did without complaint. The drink and food sellers from the adjacent market took advantage of this isolated transient group. The peaceful scene of the waiting passengers would explode into confusion as the bus came into sight amidst plumes of diesel smoke and swirling dust. The bus would be surrounded on all sides, not just a crowd by the door, with shouts and gestures between passengers and staff as to how their bags were to be placed. Bus staff on the roof manhandled all the bulkier goods aloft, while the interior filled up with passengers and none-roof cargo. The bus appeared to slip into the background as its outline blurred against the numbers of people and baggage either on the roof or standing around the windows pushing in plastic shopping bags or cardboard boxes.

Even at this stage the market food sellers were still either in the bus or handing their charcoaled maize cobs and packets of nuts in through the windows. It was a lengthy process. On all the bus journeys I took, the interior was so full of people and packages, I found it was just about impossible to move. What little access there was, the food vendors were certain to occupy. Anything I may have wanted to retrieve from my bag on the roof, would only have been possible by climbing out through the window.

The signal to leave was a series of loud horn blasts given some minutes before leaving and on the moment of departure. This was the final sign for the food vendors to depart from the bus. As the over-loaded vehicle gathered speed and headed towards the outskirts of town, the open windows provided a welcome breeze through the cramped interior amidst the multiple smells of goods and people.

From my vantage point on a window seat – always the window, as it was the only place guaranteed to receive fresh air when the bus stopped – I could observe Africa on the move.

Buses are a social experience

The long distance bus was not a place for relaxation. Along rural roads you could expect constant pounding from the truck-like suspension. This was usually associated with sudden, rapid braking to avoid obstacles and consequent fierce acceleration. Passengers were in a continual cycle of anticipated expectancy for the next sudden jolt. Through the open windows occasional clouds of red dust would blow in as vehicles passed, adding a misty transparency to the colourful interior. Passengers were used to this turmoil, and either chatted or sang while taking care of babies between eating the goodies from the food sellers. For me it was a new world, as different to a European bus journey as it was possible to get.

The effect of the wet or dry season on earth roads, largely determines the best (or worst) in cross-country journeys. But even on smooth paved roads, bus travel can always be relied upon to bring its own surprises. On a late-night bus, given the ubiquitous name of the 'night compost', on paved roads for the five hour journey between Zomba and Lilongwe I settled in to what I believed would be a routine trip. On one of the hill climbs towards the uplands of Dedza near the Mozambique border, a loud metallic crash brought the bus to a halt. The driver took the engine cover lid off and called out:

"Anyone with a torch please help out".

It appeared I was the only one, and duly assisted. Delving through the engine compartment it appeared that the alternator, or at least something which powered the lights, had fallen off. Another plea issued from the driver:

"Please everyone, off the bus and look for a large metal object".

It must have been a bizarre sight to passing motorists to see maybe thirty people in the middle of the night searching down the road behind the bus following me and my flashlight. Everyone fanned out over the hard shoulder, feeling in the gloom for a metal object amongst the stones. The bus driver shouted instructions as to what they should find, as passing headlights picked out the searchers as they combed a hundred metres or so of road behind the bus. As no metal object revealed itself, the driver decided to travel on with sidelights only. I could only see glimmers through the front windscreen, but he delivered us safely to our destination. Perhaps he was used to this, but being a bus driver in Africa brings out a resourcefulness and fearlessness which only bus drivers - and cyclists - can display.

When the bus does get going there are also delays caused by another hazard - the police or army roadblock. Delays caused by landslides or washed away bridges were monumental hazards that were always the acceptable trauma of travel. But the man-made imposition of roadblocks was different and a ripple of irritation throughout the bus showed it as though a mild electric current had been switched on causing people to shift slightly in their seats.

Papers were checked and loads inspected. Whenever there was an impending visit by a prominent dignitary, the frequency of inspections in that area increased. Or it may be that reports of insurgents necessitated investigation. Both Malawi and Zambia are landlocked countries with borders open to infiltration and together with the sensitive political climate it was really not surprising that check-posts were frequent. In rural areas with shortages of all kinds of basic goods, bribes of money or cigarettes or some other item not seen for a while, speeded-up transit through these irritations considerably.

Bus travel was therefore never a dull process. I am an advocate of using these people carriers for this insight not only into the physical process of travelling, but as a legitimate method to bring oneself into contact with ordinary people. Just by being on something as ordinary as a bus one can observe, talk, share some food and in a way be part of a community if only for a few hours. The acceptance by people of the disruption to their travel plans and the inevitability of things beyond their control, whether due to storms or breakdowns, comes across strongly during bus journeys. It is something that you do not learn but absorb by just being there. It is absorbed along with all the irritations and interruptions that you have to accept along with all the other travelling masses.

Being a traveller in Africa means you quickly accept this is the way things are. Irritations are displaced by the timelessness of the traditional way of life and the hospitality of the people sitting around like you waiting for the bus to be repaired. I came to realize that the organized and efficient western way of travel, where regulations and guide-lines cover everything from the exact number of passengers to the size of cabin baggage and the trauma exerted by being a few minutes late departing, do not count for excitement or adventure. The packaged holiday concepts of 'meeting the people' will rarely approach the spontaneity and the real life situation of an ordinary bus journey.

Like so much in Africa, what regulations do exist are seldom followed. All the chaos this brings, seldom registers in people's faces. Look at the chatting people and wide-eyed children and in the way they go about their daily activities, seems to suggest lives without the need for rules. Life is like waiting for the seasonal rains to start. People are thankful for the most fundamental events of nature, to make their lives worthwhile.

Negotiating the roads

Many of the roads in Africa have the dubious reputation of being amongst the worst in the world. Although newly hard surfaced major routes between cities can be of good quality and regularly maintained, these are still the exception. Cut price construction contracts and even more savage reductions in maintenance budgets, often lead to a road little better than it was before work started. The excellent Michelin maps were the *de facto* reference manuals, but even these could not keep pace with the rapid changes in road conditions. The ravages of deforestation with the consequent flooding during tropical storms can wash away sections of road or produce endless potholes. The continual wear and tear of heavy long-distance trucks, often over-loaded, brake up the surface still further leaving a driver's nightmare of ridges, holes, gullies and gaps where you assumed the road should be.

Maps showing unpaved surfaces are a particular cause of concern to the cross-country driver. These can be anything from smooth through to almost impassable and can change overnight when the rainy season is in full force. Perhaps if the president or his aides had been along this way recently, then you were in luck, for the surface would have undoubtedly been smoothed by a so-called 'road grader'. When travelling through remote areas, local knowledge from fellow road-users is invaluable. It could well prevent miles of travel only to find sections of road impassable or bridges collapsed. On any cross-country journey, the displays of wrecks of vehicles not robust enough to take on such a battering are a constant reminder of the hazards involved. Even on well-maintained highways there are continual examples of black tyre marks streaked across roads and the shredded remains of tyre treads strewn along the verges.

A tough truck chassis and rock hard suspension are essential to keep buses on the road. Even so it is not unusual to see them swaying lop-sided and making crab-like progress along the rural roads. Any vehicle negotiating unpaved roads (occasionally even tarred roads), require truck-like durability. In the dry season these roads turn into rivers of sand with central ridges reminiscent of the ripples on sand dunes transversing the surface. However, these ridges are rock hard and are not produced by wind, but by the constant pounding of vehicle tyres. Consequently, unless these roads are navigated at speed, with the tyres clipping only the ridge tops, the battering on any vehicle can shake it to pieces, together with the occupants.

To pass on-coming traffic it will often be necessary to veer towards the road edge and hit the soft sand, usually resulting in back-end slides with the ejection of immense clouds of dust all around the vehicle. This usually enters the interior and coats all within in a red haze. It can be virtually impossible for any vehicle to overtake safely as all around is enveloped in a swirling red haze. Approaching traffic can be easily identified a kilometre away, even when normally invisible from over a hillcrest, by the column of dust churned up, rising in the air like a whirlwind. It's reminiscent of seeing the light from a distant car's headlights as it approaches at night.

Conversely, the opposite occurs during the rains with tracks of paved roads being washed away and rural roads often rendered impassable. Where roads are passable, huge ruts are gouged out and fill with dark-red water. The spray dries like a dye on the vehicles' sides and look as if a giant has been having fun with an enormous spray can. Unless vehicles can squirm their way past these ruts, it can take rally skills to keep a vehicle on the road. Even the high clearance of buses with their double-wheel traction is no guarantee of escape from the obstacles. It is a common sight to see bogged down buses with their passengers encamped on the roadside while efforts are made to dig the vehicle out.

This could take hours and with a bus angled across the road, attempts by other road users to get by produces some extraordinary displays of skill. Roadsides are built up and branches hacked to fill ridges. Teams of drivers, and passengers from stranded vehicles become maintenance crews. With shouting, pulling and pushing, they cajole their vehicles around the obstacle and hopefully towards a clearer road ahead. But while a cheer goes up for the fortunate few, many get bogged down into an even worse quagmire. Vehicles are spread like thrown dice into a sea of mud. For the bus passengers, who are a pretty tolerant lot anyway, they sit passively by, chatting and opening their food reserves. It is well-deserved entertainment.

Trucks – kings of the road

People do not travel between cities and towns only by bus. However sturdy bicycles are, they are really not up to the job. For those who can afford them, cars and motorcycles provide the most luxurious choice of transport, especially when their transport costs can be funded by the hordes of hitchhikers found on most roads. Trucks are always an optional extra and whether full or empty of goods, will often have a second cargo of passengers either in the empty rear or stacked on top of whatever goods are being transported.

Typical of one such long-distance truck ride was when I returned to Zambia in the early 1980s with Kathy and my son Lloyd. We took a ride on a colleague's transport truck between Lusaka and Kariba, famous for the Kariba Dam, third largest man-made lake in the world. We rode with the driver in the cab, with an assistant seated on the goods in the back. It soon became apparent why the vehicle was driven so cautiously. Our passenger door would not close and closer inspection revealed it was held in place by a self-opening latch that was prone to disengage whenever the vehicle made the slightest right-hand turn. A still more disconcerting discovery was that the braking system seemed to decide for itself whether or not to operate.

The descent of hills was particularly unnerving, as the faulty brakes would not slow the vehicle adequately, which meant some bends at the bottom had to be over-shot and then the truck reversed back to negotiate the turning. During one gruelling hill climb an explosion from the rear signalled a tyre had punctured. Fortunately it was a double-wheel axle and the second tyre held. There was no question of stopping on the hill as the brakes would never have held, so an inspection had to wait until the relatively flat summit was reached. As with so much of life in Zambia the simple act of changing a wheel focussed the day-to-day problems ordinary people had to face in a country where just about anything was either not available or in short supply.

The shortage of commodities extended to a critical shortage of tyres. Locally made re-treads were not up to the demands of overladen vehicles pounding through rut and pot-holed roads. The spare tyre was a larger size than the other wheels. With the vehicle jacked up and the spare wheel in place, its larger size prevented its smaller partner on the axle from contacting the ground. But any wheel is better than none and on we went. We were fortunate to have a driver who knew the limitations of his vehicle. This hazardous route was littered with the remains of vehicles and shredded tyres, testimony to drivers who strayed over those limits.

The awe-inspiring Kariba Dam

After formality at customs, we walked into Zimbabwe across the magnificent Kariba Dam. From the approach road high above the Zambezi River we could look down upon this structure, a man-made mountain of concrete with precise geometric form bridging the ruggedness of the sheer rock faces of a natural gorge. Its curved singular biceps of stone are flexed to force back a 200-kilometre lake of fresh water for power generation. Its statistics cannot be comprehended unless seen. The dam wall is 579 metres long and contains nearly one million cubic metres of concrete. This structure can control 9,000 cubic metres of water a second and has a drainage system that has eroded a 60-metre-deep fissure in the river-bed. Kariba dams the Zambezi River and is topped by a 21-

metre-wide dual-lane 'highway' which straggles across its top and gives views on one side of the lake disappearing into the horizon.

The awe-inspiring Kariba Dam

I found it awe-inspiring enough to discover the mighty Zambezi had been dammed, but the magnitude of this construction was truly inspiring. From the opposite wall, a drop of 128 metres shows a trickle of the once mighty river. Its full majesty is only regained at the height of the rains when the sluices of the dam are opened and enormous overflows produce a raging torrent.

There are many legends that accompanied the construction of the Kariba Dam. In the upper Zambezi Valley, the *BaTonga* people were threatened with displacement by the rising lake waters. They called upon the fish-headed and serpent-tailed Zambezi River God, *Nyaminyami* and asked him to intervene in order to preserve his own environment and assist the *BaTonga* people to return to their original homes. There were two disastrous floods during construction of the dam and it was believed *Nyaminyami* was responsible. The tribespeople believe the dam separated *Nyaminyami* from his wife, and the frequent earth tremors since the wall was built are caused by the spirit trying to reach his wife. Many tribespeople believe *Nyaminyami* will one day fulfil his promise to destroy the dam and allow his people to return to their homes.

Walking across the dam wall into Zimbabwe is possibly the most impressive entrance into any country.

CHAPTER 15

Against all odds – the railways

WHEREVER THE British went the train was soon to follow. The history of railroad construction during colonial times was of immense importance in the opening up of the continent. The stories of these massive projects provide a fascinating account of the skill and courage of these early engineers. It is a testament to the determination of the construction workers in overcoming the physical rigours in what was in many areas, uncharted territory. It was not only the isolation of the country and the difficulty of obtaining supplies which made these projects monumental, but attacks by animals and the toll taken by tropical diseases were part of the price paid by these early pioneering railroad builders. It was to become the material of legends. Whether in India or Africa, railways were constructed as an economic lifeline to move goods and people across vast distances. Armies of workers were brought in to construct tracks through impossible terrain. River gorges and mountain passes were crossed using little more than the timber and stone hacked from the countryside as the line inched its way forward. One of the most infamous was referred to as the 'lunatic express', a 2,350-kilometre track running from Kampala in Uganda through Kenya to Nairobi and Mombasa on the coast. The railway transformed and opened up the territory as it went. This cannot be more dramatically demonstrated than by a service station, originally built for railway maintenance, which was eventually to become the sprawling city of Nairobi. The railway was indeed the catalyst for change.

The TAZARA railway

In recent times the only rail construction project of similar scale and grandeur was the TAZARA rail link from Lusaka, Zambia, to Dar-es-Salaam in Tanzania. The project was also known as the *Uhuru Railway*, a *Swahili* word for Freedom Railway, and the Tanzam Railway). This 1,860-kilometre rail venture was constructed between 1970-75 by the People's Republic of China. At this time both Zambia and Tanzania had strong communist ideals and saw a rail link between the two countries as a political allegiance and a means of shipping Zambian goods - especially copper - to the seaport of Dar-es-Salaam.

Existing rail and most road links from Zambia going south through Rhodesia had been severely disrupted because of border closures brought on by the liberation war in Rhodesia. Increasing sabotage by freedom fighters in their attempts to cut supply routes to Rhodesia, resulted in Zambia being almost unable to get its copper out and essential goods in. After completion, the TAZARA line was handed over to the Zambian government, but maintenance and management of such a complex structure was never going to be easy and it soon became inefficient with major logistical problems. But whatever its later difficulties, it still ranks as a major achievement in railroad construction.

The project was originally rejected by western aid agencies as being unfeasible and grossly expensive. But the Chinese, already a supplier of weapons and manpower in the liberation war in Rhodesia and always willing to gain influence in developing countries, came to the rescue. They imported everything for the project - a labour force of over 50,000 Chinese, supplies, materials, transport and an infrastructure costing some $500m, necessary to put it all together. The harsh and remote terrain took a disastrous toll on even the rugged Chinese with many deaths from disease and accidents. A cemetery exists near to Dar-es-Salaam with a marble plinth recording their heroic achievement: 'Cemetery for the Memorable Deceased Chinese Experts Assisting Tanzania'. What the Chinese achieved then, is being re-enacted in the 21st century as they return to the continent, trading building projects for access to raw materials.

Railway history being made

Although I was resident in Malawi during this time, I saw part of this construction during a visit to Zambia in 1971. I watched from the road that traversed one section of the track and saw how desolate bush land had been converted into a construction site. It was as if a giant spade had scraped the landscape for as far as the eye could see. Red dust was thrown up not by monstrous yellow coloured earthmovers so common today, but by innumerable, smaller, dark green road scrapers. Blue clothed workers so reminiscent of Mao days were scattered in endless gangs as far as one could see through the haze. The scene had a force the early rail pioneers would surely have been proud of. The view from a distance emphasised their numbers and gave a reminder of what such a force can achieve.

The heat haze made the landscape into a constantly changing, living entity with shimmering patterns of red dust through which the blue clothed workers emerged and faded. Small trucks ferried up and down the newly laid track. The trucks had split windscreens and individual mudguards with protruding headlights. They were all very utilitarian and ideal for the territory they were despatched to conquer. These were the vehicles with all the hallmarks of being made in China, long before the country became a manufacturing base for the world. Everything mechanical in that landscape was made as practical and uncompromising as the terrain itself. They could be repaired with the most basic of spares and what was not available could be made with transportable workshop tools.

Later generations of western produced trucks necessitating a support factory of skilled technicians and circuit boards, fell by the wayside for lack of simple repairs. As far as I am aware there was no attempt by the Chinese to integrate with the local population. At night they retired to their own communes and probably studied Mao's teachings while they planned what the next day's activities were going to be.

A centre for steam. Bulawayo marshalling yards

When I eventually came to work in Lusaka, I took this rail journey part of the way north to where a branch line connected to the Copperbelt town of Kitwe. I never did cover the full route, but even partway was something special. Both Zimbabwe and South Africa have longer and more famous rail networks. The rail link from Lusaka to the west coast of Africa through Angola to the port of Benguela is longer. But there is no recent construction of this scale. For such a unique piece of modern rail construction it is almost forgotten. It is not often one can travel on a track which covers nearly 2,000 kilometres across two countries and have witnessed its construction. It was a feat of rail construction made with equal quantities of both manpower and machines. Neither city is cited as a tourist destination and attracts little foreign attention. The TAZARA railway is uniquely built and is a tribute to its constructors, but this huge project was built for a political and practical purpose that has essentially been assigned to history.

Malawi railways

In Malawi the railways did not have the legends or the scale displayed by its neighbour. But as a landlocked country, there was a network that linked the lakeshore, through to the capital Blantyre and on to the seaport at Beira and Ncala in Mozambique. It was an essential lifeline to transport heavy freight, as the roads at this time were not only in extremely poor condition, but prone to be washed away - as indeed was the track, but not quite so often.

The rail links were essentially for long distances but journey times were much slower than that achieved by the hair-brained bus drivers, despite the difficult road conditions. The state of the track in any case made even moderate speed a hazard. As the route invariably went through bush areas the possibility of large animals on the track was a constant danger. In Malawi the route in the south of the country dropped into the Shire Valley, the lowest area in the country, and only marginally above sea level. It was very remote, but for those travelling through the region it provided spectacular views of the Shire River falls and rapids. It was also the poorest area of the country, incredibly hot during the rains and suffered from either extremes of flooding or drought.

The trains were driven by robust steam engines, presumably purchased from Mozambique or Rhodesia Railways, which were almost exclusively steam even until the late 70s. But slowly an influx of diesel driven machines started to make an appearance. They tended to have even more flexible timetables than the inter-city buses. The one or maybe two per day which tended the route along the lakeshore passed very close to a mission station. It was here they routinely picked up a missionary and if he were still at his mid-day lunch the train would be halted while he finished his meal.

Delays of this nature were well accepted by the travelling public, most of whom were villagers who arranged their day by the angle of sun and not by the clock hour hand. For many there was nothing that was particularly important to be done this day in any case. Even meeting their family and friends at the next stop was a flexible affair. There would be no pacing along the track or looking at timetables. They would wait around and gossip until the train arrived. It was not an empty time. Everything in Africa takes time, whether it will be for the rains to start or for the local authority to provide a village water borehole. And the wait could be put to good use with family discussions and children's playtime. The train would wait and get going when the driver thought it was good and ready.

Getting on and going

Around the carriages and platform the pent-up energy of the waiting travellers would suddenly erupt into chaotic movement as the train came to a squealing stop, its clanging bell hardly needed to warn of its arrival.

Conditions on board a train were similar to the bus, only the train had even more carrying space. The crowds waiting were larger and the number of bags squeezed through the doors suggested something inside must have been devouring them all. The fact that it was necessary to put all baggage inside instead of on the roof as the buses allowed, could well have resulted in even greater overcrowding. But somehow carriages appeared to swallow it all. Trains stayed at major stations for half-an-hour or more and this enabled the most skilful piling of baggage into the seemingly inaccessible locations of the carriage.

The steam age. Water is carried in the front tender

The packages that were handled up the carriage entrance reflected the essence of the African traveller; no designer styled carrying cases with snap-shut handles and pulling wheels. In their place were canvas bags held together with plastic cord; cardboard boxes and large plastic buckets that were once used for transporting water from the village well and now served as an open topped carrying case. Most were delivered to the train steps by sturdy women with well-balanced head loads and usually a child wrapped around their backs. Some 1950s style brown suitcases with reinforced corners would occasionally appear carried by men in suits. All the colours that the fabric stores could supply appeared to be in motion as the passengers pushed and pulled packages through the doors and windows and handed children up to out-stretched hands.

It was a scene re-enacted whenever a train arrived anywhere in the country. Passengers getting off a train needed to be quick, so as not to be crushed by those struggling to get on; it was as though the carriage would suck everything in, the people, their children, their packages and slot them into hitherto inaccessible places. There never seemed to be occasions where anyone or anything would be left behind; the train would find space and at the same time, tame the scrambling and impose an imperfect order. All the noise, colour, smells and confusion of the market place were present and showed the unique and timeless way Africa travelled. Children sold their little packets of peanuts and the charcoal smells of baked corn drifted along the platform and in through the open windows.

For the well-off train traveller the luxury of first-class carriages provided a world of difference from the chaos and crowds of the lowly third-class corridors. Second-class provided better seating, but it was only first-class with its spacious seats and even sleeping accommodation that revealed the real gulf between the ordinary and the elite traveller. Although sleeping even in first-class was often difficult with the clattering tracks and the continuous jarring of the carriage, it did provide a far better chance of a restful night than that endured by the masses in the next carriage squeezed on to wooden benches.

Anyone who may have (fortunately) fallen asleep on these journeys would find that night-time travel would be interrupted not only by the whine of mosquitoes, but by frequent and long blasts from the whistle. The hazardous nature of night-time travel prompted a more cautious attitude by the driver. I had no argument to this, as anything slower must be safer. In Africa the pace of life dictated a slow careful approach to everything, but the buses, bicycles and trucks appeared at odds with this. But it was a challenge they undertook at their peril. The ponderous, leisurely progress of the train had a comforting almost trustworthy air about it, as though you were more certain about arriving.

There were always numerous stops at places where it was difficult to determine whether it was a scheduled stop or merely a rest break. During night-time, the all enveloping blackness of the savanna night would give little clue as to what was going on outside. Getting under power again was always accompanied by more whistle blasts and jolting of the carriages as the load was taken up once more.

CHAPTER 16

Transport on Lake Malawi - the 'flame' lake
From pre-history to modern times

A LAND-LOCKED country with no direct access to a seaport must count its blessings when it contains a fresh-water lake covering a fifth of the country. Lake Malawi is such a blessing. At 570 km long and 80 km across at its widest point, this vast body of water is the third largest lake in Africa, with something over 500 species of fish. No-one is quite sure how many, and more are constantly being found. It has a depth of 700 metres in the area to the north of Nkhata Bay, with the lakebed actually below sea level. This magnificent lake provides not only a sustainable diet for the people, but also regular and cheap transport up and down the country both for people and goods. It is also the country's most important tourist attraction. So it is not surprising that lake transport figured prominently in Malawi's early history.

An early magnet for settlers

Lake Malawi is sited on the Great Rift Valley, formed in the Jurassic Age over 100 m years ago. The lush conditions must have been a magnet for invaders. The original settlers, the *Akafula*, settled on its shores around 500 B.C. They were a hybrid descent of Bantu from the equatorial forests and migrating Bushmen from North Africa. They were a race of dwarfs, their name literally means 'diggers from the soil', skilled in ironwork. The *Akafula* did not cultivate, but were a race of hunters, with plentiful game all around the lakeshore. The vast majority of these early settlers disappeared about 400 years ago, although the last remaining people were still to be found as late as 1800. The vista of the lake has changed little over more than 2,000 years and to the *Akafula* people, it must have looked like it does today. However, their idyllic life was always a fight against the blood disease bilharzia, prolific around the lakeshore, which almost destroyed them.

Other migrants followed, principally the Bantu from the equatorial forests further north. These were the *Amaravi* from the *Luba* country in the Congo basin and they appeared by the lake around 1300. Ethnic strife took its toll with the Bantu who hunted to extinction the original Bushmen settlers. The lake has experienced turbulent times.

The 'modern' explorers

The explorers from Europe were comparatively late arrivals. An early Portuguese map of 1546 shows 'Maravi' or Malawi meaning 'flame'. This probably is derived from the colour of light reflected by the lake in the setting sun. Although the lake's discovery has been popularly credited to the missionary-explorer David Livingstone, the first white man to visit Lake Malawi was a Portuguese trader, Gaspar Bacarro in 1616. The achievements of these early explorers are outstanding examples of endurance. Bacarro took samples of silver discovered by Diogo Simoes Madeira and attempted to get the discovery back to Lisbon. It is reported he trekked over 1,000 kilometres in 53 days. This was through virtually unknown territory and his survival in hostile conditions was a feat of determination against adversity. Whatever happened to the silver discoveries is not known as there are no silver mines in the country.

A difficult lake to find

Popular 'modern' history of the lake began with David Livingstone, who referred to it as 'the lake of stars' at his first sighting in January 1859. Encountering this inland sea was not his original intention, as the giant Zambezi River, his 'God's Highway', was the preferred route to the discovery of this vast continent. But it was not to be. After entering the Zambezi in 1858 in his ocean-going steamer the *Pearl*, the vessel proved too large and bottomed on the numerous sandbanks. This voyage of discovery was abandoned at Tete, in Mozambique, some 450 km inland.

A smaller steamer the *Ma Robert*, was acquired to get over these difficulties, but also suffered the small fate. It still took two months to reach the same place. Not to be abandoned a second time, the vessel was hauled through the shallows, with the stores off-loaded and manhandled until deeper water was reached. The toll from heatstroke and fever was an ever-recurring nightmare in the depths of the Zambezi valley. After a further two months of slow and exhausting progress, the impassable Kebrabasa Cataracts finally halted the expedition. These proved impassable to any ship and the termination of any further exploration.

What made this doubly infuriating to Livingstone, was that he had neglected to explore this region on an earlier expedition and had not realized that a sloping lie of the land would ultimately result in cataracts at some point. A return was inevitable. However, Livingstone had heard of this inland sea, the 'Nyasa', and turned initial failure into success. A tributary of the Zambezi, the Shire River was some 250-300 km from Tete and this would lead to 'his' lake. With the other expedition members, his brother the Rev. Charles Livingstone, Dr John Kirk and Rae George, the wide mouth of the Shire River was entered with the *Ma Robert* on New Year's Day, 1859.

Exploring the lake

It proved to be no easy sailing and another six months to sight the lake. The party were stopped once again by impassable rapids, named by Livingstone as the Murchison Cataracts, after his friend Sir Robert Murchison. This time by-pass roads were built. After passing through the smaller Lake Malombe, the goal of entering Lake Nyasa was reached. The 'modern' exploration of the lake followed in 1861 and continued over the next few years.

With such an expanse of water, other ships were soon deemed necessary for essential transport. In 1863 the *Lady Nyassa* was brought out as deterrent to slavery in 1863. This necessitated intercepting the slave boats on the lake. It was dismantled for the journey by sea and transported through the by-pass roads before being reassembled. The engineering skills necessary to complete these assignments in such remote locations, just a few years after the first explorers arrived, are a testimony of the skill and workmanship of the British builders and the local workshop teams. It was not just the hazardous terrain itself, which was treacherous enough, but there were constant attacks from wild animals and fatalities from a myriad of tropical diseases.

The first complete circumnavigation of Lake Nyasa was completed in 1875 with the arrival of the steamship *Ilala*, named after the district where Livingstone died. This was a truly geographical survey, completed by Young and Laws and another five European expedition members. During this survey they came across evidence of the Arab slave trade. The next few years were to see considerable fighting to eradicate the traders from the lake. As they discovered the numerous bays and mountain ridges which crowd the lakeshore, they were given the names of friends and relatives, all remaining established for years, until systematically replaced after independence.

Lake Malawi is notorious for its treacherous storms. The fragile steamboats first used by the missionaries were a risky means of transport. Their sailing boat the *Sheriff* was overturned in a gale in 1895. But it was not long before more substantial steamers were to make their appearance. The *Mpasa* provided a service throughout much of the early 20th century, but with increasing demands of freight and passengers and even in this early period, the first tourists, a replacement was urgently sought. Finally, in the early 1940s, a suitable ship was found, despite the Battle of the Atlantic still being waged. The *Vipya* was delivered from England in sections and landed at the port of Beira. Like a mechanical jigsaw puzzle, the pieces were brought by river freight and hauled overland, for reassembly at Monkey Bay on the lakeshore. Once again, an achievement for the engineers concerned.

By 1945, she was the largest ship to sail the lake. But the *Vipya* was doomed to follow the fate of other, smaller craft that had challenged the lake's ferocity. There had been concerns about her safety and high superstructure, which would make her top-heavy. Within a year she lay at the bottom of the lake after attempting a crossing in appalling storm conditions. There was considerable loss of life and a court of enquiry set up to investigate the cause. No blame was ever established and there was a feeling the tragedy had been covered up to avoid recriminations towards the local colonial rule. Even reports of recovering the bullion reputedly being carried were never investigated. The memory of the *Vipya* incident has faded into the lake's history.

The *Ilala*, **flagship of the 'modern' fleet**

From the 1950s, a new small fleet of steamers plied the length of Lake Malawi. The flagship is the replacement *M.V. Ilala*, constructed by the Glasgow shipbuilders, Yarrow in 1949. With a weight of 620 tons, a length of 172 feet and a beam of 30 feet 6 inches, the *Ilala* is by far the largest vessel on the lake. As with all the ships, starting with the earliest missionary vessels, the *Ilala* was transported by the same exhausting route. Due to her size, the challenges were that much greater. She was shipped out by sea and rail, to Monkey Bay via the Mozambique port of Beira. It was another feat of engineering as the ship was broken down into eighty crates, the heaviest weighing eighteen tonnes. I wonder whether those northern shipbuilders ever stopped to marvel at the journey their offspring was to make and how durable she proved to be. In the 1940s, such a remote destination in the heart of Africa was to most, a truly distant place and one few would ever visit.

She was launched on 6 September 1951 with a grand show presided over by the Bishop of Nyasaland. The *Ilala* is a sturdy workhorse and after several refits and despite the abuse of tropical storms and daily service, still plies the lake today. Her original steam engines were replaced by modern diesels in 1995. These are preserved in a lakeshore museum. After a refit in 1972 some of the original superstructure and the funnel were replaced. The new fittings gleam awkwardly against the weathered steel of the old hull, which now displays the wrinkles of old age like any lady of this vintage. Some fittings are still retained, like the original Shanks plumbing in the main cabins.

The ravages of time now show its effects after decades of the constant unpredictable lake weather and the battering endured by transporting an assortment of cargo only Africa could produce. The steel plates of the hull are now displayed as a concave series of ripples, with the original internal frames projecting every metre or so like ribs. Now and then, new plates are welded into place, but the battered hull, still intact after being riveted together more than half a century ago, is testimony to the craftsmanship of its builders.

Essential transport

The demands of reaching isolated outposts on the lakeshore, especially in the north, resulted in two other vessels being brought into service. The *Nkhwazi*, built by Yarrow Shipbuilders in 1956, together with its cargo-only companion the *Mpasa*, reach every settlement, many isolated from roads. These 'modern' lake steamers are only a century older than the first ship to ever enter the lake. A time when the northern reaches were still ravaged by Arab raiders and battles by *Angoni* warriors. It is difficult to contemplate what has occurred within this relatively short span of time.

The contrast of African lake travel to its western equivalent is emphasised in the passenger distribution. Eleven cabin class passengers occupy top deck luxury. This descends into a turmoil of humanity as the main deck is approached. First come the 28 second-class passengers and finally the 320 (at least officially, but probably more) third-class passengers on the main deck. Together with their *katundu*, people of all ages sit, sleep, walk, comfort babies, prepare their meals and attempt to find whatever shelter can be found. The cacophony of noise and colour that the travellers display is only equalled by the dazzling colours of the lake and the beauty of the lakeshore.

As the ship slowly leaves harbour amidst numerous horn blasts, one wonders at the sheer variety of life and assortment of cargo that has been swallowed up in the ship's cavernous interior. On stormy crossings as the ship rolls and waves wash over the handrail, shelter is a rare finding. The journey on the *Ilala*, for most people, is more than just getting from place to place. It is about life on the move, with ordinary people often carrying most of what they own, returning to a home they left long ago, perhaps to find work. The ship unites families.

The image of the lake is captured by possibly its greatest exponent, Oliver Ransford, in *Livingstone's Lake*:

'Ilala II' is more like a yacht than a ship, and all sense of time is lost during the sunlit idyll of her voyage. The days dissolve into a kaleidoscope blur of gold and blue and green; the tourist guesses the time by his appetite, and recalls the date only by scheduled calls at out-of-the-way places that have the most tenuous connections with the outside world. . . .

Each day on board, amid the excited bell ringing, siren shrieks and hooting that seem inseparable from all maritime arrivals and departures, laughing crowds of Africans line up on the Ilala's decks to disembark, cluttered up with baggage that includes bicycles, cages filled with squawking fowls, sewing machines and even tethered goats. They are ferried ashore in lighters to return an hour or so later crammed with another batch of passengers who quickly settle down in the cramped quarters to cards and singing and sleeping and the preparation of meals in little cooking pots.

Around the lake in seven days

The *Ilala* covers over 1,000 km on a seven day round trip, carrying cargo

**Visitors are rare in Usisya on the shores of Lake Malawi.
Kathy with excited children**

and passengers to twelve destinations. A number of isolated locations in the northern regions of Lake Malawi are so remote, it is their only viable means of contact with other areas of the country. No moorings exist in many of these stops; the ship drops anchor some hundred or so metres off shore. Such a location is the lakeshore village of Ruarwe, cut off from the interior of the country by the mountains of the Great Rift Valley to the west. As soon as the ship is sighted, dugout canoes paddle from the shore as the supply boat is lowered for its weekly delivery. Children swim in the warm waters and wave excitedly as the ship passes. It may be the last time they will see visitors until its return.

As business is conducted from canoe to ship, the scene is reminiscent of those 19th century encounters of ships visiting remote South Sea Islands. The scramble for the rope walkway is intense, as people, baggage and babies, push to off-load and arrivals struggle to get on. The stay is officially one hour, but like most activities in Africa, is dependent on whatever seems important at the time.

Provided you can reach the gangway, the canoes will happily take you ashore. These are precarious craft, with naturally round bottoms, they roll, sway with what seems to be the slightest provocation and one wonders at the paddlers skill in keeping them upright. These centuries old craft still maintain a relationship that is inextricably linked to the traditional villages that line the lakeshore. When Kathy and I voyaged around the lake, this was the usual ship-to-shore transport we chose. In any case, it was a unique experience to travel in such craft. Just sitting required a particular skill. It is rather like balancing on a log while the gentle motion of the water seems determined to throw you overboard. But I had little doubt that the seasoned canoe captain was capable enough to navigate his craft through anything but the worst storms.

On the beach this is carnival day and the whole village appears to be delighted at the ship's arrival. It transforms their lives for a couple of hours each week. As a rarely sighted white person, children arrive to dance around you, to touch a strange fair hand and giggle their few English words in welcome. Looking around at Ruarwe from the beachside cove, it appears as an isolated world, cut off by the lake and the mountains. No roads penetrate here and if it were not for the two hourly lake steamer visit, it would feel like the place time had forgotten.

Life on board for the cocooned first-class travellers, safely isolated from the masses packed onto the lower decks, was, and still is, an oasis of space and serenity. With their own restaurant, bar and top deck space, the lake cruise is the closest one could imagine to that rosy idealized world the early 20th century administrators would embark upon. The bridge is more or less open at any reasonable time for visits and progress reports. It was almost impossible not to become familiar with many of the officers and crew on a 620-ton vessel. The first engineer was always delighted to show off the new diesels to anyone interested. After one of my visits, his

Indian second in command told me about the early morning drinking routine of his boss.

"In the morning, after his late night drinks, his hand would shake so." He held out a trembling hand to demonstrate.

"Then, after a shot of brandy, everything fine!"

He held out his hand again, this time as rock solid as a mast. His white teeth gleamed into a wide smile before bursting into a bout of infectious laughter which brought us both doubling over.

The *Ilala* departs Monkey Bay at the southern end of Lake Malawi at 8 am in the morning for its weekly round trip. The first scheduled stop is at Chipoka, just three hours sailing distance, but strategically important, as this is the only rail junction on the lake service. This is the terminal where freight is transported to and from the port of Nacala in Mozambique, making it a lifeline for goods traffic.

The stop is for at least eleven hours to allow for the transfer of freight from the rail wagons alongside the jetty. The sophistication of containers is not part of the *Ilala's* transport system. And anyway they would seem out of place on an old lake steamer. As the day progresses, the passengers haul up the thin walkway on to the passenger deck an extraordinary assortment of carrier bags and boxes, doors, window frames, fruit trees for a new garden and practically anything able to be moved. There appeared no limit to what was acceptable on board. Anything larger was the task of the deck-side crane.

Moving heavy cargo

The winding gear used a combination of pallets and rope slings, with railway staff and deck hands climbing in and out of the hold in a constant, confusing jostling of movement. Hanging on to the rope slings as the next carriage of boxes was slung over the sides, a deck hand would deliver a never-ending babble of instructions shouted to the winch crew. There appeared to be people everywhere and everyone seemed to have something to say about what should be moved, how it should be moved, where to and by what means. This frenzy of activity never ceased all day and brought spectators to every vantage point around the dockside to view the spectacle as enthralling as if a local circus had come to town.

But as in every circus performance, the star of the show is put on last. It was as though all the spectators knew and were waiting in anxious participation for the final act. The ship was not due to leave until 10 pm, well after dark and it was already running late. There was a large tractor still to be lifted aboard by a rather ancient steam crane anchored to the dockside. Preparations in the form of lifting tackle and heavy rope attachments were carefully put into place. The crane was either painted black or covered with decades of soot, which had attached to every working part. Its structure was as elaborate as anything its Victorian creators could have intended, with a durability to survive anything the rigours of a tropical climate could inflict.

The centre of activity now moved from the ship and freight wagons, to the firing up of this blackened dragon. By the minimal glare of the dockside lights, shadowy figures could be made out stacking timber and prodigious quantities of water into the cavernous interior of the sleeping beast. As the cooling night breezes drifted in from the lake, flames and sparks from the crane's interior began casting flickering images of its attendant servants against the storage sheds walls. As the beast stirred into life, columns of steam began adding drama to the night sky. The noise of grinding gear wheels almost drowned out the shouting of the deck hands instructions. Amidst a conflagration of sparks, flames and steam, the winching arm of the crane took the strain. The waiting audience cheered. The ropes creaked and groaned as the tractor shifted its position.

Just clear of the *Ilala's* deck rail and within clear distance of the cargo deck, the beast would have no more. The tractor sank back to earth. The crowd groaned.

More attempts ensued, with ever louder instructions being shouted between the crane operators and the deck hands. It appeared greater supplies of timber and water were necessary. After a short anxious delay, a pick-up truck arrived, fully laden. The beast was fired up to its maximum capacity

and the ensuing firework display lit up the dockside with red and yellow streaks of colour. The steam whistled and hissed amidst a force of sparks which seemed as though they were generated from the very bowels of the earth. The winch arm took the strain and amidst clanking of lifting tackle the tractor was slung safely into place on the deck. The cheering crowd was well pleased and dispersed back to their homes with tales of a sleeping monster they had seen come to life.

The *Ilala* sailed late that night, but with a crew who were proud of their achievement. It was an insignificant event in a remote corner of the world, but nevertheless one from which memories are made.

CHAPTER 17

Into the savanna

W HENEVER ONE travels across country in Africa there is little between towns except traditional villages and vast areas of countryside. In the 1970s the number of white travellers in remote locations was fairly minimal and stopping near a village would often attract attention. Word would quickly spread and within minutes you would probably be the centre of attention, surrounded by wide-eyed children giggling and chattering, trying to touch the strange pale arms of this new arrival. I got into the habit of carrying some sweets and ballpoint pens as presents for these occasions. The only time I can remember diverting attention was by giving out a glossy magazine, full of fashion catwalk scenes, flashy advertisements and the usual exotic pictures.

I am sure it was the first time anything like this had been seen by these children, for they became subdued, attentive and riveted as they gasped and giggled at page after page of colourful extravaganza from the rich world. It was for them a tiny glimpse into something quite unreal, something they would probably never see. As I looked into their excited faces I could only reflect on how little they had and how such a simple gesture had transformed their lives on that afternoon.

The city kids were more streetwise than their country equivalents, for they were used to the cars and bustle, where office suits rubbed shoulders with market traders. But when the first pedestrian escalator was installed in a supermarket in Blantyre, they behaved like children with a new toy. They rode up and down all day, proud of their ability to accommodate the new technology. Their friends at the door stared wide-eyed with disbelief, before their own first attempts. A harassed store assistant tried in vain to clear the entrance.

Savanna shops

Even in remote areas the traveller will find little supply stores just off the road and reached by a dusty track. In Malawi and Zambia they are described as 'grocery' or 'bottle' stores and are usually owned by some enterprising villager who lives nearby, or even in a room at the back of the store. They are usually built of mud blocks, some painted, with a grass or corrugated tin roof and usually a small veranda where the owner sits awaiting passing trade. These places are the equivalent of the city corner store and like the bush bars, seem to appear in locations as though they had somehow taken root. There is usually be a name, perhaps on a board above the door or daubed on the wall. Sometimes it is simply the owner's name, such as 'Mulanga Store', or an even quite improbably grand name 'The International Bottle Store'.

The interiors are as stark as the outside, with only a counter and a few shelves behind. On a good day paraffin and cooking oil can be found.

Small business.
Hairdresser near Harare

The absence of electricity means there is little probability of any cooling and usually no running water. Luke warm bottled drinks of Coca Cola or Fanta are available, provided the supply truck has arrived with a recent delivery. These drinks are usually so cheap that even the local villagers can afford a bottle. When break time arrives their gleaming white teeth will make short work of removing the metal cap.

There are few crippling dental problems as refined sugar is still a luxury. At harvest time sugar cane in its natural form is purchased from the producers and carried in ten-foot stalks back home to the village. Along the way the carriers will strip the tough outer casing off with their teeth to extract the natural ingredient inside. Their trail is marked by ripped off sugar bark that litters the road and follows them home.

One of the products always available in these roadside stores are small tins of sardines imported from packers often located in the Far East. Not only are they cheap - they had to be for country dwellers to buy them - this commodity appeared universally plentiful. It always seemed a mystery to me why an imported tinned product should be found in such remote places. Naturally it would not go 'off' under a baking tin roof and had a long shelf life, but with such an abundance of village produce available, why this single popular product above all others? It never seemed a popular item in markets because of competition with fresh products, it only seemed to surface in bush bottle stores. There invariably seemed to be little shortage, as though the suppliers had to off-load surplus stock and dump them at rock-bottom prices in any remote store that could be found. Bunches of bananas you would expect, but stacks of imported tins of sardines always appeared to me as out of place. But perhaps this could be applied to the strange locations of the stores themselves. Whatever the paradox of tins of sardines found in remote bottle stores, they would become the mainstay for many of my camping meals.

Raw sugar cane is great for energy, but requires strong teeth.
In the background, a woodcutter descends the plateau carrying firewood

Rest houses

Although most journeys by intercity buses are scheduled to stop overnight in large towns or cities, there are places to stay outside these main centres. These are known as 'rest houses', either run by the local council or by businessmen. The best places are usually the government establishments, clean and well organized with correspondingly higher prices. Some are quite luxurious, comparable to quality hotels. The local council and independent rest houses are mostly at the lower end of the market. Their standards of accommodation vary from mosquito-infested fleapits, with a low price for the budget traveller, to places approaching the standards of government establishments. Although these places can be found within small towns, possibly near a small village or bar, the majority are quite isolated.

One common feature of most rest houses is the resident cook who takes orders for breakfast and evening meal, as there are usually no local eating-places nearby. It is necessary to provide him (it is almost always a male cook) with all the ingredients. Rest houses do not as a rule supply any food, let alone a menu. If one arrives with no food it will usually mean no meals! The cook is often in charge of the place together with a cleaner. His other task will be to get the bath water heating organised. Outside of main centres there is little electricity and this usually requires a somewhat ancient wood-fired boiler to be stoked into life. One of these I particularly remember was a 19th century cast-iron monolith with the maker's plates attached, indicating a foundry in the industrial heartland of England. It was a tiny piece of working history. This was a link with a colonial past now consigned to history, but living on and functioning as efficiently as the administration which put it there.

Because of the lack of power, lighting is supplied by storm lanterns, which gives the whole place a sort of frontier atmosphere. It also encourages early nights and early mornings. The numbing night-time silence of these places invades all of your senses and demands a certain compliance. The only sounds are the chirping of insects and perhaps a distant howling of dogs. The occasional village bar may be over the next hill, with late-night merry-making being the only human sound to interrupt the insect life. But for most rest houses, once darkness falls, the ear-numbing silence and the absence of any artificial light adds a surreal quality to the overnight stay.

There are areas of the country where even rest houses cease to exist, usually because of the remoteness or because most travellers made the effort to reach the next town. Any travellers who found themselves stranded in such places, either because their car broke down, or hitchhikers who have run out of lifts, have a strictly limited number of options. It is possible to simply find a clearing in the bush and stretch out for the night. Sleeping in the bush can be thought of as a safe option. The chance of coming across anyone else is as remote as the location. Villagers in any case are an honest community. I gave a lift once to a hitchhiker who did this on a regular basis. Apparently this enabled not only saving him the incredible small costs of a rest house, but because it was so much safer than sleeping rough near to towns, where the possibility of attacks from the urbanised community was far greater. But to sleep easy with the night-time animal kingdom would certainly require some resilience.

The mission stations

In all parts of Africa the traveller will find mission stations, established by the major Christian religions from the time when the first settlers established a foothold on a particular territory. Their central role was and is, spreading the gospel in remote locations, however, a major part of their ministry is involved with supplying facilities where either none exists, or a quality alternative. Schools and hospitals are essential parts of this ministry, together with rural industries as diverse as joinery and farming. The traditional image of missionaries pounding their message to heathen masses through fiery sermons is a misplaced movie image. From quite early times the message was spread in diverse and essentially practical ways. This meant their ministries are to be found both within towns and in the remotest outposts with, in many instances, only rough tracks providing access.

With the essential role of missionaries being of an evangelical nature, there will always be a regularly attended church attracting a congregation from the mission itself and the surrounding population. I found them to be no more zealous in their search for numbers than an equivalent grant-aided denominational school in Britain. The high standards of mission schools and associated hospitals are well known to the local population. They attract either so many pupils or hospital patients, it often overwhelms their facilities. The small fees charged for education or health treatments are enthusiastically scraped together by hard-up local people for the superior standards compared to the government-run equivalent.

As I was part of the expatriate community it was not long before I got to know several of the mission workers both in the immediate area and those who were stationed in quite remote outposts. Many had spent most of their lives in Africa and had an affinity for the country and for the community they served. They had a practicality and resourcefulness that was honed by the harsh climate. At the same time they were an easy target for political propaganda and had to weave an invisible path by avoiding confrontation at all costs with government personalities and policy. As long as they provided much needed resources and remained neutral in all matters relating to the running of the country, the government would leave them to their evangelical crusade and to the services so much admired by the population at large. Apart from their own community the missionaries had to rely upon their own resourcefulness to solve problems, especially in remote locations where road conditions might cut them off for weeks at a time. They were generally wellknown in their locality and highly respected.

A mission community grew up in an area where its founding fathers considered it to be of most use. This may have been near the villages to be administered to, or isolated for spiritual contemplation. The largest with well-established schools and clinics with fairly large numbers of staff are closest to main roads and easy to find. But the small stations with perhaps only one or two missionaries are often located in remote areas at the end of barely negotiable tracks, ideal for relating to a local rural population. Whenever we travelled across country it was always a delight to stay the night at such places and share our provisions. Visitors are always welcomed. It provided a break from the missionaries' routine and a chance to entertain new faces. After the evening meal, while the generator still struggled with a hesitating power output and the moths flickered onto the mesh window screens, there were remarkable stories to be told.

Mission stories

On one of our brief stays at a mission station some way from Kasungu in the central region of Malawi, a white-haired priest with a trim beard giggled with glee as he related the story of a wild black boar he had rescued. It was little more than a baby and took to his new master like a puppy. It quickly became the mission pet and took to sleeping under his bed. As the months passed and its size grew to quite gigantic proportions, squeezing under the bed became impossible. The solution was to gradually raise the legs higher on blocks of wood, to allow the creature access. Eventually the bed became so elevated that the missionary himself had problems climbing in. At this point the now huge boar was assigned to sleep in the living room.

He took to roaming around the mission grounds rooting for food, but terrified the local villagers who came in throngs every day. As they besieged the hospital, word would spread of this black creature and its terrifying exploits and when it eventually appeared something akin to panic spread. Apparently its fame grew and stories of its deeds were something of a legend in the area. I can only imagine this story was retold with ever greater embellishments.

Many of the children had never seen the magic of the silver screen and stared wide-eyed, not knowing whether to clap or shout

The missionaries not only provide religious teaching through their churches and schools and highly regarded hospitals; they provide practical help to local communities through building and agricultural projects. Apart from these projects that are at the heart of their services, purely recreational activities are also included to give local communities some entertainment in their leisure hours. Most small towns are without cinemas and to provide what is perhaps the only entertainment, apart from bars and occasional football matches, missionaries often arrange free film shows in their own community hall. On film nights the excitement around these places will reach fever pitch. The films are always directed to a young audience with plenty of action and clearcut plots where the villains get their cum-uppance and the hero gets the girl.

Whenever I looked in, the hall would be packed with the benches filled and even more expectant faces straining to see in the doorways. Many of the children had never seen the magic of the silver screen and stared wide-eyed, not knowing whether to clap or shout. As the projector whirred in the background the audience noise never abated but went in feverish crescendos of boos and cheers according to whether the hero was getting into or out of a tight spot. It was an entertainment to see such vivacious audience participation and a good feeling to see that with such little cost such pleasure could be given to so many. Even after the show had finished and the crowd dispersed, the laughing and discussions rose into the night air. A little piece of magic must have been carried back home by each film-goer, and for just a few hours, lightened the dusty streets so distant from the silver screen and gave their lives just a little bit more enjoyment.

Such film shows set-up in ordinary village or mission halls are a feature in poor communities wherever mission stations are to be found. Young and old will wait in anticipated excitement for the action to start. It is a scene played out on practically any night, and the simple pleasure it gives stays in the memory. There is nothing special about the plain and rather shabby hall, the backless benches crowded with ordinary villagers; the second-hand 16 mm projector whirring its image onto a makeshift sheet and the whoops of delight as the first scenes start to appear. But like a child's first Christmas party, there is a spontaneity that affects everyone present and the sheer delight from the shrieks of children's laughter to the chuckles of the old men is something infectious. These occasions give a respite from the everyday toil, which is so much a part of ordinary rural life. After the evening's film show the essential daily struggles are perhaps just a little easier.

Personalities

There are missions representing almost every area of Christian teaching. A solitary priest, Father Shuff, from the White Father's order ran a mission in a quiet area some hundred miles north of Lusaka.

Father Shuff, of Nyimba Mission, Zambia

It was a place of peace and tranquillity and Kathy and I visited it several times. He was originally from France, a large man who visited the villages on his tiny motorcycle, always clad in his flowing white robes. When he arrived in his centuries old attire amongst the traditional villages it was as though a scene from the early settlers was being re-enacted. This peaceful settlement was only a few hours drive from the lawless concrete sprawl of Lusaka, but his motorcycle was always left with the key in place and the mission doors were never locked.

Already past retirement age, he had tried to retire to a mission in France, but a lifetime in Africa had made him realize his attachment to the local villagers was equally as strong as his religious convictions. There was little he could relate to in his 'home' country any more; it was true there were more facilities and creature comforts, but the TV sit.com. shows and the consumer society soon lost their appeal and anyway they were not part of Africa. He had to leave, to discover that he had an adopted home. It was an intangible relationship borne of something about simplicity and a dependable life cycle in a place he could relate to. He returned to the only life he really knew.

Expatriate children

The children of expatriates living in Africa, had a life-style that resembled the migratory habits of birds. They often attended boarding schools in their home countries and made the journey from cold northern climes to the warm tropics and back again, not once per year as with the birds, but two or more times. Most were on specially chartered planes, known locally as the 'lollipop' flights. As the school term ended and the holiday period started their migratory lives got into gear. It was a life-style many would adapt to, but those with a permanent home would not understand.

One of the perks of the expatriate life-style was the supplement awarded to keep their children in private boarding schools in their home country. It was a bonus many could not have afforded and was an extra many considered worth the long absences their children spent away from the parental home

For children of their age group, there was generally little provision in an expatriate community geared towards the pursuits of their working parents. They spent a great deal of their time hanging around the colonial clubs, where for a few months of the year the unexpected noise and colour of teenagers changed the atmosphere. Outside of their homes and the clubs' environment there was little in the way of entertainment. Even in the larger towns, the cinemas were either non-existent or rather dated in both appearance and listings. They hardly had anything in common with the local population of their age and this meant they generally kept to their own groups and made their own amusements.

In an effort to keep them entertained, the club would try out all sorts of initiatives, including pool games and the inevitable teenage discos. At the end of the holidays an almost eerie quiet would descend upon the expatriate environment, as flights of teenagers would migrate once more back to their boarding schools in the western world. There was both a sense of relief at the restored calm and at the same time some regrets at the liveliness the places had lost. These migratory kids were able, in the majority of cases, to keep a balance between their split lives and generally switch-gears between life in the boarding school and their sunshine holidays. This was not always so easy with the kids permanently living the 'expatriate' life, either in towns or in the mission stations.

In the larger towns, private schools were generally good and staffed with expatriate teachers. For the younger children of expatriates and those of the wealthy local middle class, this provided an alternative to the divided, migratory life of the older teenagers.

The 'miss-kids'

The name 'miss-kids' was applied to a varied group of mission children, brought up in religious schools in Africa and then suddenly and abruptly taken to a new life, to continue their education, in a chilly and alien northern country. Their schools were essentially self-contained with excellent facilities and hospitals, but in often remote, sometimes isolated communities. It was no surprise that such children, brought up in the somewhat artificial life of colonial Africa, developed problems of adjustment when they were relocated overseas for their higher education.

They often developed a sort of 'split personality' not really belonging to their former colonial or mission years, yet not adjusting to the strange new life in their new environment. For many their religious upbringing became a strength that supported them through difficult years of adjustment. There were often strong relationships formed with others of a similar background with whom they could easily identify.

The 'miss-kids' were perhaps like a much younger version of older colonial personnel who had spent most of their working lives in the fledgling countries to which they had been assigned. When they retired, after a lifetime away from their 'home' country, they had little in common with its strange new ways. It was no more than the country of their birth. Those that did settle called their seaside bungalows after some remote landscape they could only dream of.

When in later life the 'miss-kids' were asked about their early years, many had formed a shield against a culture they had little preparation for and difficulty in understanding. They decorated their western bedrooms in the style of their previous home, now so remote. Their difficulty in relationships became apparent in many small but significant ways, like lacking a style of dress, which most young people seem to instinctively possess. Most relationships were both better and longer lasting with those who had had a similar background.

The 'miss-kids' brought with them part of a previous life which had not only formed their view of the world, but was something they would keep forever. They were a product of a time that was rapidly disappearing, as increasingly fewer expatriates and their families are committed to a lifetime in a foreign land. As the empire ceased and the armies of long-term administrators retreated, so the 'miss-kids' became a living part of that history.

CHAPTER 18

Crossing borders

CROSSING BORDERS is one of the inevitable consequences and at times an extremely irritating necessity, of living in land-locked countries. This is especially so in Africa, a continent with so many borders, any extensive land traveller will encounter, sooner rather than later, the infamous sign 'Caution, border crossing ahead'. This is not to suggest this sign should strike fear into the heart of those who suspect their papers are not in order, but the crossing of some remote borders should really be approached with a great deal of caution. Indeed many borders usually require a degree of diplomacy and not a little courage, to ensure a smooth transit.

On route to a border post. 'International' is a name often exaggerated

There is a special code for travellers in remote territories, which although may well be adopted in western countries, certainly does apply in developing countries and also to the Far East. That is of course if the idea is to get through customs boundaries with the minimum of trouble. This 'code' is not likely to apply to the package dealers who are disgorged by the jumbo load in the Greek islands or similar destinations.

But it certainly should be taken note of by individual travellers, especially those approaching isolated customs outposts, especially when one is a 'foreign' arrival in a less than touristy destination. Anyone who has tangled with the rather special bureaucracy displayed in these frontier posts will know, or will soon find to their cost, they are not to be messed with!

During my years living in Africa there were many occasions when I travelled through customs posts and the consequences were as far from an arrival at London's Heathrow as one can get. One of the legacies of the colonial era was the association of an individual's appearance with the idea of what constitutes something tangibly close to respectability; i.e. honesty, fair play, a sense of traditional values associated with gentlemanly conduct and the implication that one may be trusted. This rather dated visual value system should not be made light of. The local inhabitants expected an association of respect and trustworthiness from the Europeans who were the *bwanas* and *donas* of colonial times. The isolation of the continent and the regime of colonisation were all bound up with the idea of traditional European values.

It was expected that the European kept his word and could be relied upon. His word was his honour with all the associated values it implied. The extravagant 'hippy' culture of the 1960s was frowned upon by several African states as being associated with liberal ideals, drug culture and a general apathy towards the established regime. This was antagonistic to regimes in Africa who undoubtedly saw this lifestyle as a threat. In Malawi there was zero tolerance to both a 'dishevelled' or a non-conformist outward appearance or any association to an 'alternative' culture. Arrive at a border decked out in 'alternative' clobber and you simply would not get in.

Customs etiquette

Whenever travelling through Africa and the warning sign looms up that a customs crossing is just ahead, it is time to smarten up. Attempt to look clean - although after travelling through the bush for a week this may not be easy; have respectable clothes, although do not be over-dressed. Even in the 21st century this approach can still produce results. The emphasis on appearance tends to convey this all-important atmosphere of respectability and a statement that one does not arrive posing a potential threat. Also travelling as a family helps - families are seen as being more respectable.

Whenever I was with my wife and young son and traversing a customs post, there were always fewer delays and even a hesitant smile from the man demanding passports. Perhaps a family unit was seen as less of a potential problem or a child's smile could even momentarily enrich a customs officer's boring day. Whatever it may be, it often worked.

Being in the employ of the government also seems to help. Whenever I travelled my passport revealed I was a civil servant from Malawi - and later Zambia. All government employees seem deemed to belong to a fraternity where a vague law exists to give an easier passage through the red tape and acquire the right stamps. And if you are lucky, the necessary papers will be returned with an all-clear smile. Customs officials rarely smile. It can be a fragile line between a major incident and a seamless transition between borders. Most times it will be smooth, but fail to follow correct procedures at one's peril.

Some of the staff manning these outposts can be the most truculent ever to sit behind a desk, and need tactful handling. It is not necessarily their intention to delay and harass, after all it interrupts their day as much as yours. But a combination of intangible occurrences can trigger a trail of consequences that can leave the less experienced traveller in a state of frustration, nearing to despair. There is a learning curve to negotiating customs posts in developing countries, or politically sensitive borders. There were certainly times when I have encountered the most mindless bureaucracy.

Politeness is a prerequisite, even in the face of what appears to be provocation. It is essential not to be put off by such trivia as, for instance, when the desk staff having had so much to drink, the stamping of a passport becomes difficult. This occurred to me at the remote Nyamapanda crossing from Rhodesia into Mozambique. My papers had not been correctly stamped. After travelling through some miles of no-man's land to the next post at Changara, I was sent back to obtain the all-important stamp. The process of getting the officials, who by now were barely standing, to realise why I had returned and what document needed their attention was a lesson in diplomacy.

It should always be remembered that rules in Africa are flexible and made to fit the circumstances

At another border between Rhodesia and Malawi I arrived to find it had closed early and the guards/staff were singing in drunken abandonment in their quarters nearby. The ability to consume plenty of drink at customs posts is an on-going part of the job. Camping at the road barrier was all that could be done until the clear air of a new day enveloped the customs staff in an early sobriety.

Customs strategy

As with all government staff in developing countries, customs officers are notoriously low paid, and if the regime is corrupt enough, are easily bribed. In fact some level of corruption is so endemic in many countries it has become almost a way of life. In order to get things done at any level bribery has become an accepted part of the process and as a means of transit through customs, is no exception. But this is something that one must know in advance and trading customs know-how with trail-hardened travellers can be invaluable. Discovering how to negotiate a particular transit crossing is a valuable piece of information. A wrong move in attempting to 'influence' a straight official may well turn, if not nasty, then incur delays, seemingly endless form filling and telephone calls, while the 'innocent' mistake is sorted out.

It should always be remembered that rules in Africa are flexible and made to fit the circumstances and bureaucracy can simply be a way of officially sanctioning that flexibility. Rules are interpreted in whatever way suits the officials' objectives. While the objective is usually to extract money, or some scarce commodity, dealing with such officials must be done with some degree of diplomacy. It has to be as though the process of 'lubricating' the bureaucracy is a natural part of the process. During my time in Zambia, I was involved in numerous dubious dealings with authority. This often had to be, because it was the only way to get things done. It was as though corruption had become an official part of the process. Incurring this 'flexibility' was an inevitable part of border crossings.

When leaving the border post of Chipata, Zambia for a destination in Malawi, I declared an amount of local currency, the Zambian Kwacha, slightly in excess of the amount allowed for brief visits. I was allowed through, the officials knowing I was returning in a few days. Right on cue the error was discovered upon re-entry and the penalties made clear. With a plentiful supply of staple goods in next-door Malawi and chronic shortages in Zambia, the procedures for 'extracting' goods from Malawi travellers were well established.

However, even in corrupt regimes some degree of rule exists. It is as hazardous for the officials to ask directly for some 'compensation' as it is for the traveller to offer a bribe to smooth formalities. Each side is as apprehensive of a set-up as the other. One develops a feel for the situation and can make slanted suggestions. In my case after a customs inspection of my car, I suggested they must be short of certain commodities I had brought back. Much indecision seemed to suggest they had extracted a goodly amount already that week of what I was carrying.

Having no more 'hardware' commodities to barter, now the delicate process of cash transfer had to begin. This is always difficult to judge as it depends on one's assessment of the severity of the infringement incurred and what the going rate is going to be to get it lifted. After some weighing-up, I decided the appearance of K20 (twenty Zambian Kwacha, at the time something like £15 at the official rate) should do the trick.

"Perhaps you could take another look at my passport."

I tentatively offered the document together with the cash just showing over the cover. The official quickly removed the worn paper notes and stamped the passport as though it was just another routine exercise.

"Well sir, we will forget about it on this occasion, but please remember in future."

With the all-important stamp and a friendly wave all formalities were concluded. Such procedures really only occur on quiet rural crossings where time and opportunity for such shenanigans is available, rather than at major terminals where busloads of travellers appear all together.

Border nostalgia

There is a long border between Malawi and Mozambique, which extends all along Malawi's southern tip and around half of its western territory. In fact the road north to Dedza actually runs on the actual border for around twenty kilometres. Stopping over in the picturesque mountain scenery at the Dedza Government Rest House was a pleasant break. Apart from the ideal setting of the rest house amidst the blue gum trees, no other bar or restaurant existed.

It is possible to walk across the road and enter Mozambique. The border post is several kilometres away at Villa Coutinho, so although this is officially Mozambique territory there was no sign or anything to officially inform you which country you were in.

Bar Domino was in this no-man's land territory, yet just fifty metres off the recently tarred Malawian road heading north. It was owned and run by white Portuguese settlers - whom as far as I was aware had been in the country for several generations. The building was basic with ant-proof concrete floors and concrete blocks for the walls. It was painted with swathes of contrasting colours that had a hint of Iberian influence, with garish woven wall hangings depicting African scenes. For such an isolated place the bar was amazingly well stocked with imported Portuguese wines, spirits, liquors and cerveza.

It was here on many trips north I would stop over to spend an evening at the Domino. It was a magnet for the white Mozambique settlers who had businesses nearby or were just passing through. It was inevitable that conversations with this diverse group from lonely outposts would be struck up. The evening was pleasantly passed sitting on bar stools sipping the only cerveza to be found for miles, by the light of a few solitary electric bulbs fired by a slightly throbbing generator somewhere out in the yard.

The war between the Portuguese government forces and the anti-colonial Frelimo liberation army, still gathering momentum out in the central regions, was almost forgotten in this isolated corner of such a vast country. In this place the conflict may have been a million miles away. But the war did catch up. By the late 1980s thousands of displaced people were forced to seek sanctuary in Malawi and crossed the border at this isolated place to join yet another refugee camp.

It was in 1986 when I returned to Malawi again with my wife Kathy and son Lloyd to renew acquaintances and to see how the country had changed. We passed through Dedza and stayed at the same government rest house. It still resided amongst the blue gum trees and the pot-holed road to its entrance had not been repaired. The old cast iron boiler still provided the wood fire heating and the gentle roar of the paraffin lamps was the only sound disturbing the night.

The war catches up.
Rocket damage in Dedza on the Malawi/Mozambique border

In the late afternoon I walked along the road opposite the Domino Bar. The war had indeed reached here. The rocket-blasted building was a shell of its former self. As in so much of this battle-scarred country a battle had also raged here in this tiny outpost. Or perhaps the buildings represented a symbol of the colonial past and a rocket attack was the stamp of the new regime. This country was littered with land mines. I wondered as to whether even this isolated bar had any of these death traps planted outside its walls. These indiscriminate maiming and killing devices had wreaked havoc on the local population and had as a consequence, initiated publicity and charities to aid its victims.

I hesitated at the rain ditch near the roadside looking across this no-man's land towards the burnt-out building, wanting a last look and debating the risks. Children were moving their hump-backed cattle past the entrance, so I decided to face the hazard and walked up the dusty track to the remains of the bar. As I stepped over the rubble and through the shattered wall, it was impossible to dismiss the memories of this place from sixteen years ago. The walls still held the faded paint, now strewn with machine-gunned score marks and so too was the curved bar with its hard timber surface. It was as though the ghostly figures of those Mozambique settlers could have still been sitting there on those bar stools sipping cerveza. When one returns to places like this after so many years, it is often to find that the old has been swept away and something new has replaced it. One is left with only memories of what the place had once been. But here everything remained; only the ravages of regime change had left their mark.

CHAPTER 19

Across southern Africa
Borders and wars

MY SECOND contract in Malawi began in October 1973. The return was planned as a journey that would have been contemplated by some 19th century explorers, as the immensity of the distance defied my sense of reality until it actually started. It was not just the trauma of crossing borders, but a war was raging across two of the countries I had to traverse before reaching landlocked Malawi. There was no other way around and it seemed a hugely illogical oversight verging on either irresponsibility or not a little insanity. How can such an outrageous planning error be accounted for? Whatever lack of planning was responsible, this was to be the route for Kathy and myself - by sea and overland.

Pendennis Castle, **ready to sail from Southampton**

We sailed with our twelve year old Morris 1000 Traveller safely stowed aboard the *Pendennis Castle,* one of the last of the famous 'White Line' Cunard regular passenger sailings to Cape Town and on to Australia. These were not pleasure cruises as such, but transit journeys for business people and those returning home, or starting a new life. South Africa was regarded as part of the 'new world' and a popular destination for numerous immigrants. These twelve-day voyages to South Africa are now the stuff of history, shown on marine archives with the traditional streamers and funnel blasts as the ship departed. Our route was to take in a crossing of Africa that would entail a distance of a quarter of the continent from south to north. This would encompass a complete transit through the whole length of both South Africa and Rhodesia, including Mozambique, before our final destination into Malawi. The enormous scale of the journey with much of it in extremely isolated districts in a twelve-year-old vehicle did not appear to be a concern to us.

The unique opportunity to embark on a journey of such proportions was something not to be missed and without doubt our enthusiasm quelled all practical obstacles and banished any concept of the hazards undoubtedly involved. It was a journey of a lifetime that had to be seized and with it any suggestions as to the dangers in traversing so much of this vast continent must be dismissed. It was as though Africa had already infused into us something that had inspired those early explorers. There has to be a readiness to trust the future without any guarantees, which in retrospect such guarantees are just too much to expect. Like waiting for the rains, it is a kind of act of faith. Something of this was merged into this journey, a curious kind of homecoming from a continent you cannot entirely escape from.

Landing in Cape Town

Our car emerged from somewhere in the hold in a sling made of rope. We watched as the hoist from the *Pendennis Castle* lowered it gently on to the quayside. Once formalities were over, I drove out into a blazing afternoon sun. The Morris would in later years become revered as a go almost anywhere vehicle and to become the stuff of legends, but perhaps the overland trek which lay ahead would create an altogether new dimension in its achievements.

Our English licence plates created a curiosity at a police check in Cape Town when the officer learned of our intended journey and mused:

"You're expecting to go where?"

I'm not sure whether he took my intentions seriously. He probably only knew of overlanders with four-wheel drive monsters sporting go-anywhere tyres and sand shovels strapped on to the roof. Perhaps being on a bicycle would not have produced any more of a startled reaction.

"Surely you don't expect this thing to get you that far?"

He stared in disbelief and eyed our vehicle suspiciously. This is not surprising as many in South Africa, at this critical time in their *apartheid* era, would view anywhere north of the Limpopo River to be embarking on a mission impossible.

It was all the same, the first time anyone had offered some serious misgivings about our audacious travel plans.

"Whatever you may think, it's a risk we're prepared to take. We'll get around the trouble spots."

It was a half-hearted response, but the best I could muster. He waved us through still doubting our sanity. Perhaps he knew something about the war enveloping Rhodesia and didn't want to say.

**The Morris heads north into Rhodesia (Zimbabwe).
With the author at Providential Pass**

The journey started at Cape Town and followed the south coast 'Garden Route' to Port Elizabeth, before heading north. This was an area of unparalleled beauty, with the rolling surf on the south side where the Atlantic Ocean meets the Indian Ocean and the beautiful landscape of lush meadows to the north. And as a backdrop, the blue-grey mountains of the Little Karroo were framed against a cloudless sky. Even farther inland lies the Great Karroo, the dry plateau forming a protective barrier for the lush coast.

After Port Elizabeth the road turns in a few kilometres from the coast, before returning to the sea at East London. The orderliness of the landscape, the manicured fields and the neat rows of vines with the old pastel coloured colonial Dutch residences were too precise for the Africa I knew. It was a vista of Switzerland and held no preparation for the arid terrain that would soon follow. Once again the road turned inland; miles of black-paved surface stretching on to the coastal resort of Durban.

The *apartheid* system was fully entrenched and only racial politics cast an uneasy atmosphere over such beauty. The squatter townships and traditional villages were well away from inquisitive eyes.

"What do you think about the future of South Africa?" I asked a weather-beaten Afrikaans man at a local filling station on an empty stretch of road some miles south of Durban.

"We built this country and we're going to keep it!"

His determined reply was borne of a deep-rooted attachment to his land. He believed without question, as if as an article of faith. Perhaps he still owns his patch in that vast expanse and to all practical purposes perhaps his own world has not changed. But twenty years later the world and South Africa would move on. Even after the regime changed, for some white South Africans born and bred here, knowing no other life, their cocooned world in the hinterland far distant from the cities has changed little.

Into the Transvaal

As we continued north, driving some 30 kilometres parallel to the shore of the 'Wild Coast' to the east, the gentle green of the temperate climate started to fade. The air became noticeably warmer and the terrain became dryer. As we approached Durban, the jutting mauve peaks of the Drakensberg hills to our west, formed a barrier to the flat lands of the Orange Free State in the heartland of Boer territory. Our route turned inland and west to Pietermaritzburg and on to the largest city, Johannesburg. This gigantic city built from gold-wealth is still an extraordinary testament to the determination of those early settlers. Like a western city with all the trappings of wealth, it seemed unreal with its shopping malls, and glass towers. But a few kilometres away, almost out of sight, are the shantytowns of cheap shacks, housing the thousands of workers who supported this edifice, simmering as an alternative city.

Now our route turned almost due north through the capital Pretoria (since changed to Tshwane) and the Springbok Flats. The roads of black asphalt were well built and virtually empty of traffic. We were now crossing the Transvaal and heading towards the border with Rhodesia. The countryside alternated between dry savanna bush and miles of beautiful dense forest. The temperature was rising every day. As we crossed the Tropic of Capricorn the terrain was giving way to the interior savanna lands. This was hot, dry yellow-red earth with distant acacia trees. It was terrain we knew so well.

Rhodesia from the south

After crossing the border at Messina and entering Rhodesia at Beitbridge, the empty lowlands were now parched with the late October heat that precedes the start of the rains. The smell of dried grass mixed with distant fires tainted the air and the hot wind blew in red dust from a now increasingly waterless interior. All Africa was in the air and the landscape framed within a deep blue sky, took on a familiarity we had become so accustomed to. It was the essence of this vast interior, between the jungles to the north and the manicured vines so far to the south.

The inspiring Great Zimbabwe ruins

It was possible this territory could be mastered and the scattered farms we saw showed what was possible. But it was only possible with the relentless determination of those who built these places and knew that if this devotion relaxed, the wind and the sun would claim everything back. As you looked at the endless miles of thorn bush and dried riverbeds, the land itself defied change and you appreciated it for what it was.

Great Zimbabwe

The crossing of the isolated south of Rhodesia was flat and hot and continued until Fort Victoria and the famous antiquity of the Great Zimbabwe ruins. The magnitude of this mysterious city from an early civilisation is inspirational. This monument is one of the oldest and largest structures south of the Sahara and was built in the 11th century with construction continuing for the following 300 years. This great monument rises out of the surrounding savanna like an island from the sea. The Great Enclosure with its eleven metre high walls, extending for 250 metres and conical tower, all built from the local stone, dazzles in the brilliant light and is an awe-inspiring sight. The first Europeans to discover Great Zimbabwe were Portuguese traders, although Chinese pottery and coins from Arabia have been discovered suggesting that the city formed part of a vast trade network. Adam Renders discovered the site in 1867 on a hunting expedition.

These ruins cover 1,800 acres with a Hill Complex, used as a temple and the Valley Complex occupied by its citizens. The huge Great Enclosure was the domain of the king. It is still a subject of conjecture as to what initiative was responsible for such a structure. However, it is generally believed an early *Shona* speaking people, probably from the *Lemba* tribe, built the city. To early African travellers, this city must have appeared as though they had been transported to another world. They are as impressive now as they must have been during this chance discovery.

Still looking splendid. An example of Bulawayo colonial architecture

We followed the road north into Salisbury, an organised and pleasant city cited on a high plateau where it escapes the heat of the plains and the air has a vibrant quality all through the year. It was here where we discovered that the liberation war had taken a turn for the worse. There seemed scant news about conditions north of Salisbury towards the Mozambique border in this truly isolated and thinly populated region. The area in fact, I had planned as the most suitable route to Malawi. All information, from either official news to local gossip, pointed to the region to the north as being either a war zone to at best 'unstable'. Politics were against revealing that wide parts of the country were either no-go areas or extremely dangerous, as the Rhodesian liberation forces based in Mozambique and Zambia were engaging with the Rhodesian military.

There were also serious confrontations between the Portuguese forces and the 'Frelimo' liberation army who were only a couple of years away from ousting the Portuguese and banishing the colonialists. The situation was constantly changing on an almost day-to-day basis and this together with the time it took to get news out made advanced planning near impossible.

Where to cross next

We were now in the heartland of Africa where knowledge of local conditions is as indeterminable as the date when the first of the season's rains will start. Now we were fully aware that our route from Salisbury through the desolate northern terrain towards the southern border of Mozambique and thence into Malawi, was out of the question. The road that leads up to the town of Tete, in Mozambique on the banks of the Zambezi was a nightmare of ruts, sand and boulders.

We had traversed this section two years earlier, just prior to it being closed to civilian traffic. It had been land-mined by the Mozambique liberation armies and traffic was eventually escorted through headed by a Portuguese military mine detector. It was not possible to know whether the road was even open.

Looking back now I'm not sure how this scenario had escaped our planning. Perhaps the enormity of the previous distances had led to a loss of focus on this final but intractable part of the journey. Our knowledge of Africa was enough to know of the dangers inherent in remote cross-country travel. To risk war zones in this unpredictable continent was not for the faint hearted and not for us. We had to look at the options of escaping from a city surrounded by a war situation.

But there were other options and Africa can always surprise with its diversity. Chaos and insecurity in one location could be calm and peaceful in another only a few miles away. I started to put together an escape plan. There was a less direct route to the coastal city of Beira, linked by a substantial tarred highway crossing through the picturesque town of Umtali. Tarred roads are difficult to mine and in the dry season a lack of vegetation cover makes an ambush difficult. From Beira there were both road and rail links into Malawi. We had to assume either one at least must be open. And so instead of heading north our route now headed south-east towards Beira and the Indian Ocean.

Into Mozambique

The 550 or so km to Beira in Mozambique was a delight to travel. The hilly sections around Umtali, close to the border are designated scenic routes on the Michelin map of the area. And this authoritative map/guide, so indispensable on journeys such as these, was proved accurate once again. The border crossing into Mozambique was at Vila de Manica and once more the unpredictable nature of the remote customs post lived up to expectations. We camped on one side of the border, with the barrier firmly closed, while the merry-making officials boozed the night away and competed with the night-time savanna sounds for supremacy.

A Rhodesian landmine protection vehicle.
Used on bush roads during the independence war

Upon arrival in Beira it transpired the difficult gravel road into southern Malawi was also dangerous due to land mines planted in the sandy surfaces to avoid detection. This treacherous route, some 280 km long, which transversed a particularly isolated southern region of Mozambique, was once again an impossible route to follow. Apart from the Portuguese military, it would be doubtful if any other vehicle ventured on to this piece of road. Only one or two tiny towns appeared on its entire length and anyone who reached its junction with the mighty Zambezi, would heave a gasp of relief. Even without the prospect of land mines, to tackle this wilderness track, neglected for years, would demand an act of faith.

The Mozambique liberation army – 'Frelimo' scented victory and isolating supply links from land-locked countries - notably white ruled Rhodesia, but also Malawi - could only further their cause. Once again, the diversity of Africa was to show itself. There was a rail link to transport goods and people into land-locked Malawi. This was the only route and it was fortunately open. Occasionally road and rail links run side-by-side, one possibly supporting the other. This was one such link, with the land-mined road often within small-arms attack distance of the train. Was it possible the liberation forces had overlooked such a strategic opportunity? Apparently not, as we were to learn the train was still a somewhat hazardous option as track sabotage was common. Frelimo passed their days by machine-gun attacks on the train. The train drivers had courage surpassing that of the Lusaka mini-bus operators.

Dondo is all trains

We had no alternative option and left our car to be shipped from the main commercial freight centre of Dondo - a few miles inland. This large complex was organised and staffed by the Portuguese colonialists who seemed to do everything from issuing tickets to driving the trains. We stayed in Beira overnight and travelled to Dondo the next day to await the train to Blantyre in Malawi.

The rail centre at Dondo, Mozambique

Dondo is a maze of railway lines that cross each other with no apparent order. It was as if they had been thrown out upon the terrain like lengths of intertwined ladders, in some outrageous artistic experiment, rather than a plan to move freight. They vanished into sidings or disappeared into a heat haze that engulfed everything into a premature horizon. It was a confusion of wagons, carriages and steam locomotives all in a fusion of hissing steam, belching smoke and shrill whistles. These mighty clanking machines had nameplates mainly from factories in England, many of which must have seen their glory days long ago in the 1930s and 40s.

The friendly Portuguese drivers were delighted to have me in the cab while they shunted freight up and down the depot. It was all a rather bizarre setting. Whether they knew it or not their whole colonial legacy with themselves as an integral part of it was on the verge of being handed over to the new Marxist rulers within a couple of years. With the hand-over of the rail system they would all go too, even though for many, they had been brought up in the country and knew no other life.

There was a guerrilla war just north of the depot and as far as I could tell no visible army protection within sight. Such a strategic rail centre would surely be a possible target. Yet here we were shunting freight up and down the depot. I was playing out my childhood dreams of being fireman-assistant in an almost forgotten age of steam. The train hissed, chugged and whistled as the driver laughed and shouted instructions in a broken Portuguese dialect. Perhaps this was a tiny part of the endearing yet contradictory nature of this land. There is nothing planned, it just happens and becomes another memory.

As our train steamed northwest through the tinder dry lowlands of the Zambezi valley towards Malawi, the October heat was stifling. On one of the few stops, two nuns boarded from a local mission. They said the temperature on their porch had been 45° C that morning. Perhaps the conditions had also deterred the guerrillas in their bush warfare. The journey was without incident. Even our car arrived dent and bullet-free after a few more days. But when the rains arrived and with them the camouflage of the tall grass, the attacks on the rail line occurred again.

CHAPTER 20

Roads and rivers

ROADS IN south Saharan Africa in the 1970s could be anything from a rough clearing through the bush to, in exceptional circumstances, a well-maintained tarred highway. Even in the 21st century, with major improvements, there are large areas of countryside where roads can still range from the good to the almost impassable. The authoritative Michelin maps/guides list road construction from 'transcontinental' through 'improved', 'partially improved', 'earth', 'marked tracks' and 'dirt'. And even this list is broken into what are euphemistically known as 'obstacles'. These range from difficult or dangerous to impassable in the rainy season. Some roads I have used could well extend this description still further.

During 1971 we took a journey from Malawi, through Zambia and Rhodesia, returning from Salisbury to Tete in Mozambique. The first 150 km north of Salisbury (now Harare) the road was tarred as far as the small town of Mtoko. My map then reported the road as 'improved', before downgrading it to 'partially improved'. These descriptions were, I'm sure, designed to instil a sense of hope to the cross-country traveller. Admittedly the car was an Austin 1100, not a vehicle of choice, as its modern gas-filled suspension was more suited to western motorways than African savanna roads. Its fatal flaw was the low clearance resulting in the underside enduring continuous encounters with rocks and sand ridges from the notorious 'partially improved' tracks.

From Mtoko to Tete the road deteriorated rapidly as it approached the Mozambique border. From the crossing point at Nyamapanda the road was a nightmare of rocks, ruts, stones and holes, with sections that could have been specially created for the sole purpose of destroying anything on four wheels. But right in the middle of this section of Mozambique, the road is interrupted by the massive Zambezi River, a natural barrier dividing the country and virtually cutting it in two. Getting across this mighty river I will come back to.

The worst of roads

This particular journey through Mozambique and the Zambezi Valley represented the epitome of African savanna travel. For a traveller seeking the final level of road impassability, without a road being only passable to tractors and tanks, this was as good as it gets. The terrain was a combination of obstacles strewn with gutted channels, which although now dry, would be awash during the rains. The surface was not only pot-holed, but was strewn with boulders which projected from the sand-surface and always seemed adjacent to deep channels.

A vehicle that had the misfortune of bottoming into a hole would have the added trauma of hitting a jutting rock upon exiting. The side of the road disappeared into deep sand and a combination of road boulders and thorn trees. Getting off the road to pass obstructions was as problematic as keeping on the road in one piece. Occasional stretches lost the holes and boulders and appeared almost flat, as the road disappeared into a desert-like mirage shimmering in the valley heat. But this was a false relief as the road was traversed by some of the deepest corrugations I have encountered.

The combination of road conditions and blistering heat were together unforgiving in the relentless mile after mile of destructive capacity, exacted on traveller and vehicle alike. In the dry season before the rains are due, the temperatures reach 45° C and above. In the rains this territory would demand even greater displays of cross-country determination and if passable at all, would require the best of four-wheel vehicles. There was to be another 400 kilometres of this road before the river crossing at Tete was reached.

The road as a challenge

It always seemed to me this was what travelling in Africa was about. On these roads you were in the terrain, became part of it, as though the road with its rocks and gullies was, for the duration of the journey, very close to you. You smelt the heat and tasted the red and yellow dust as it stuck to your face sweat. This was a challenge between you and the road as if it had a lifeforce in its ever-moving sand and channels. There was no way either you or your vehicle could escape. The road had to be endured until your destination. And if you survived, it would be like all challenges, in celebrating a victory with stories to be told. Paved roads with savage scenery as a backdrop were not the same. You did not have the same intimacy and the stories of it could never be as dramatic.

View from the road

Both on the road and across the savanna, hot swirls of rising air make funnels of red dust swirling up and racing across the landscape carrying broken stalks of yellow grass. The dust clouds provide an additional intensity to the haze and for two hours prior to sunset, filter out the intensity of the blazing sun, reducing it to a pink ball. As the sun descends almost vertically into the ever-denser haze, just for a brief time, a customary quiet descends. The smell of dried vegetation like sweet potatoes drifts in before the sounds of the night commence. The hot air becomes still, except for gentle evening breezes that entice small birds from the protective shade, to enjoy a dust-bath on the road surface.

The vegetation becomes paralysed in the unrelenting sun. The trees grow into grotesque angular forms as nature struggles in the task of conserving what little moisture remains. The leaves disappear, drying to a crisp. The foot and bicycle trails leading to the villages, which during the rains would be like canyons between the high grass, now appear like red streams, devoid of vegetation. They are now clearly visible meandering between the rocks and thorn thickets.

Some bridges in rural areas are simply two wooden planks wide enough to take the vehicle's wheels

Lush tall grass from last season's rains now become waving yellow stalks, dazzling in the clear air. Where the grass has broken off, the sun burnt stalks are brittle and sharp. There is no softness in this landscape. The river-beds become a carpet of sand and the few remaining waterholes become magnets for wildlife. The air takes on the scent of dried cedar as the distant grass fires add their own perfumed aroma to the air that can only belong to the dry season.

On to the Zambezi

There are many rivers and streams feeding into the mighty Zambezi. They all must be crossed and bridges are an inevitable part of savanna travel. Without them, everything stops. In rural areas, bridges that appear to have been neglected from the time they had been built, are often patched up with just enough repairs to keep them from total disintegration. Such bridges must be approached with caution. In the rains it is quite possible for a bridge to be washed away so completely, it appears as if none ever existed.

Once a bridge has been destroyed by sheer force of water, all transport comes to a standstill. Roads can often be navigated in more or less any condition, and in most cases, some way of getting around the ruts or landslides can usually be found. But without a bridge able to support the weight of a vehicle, the route becomes impassable. Whatever driver is bold enough to test the capability of a suspect bridge has courage surpassing the cross-country bus drivers and is something of a road-hero. There are wrecks littered around many river crossings bearing testimony to those who did not make it across.

Therefore, irrespective of road conditions, bridges are generally in good condition, with many even boasting a short tarmac stretch of road as an introduction to their smooth surface. Some bridges in rural areas are simply two wooden planks wide enough to take the vehicle's wheels, laid across a few supporting steel girders. As the vehicle's weight is taken up, there are disconcerting creaks and rattles, with even visible movements of the boards as they take up the strain. But such structures are generally the exception. Admittedly these bridges would give anxious moments when crossing, but as long as there were no actual holes in the structure it was generally safe!

All hauling by manpower. Luangwa River pontoon crossing

There are still major rivers without bridges either because it is too expensive to get them built, or because traffic volume is insufficient. There was one such crossing on the major link road between Rhodesia (Zimbabwe) and Malawi, a crossing point every traveller in the 1970s and 80s had to confront.

From the hilltop looking down at the river town of Tete, I saw the kilometre wide shimmering waters of the Zambezi fading into the dust-laden horizon and knew the same as any other traveller, this was the only route north. The road finished in the town and the only way of continuing north was by means of a rickety wooden pontoon able to carry around two cars or one truck.

Most freight into Malawi either arrives through the Mozambique port of Beira and thence by rail or is routed through Lusaka by truck along the 'Great North Road'. The town of Tete was the gateway north from Rhodesia into Malawi, a town in the middle of nowhere, isolated in the savanna lowlands with only one barely passable road in. Its importance was its pontoon. Presumably at this wilderness out-station there was, at this time, no necessity for any better river crossing.

This was another enigma of Africa. The pontoon, a construction of wood, floating on what must have been oil containers tied together, was the lifeline link to the north for the whole of this region. As it bobbed at the riverbank, a ramp was attached to this unique crossing craft with instructions to drive on. As the weight of the car hit the ramp, the pontoon lowered at that end, the opposite side lifting out of the water. This switchback process continued until the car was as near to the centre of the pontoon as possible. The two operators surveyed the proceedings with that calm sereneness I had only observed in the Lusaka mini-bus drivers.

The pontoon was hauled across the river by ropes, which either floated or disappeared below water before reaching the other side. The two operators hauled on these ropes and the craft made for the opposite shore with much creaking and flexing. [A rather grand modern bridge has now replaced the pontoon.]

Light relief in a war zone

After the pontoon crossing, the same vehicle-destroying road recommenced and carried with it the same destructive force as it had shown all along. But this stretch of the journey across Mozambique and onwards towards the Malawi border had become one of the first targets in the terrorist war to isolate Mozambique and its land routes.

This was in 1971 and the guerrilla war between the Portuguese colonialists and the 'Frelimo' liberation army was starting to get publicity on the world's stage. In 1975 it was all change, with the ruling Portuguese colonial power under General Spinola being ousted. The army was in no mood to continue what it saw as a losing war and staged a coup. Within a year, in 1976, Mozambique was under the Marxist control of Samora Machel and by March, the border with Rhodesia was closed. With the Soviets giving their support with logistical supplies, Mozambique joined the 'front-line' states in the liberation war against Rhodesia.

But in 1971 no one took this apparently rebel liberation movement seriously. Frelimo was starting to flex its military muscles against the

Portuguese colonialists using traditional guerrilla tactics and laying land mines on isolated bush roads.

I was not surprised to find this dusty, rock-strewn road through Mozambique was quiet, but in fact it was almost deserted. Upon arrival at the Malawi customs it transpired that the Portuguese authorities had banned civilian transport, as several vehicles had been blown-up by land mines a few days earlier. In those days changes in political and military strategy took time to filter through to the cross-country traveller.

Whether the authorities would consider it necessary to put up warning signs along such an isolated road, that a full-scale war may be under way and the road extremely dangerous, is doubtful. Like us, many innocent travellers had already been through, unaware of the danger. Travel through Africa at this time was always going to be hazardous. However, once on the road, it was probably better not to know that you could be blown up at any moment.

It did go some way to explain the Portuguese army troops all around the town of Tete and the large army base some way north of the Zambezi. I had driven in to this base without being challenged, to get a replacement spring for the car's clutch return. To get into such a place sited in a potential war zone in the 21st century would be virtually impossible, with at the very least, thorough searches and much questioning.

However, I do remember a diversion had occurred, which had taken all attention off guerrilla warfare. A Portuguese glamour girl, who had just arrived, had indeed taken over the troops' attention and nothing short of an attack by Kalashnikov-welding guerrillas was likely to get it back. Perhaps Miss Portugal was on a morale-boosting entertainment mission. Or perhaps she had taken refuge from the nerve-shattering road outside the camp's perimeter? All I could see was her shapely form waving from the rear of an army truck amidst cheers from the admiring soldiers.

As I drove in through the barbed-wire entrance to the camp, a bronzed platoon leader diverted his attention from Miss Portugal and surveyed me through eyes squinting against the mid-day glare.

"Please, may we help you?"

I got out of the car and we shook hands. For what must have been a rare encounter with two English cross-country travellers, he seemed able to reduce any resemblance of surprise to an unconstrained daily routine.

"I have this problem . . ." which I demonstrated under the car's bonnet.

"We will fix this."

"Any help will be most appreciated."

Bits of springs appeared from spares boxes and were applied to sort the problem out. Meanwhile across the sandy stretch of parade ground, the Portuguese glamour girl was still in the rear of the army truck surrounded by adoring fans. Her flowing black hair and lilac dress were catching the early afternoon breeze, creating a movie-style image, which seemed out of place in this harsh terrain. It would have been a tantalising, perhaps surreal occasion, if she was just the start of a road-show for the troops in this sand-blown waste-land, so far from all of their homes.

I found a spring that was good enough for a temporary repair.

"I appreciate your regiment's assistance", I gratefully acknowledged. The platoon leader gave a gesture, half-salute and half-wave. His attention was returning to the Portuguese glamour girl with the flowing dress blowing kisses from the back of the truck. As I drove out, she was descending the truck's steps to cheers from the soldiers. The camp disappeared behind the dust cloud as the car took up its own personal encounter with the road.

The next day, I learned, civilian vehicles would be taken through in convoy, with a military mine sweeper leading the way.

Within five years of the time I had driven into this Portuguese army base in a desolate area of Mozambique, the army would be gone and the country would have a new government. Peace however was still elusive and many years away.

The stone covered road to Kariba Dam

CHAPTER 21

Lusaka, the city built with copper

IN POST-INDEPENDENT Zambia in the 1970s, its capital Lusaka outshone just about all the capital cities in newly independent countries throughout southern Africa. It was new and brash with high-rise buildings and sidewalk hustlers. It was built on copper wealth with the metal from the huge reserves being mined close to the northern towns of Kitwe and Ndola. Copper from Zambia found its way into electricity cables and building sites around the world.

The metal was not forgotten at home either. The dome of the national assembly is built of it and copper is fashioned into thousands of crafts and curios in shops throughout the country. It produced a rich country with the world's second highest deposits of the precious stuff, enough wealth for most luxuries to be imported and to be affordable (at least by the growing numbers of the rich middle class). There was money aplenty for imports of luxury foods and even some designer labels from western fashion houses.

The drive to make this city compare with its southern neighbour Salisbury, or something resembling a European city in the sun was not without cost. The waste of resources that this produced was excessive. Supermarket shelves were lined with imported breakfast cereals and jars of dinner table niceties for those who could afford them. And there were many who could. It was not just the well-paid expatriates, but also the growing ranks of the indigenous population.

The well-off city dwellers filled their shopping baskets with such goodies as much for status as nutrition. One shopping trip would be a couple of month's income for the boy outside guarding the car. The gravy-train rolled until the oil price shocks in the mid-1970s hit commodity prices with the consequent catastrophic decline of the copper price. For a city built on one commodity, it was a sudden shock that would change its way of life.

Lusaka landscape

Lusaka is built on a high flat plain and its tall central office blocks can be seen for miles. Any traveller who had traversed hours of virtually empty savanna countryside would have a vision of grey towers emerging like pointed fingers against an almost featureless skyline. Everything in nature on this yellow savanna was identified with curves and irregularity, a product of the forces of sun, rain and wind. The Lusaka skyline appeared angular and vertical. This was a testament of how humans could transform the landscape. The traveller would not just see the growing towers; this was not a powerful enough description. This was an experience, almost surreal and it grew like a mirage upon the flat straight line of the horizon. At night its glow cut into the near black sky. The whistle of diesel trains disturbed the stillness. All roads led into the city. It would be less than an hour after seeing the beginning of this burgeoning cityscape until the traveller entered the four-lane dual carriageway known as Cairo Road.

Its presumptuous name was coined from its Northern Rhodesia days when Cecil Rhodes, the country's founder, had visions of a highway linking the country to Cairo, capital of Egypt. This mile long arrow-straight thoroughfare passed the high-rise buildings towering like concrete and steel monuments above the walkways, shaded by the jacaranda trees. No wonder its contrast with village life would fire the imaginations of the rural young, migrating here for a better existence. But as is so common in developing countries the world over, the reality for many is a life as tough as what they left behind. But stay they did, in a mushrooming shantytown complex which grew for miles in a chaotic spread from the city perimeter and into the bush beyond.

The dark days

With little foresight and no infrastructure to produce homemade goods, plus a shortage of foreign exchange, suddenly all this affluence dried up. By the late 1970s it was like a one company town in which the company suddenly went bust and closed. The capital and copper-belt towns of Ndola and Kitwe had been built from copper and now the market price could barely pay for the overheads. The western-style supermarkets looked like a suburban desert and even the side-street shops were empty. Everything disappeared off the shelves, even basic foodstuffs like maize and cooking oil vanished. The market traders, normally a force of last resort in times of hardship found their supplies difficult to come by.

The country became a focus for corruption and mafia-style crooks as the demand for goods, taken for granted for so long, became suddenly scarce. For the urbanised wealthy their custom oiled the illegal markets that sprang up to meet this new demand. Cigarette pimps and kerbside bread sellers became for many the last resort of supply. This entire catastrophe established itself like a virus within two years in the mid-1970s.

And catastrophe it was, a tragic contrast to the days when smart suited office workers pulled trolley loads of imported prizes from city centre supermarkets. But ten miles outside Lusaka, outside the perimeter of cornflakes and imported shirts, the inhabitants of the mud and thatch houses of the villages were also caught in this now confused country. The people from the surrounding townships could never aspire to own the fashionable imports; they would be forever beyond reach in a city where the rich and poor walked the same streets. But now simple staple goods like cooking oil and maize flour, bread rolls and margarine disappeared. But as if this was not enough, Zambia had become a 'front-line' state in the war with neighbouring Rhodesia and was both a supplier and safe-haven for the so-called 'freedom fighters' who made guerrilla raids into this colonial territory. Zambia became a target for retaliatory attacks by the Rhodesian army.

The natural border of the Zambezi River was no barrier against lightning attacks targeted at both the 'freedom fighter' training camps and political strongmen. The country's problems were compounded further by internal strife and rivalry, brought on by the war that many people did not care about and considered it was not their concern. They had concerns enough. President Kaunda was under pressure from rivals within his own political group UNIP - United National Independence Party. The *Shona* people dominated his power base. The antagonistic western province was yet another political problem. The *Ndebele* tribal group controlled this area and they had leadership aspirations of their own.

My arrival into a city of sunshine and confusion

As a seasoned expatriate I was expected to allow this chaos to remain in the background, after all it was none of my business. I had to get on with the job in hand. But to live in a country like Zambia and especially its chaotic capital and to ignore what's happening on the streets, must be approaching surreal. From street demonstrations and food riots to attempts on presidential power, and the effects of rocket attacks from Rhodesian forces, was starting to be part of life. It was a powerful backdrop and had become part of the Lusaka way of doing things. Life did proceed with some sort of normality, as people learnt to get on with what they had and in Africa there is a spirit of survival that is found everywhere. But there was an undercurrent of discontent that surfaced in frequent street protests as shops became empty as essential goods and food became difficult to get.

My new contract with the Zambian Government started in June 1977, although the lengthy negotiations had started months earlier while I was still living in Malawi. Whatever the country's internal problems it had no affect on my recruitment and as far as I remember was not even referred to. My recruitment procedure seemed to acquire something of the surreal dual-nature of the country. Life at one level was calm and normal, but just below the surface a war scenario would show itself before normality returned once again.

My application to the Government Printing Department was for a training assignment to introduce new computer-aided composition equipment. The machinery had not yet arrived in Zambia and no one knew where it was, indeed, even if it still existed. The system was state-of-the-art, and would, it was hoped, propel the department into the latest technology. The Zambian High Commission in London seemed in no hurry to get me out there. This was just as well as my cross-country travelling after leaving Malawi in 1976, had been already planned and I would be out of touch with civilisation for at least a couple of months.

My eventual interview with the Zambia High Commission in London was a seemingly rubber-stamp affair. The fact that I had survived in an adjacent part of Africa for six years already seemed qualification enough. I knew the life and by definition was a survivor. Lusaka I was to find, needed survivors. But perhaps other candidates knew something of the disturbances brewing out there and the possibility of a life-threatening situation did not appeal. Before taking up the appointment, I went through a costly training scheme in England and came out all set with manuals, notes, plans, back-up procedures, tools needed and every source of information to get it all going.

Within a couple of days of my arrival, it transpired a possible coup was in the offing and a dusk to dawn curfew was imposed with compulsory blackouts.

I duly arrived in Lusaka in June 1977. Kathy and Lloyd, then just two months old, stayed behind for family visits to Canada. My Zambian Airways flight became first class - apparently an overbooking error propelled me into this booze-laden executive area. The plying of drinks was an on-going speciality and proceeded into the overnight hours, by hostesses determined to off-load the on-board consignment of their liquor store, presumably to make room for replenishments on the return flight. This proved to be a perfect introduction to the local life-style. It was easy to muse about the life on board the national flight carrier with free unlimited booze swamping the executive suite and the local inhabitants unable to obtain cooking oil. This tiny example of the inequality of life so commonplace in developing countries becomes ever more poignant when the distinction between the have and have-nots is experienced daily on the city streets.

Lights out at night

It was sobering reality to land in the crystal-clear air and dazzling blue sky of dry-season Lusaka. I was met at the airport by one of my department's expatriate staff and dropped off at an apartment which was to be my temporary home for a couple of months while something more permanent was being arranged. Within a couple of days of my arrival, it transpired a possible coup was in the offing and a dusk to dawn curfew was imposed with compulsory blackouts. Such procedures are the typical response from a head of state when whispers of dissent are colouring the political atmosphere.

The apartment was situated within walking distance of the city centre and had a small balcony, not really a *khondi,* but large enough to sit out in the cool night air. It was here I would sit during the blackout hours, late into the evening watching the troop patrols in their open backed pick-ups, sirens blazing, speeding through the deserted streets. Anyone violating the curfew would certainly be arrested and would probably be shot on sight.

The city centre office blocks showed solid black against a lighter moonlit sky. It was a strange sensation to see a city so quiet and dark, as if at any time a switch would be thrown and all the lights would suddenly come on. I wondered whether there were hundreds of other eyes staring through darkened windows, listening to the sirens and distant rifle shots. Perhaps they wondered whether a new leader would be addressing them in the morning. But the president was a survivor and with an apparently loyal army it would take more than whispers to replace him.

Shortages and Corruption

The decline in revenues from copper had a gradual but inescapable effect on goods brought in from outside the country. There was an inevitable shortage of foreign exchange. The poorly developed manufacturing infrastructure was incapable of producing even the most basic of commodities and shortages became endemic. The once quite splendid and well-stocked supermarkets became eerie wastelands with shelves completely empty, stretching from the front of the store and covering every aisle. Occasionally shelves would appear with a bizarre selection of non-essential items, like jars of nutmeg or low voltage light bulbs. These would be carefully placed in a single-line along the front edge of the shelf with an almost military precision.

Nothing was on top or behind the isolated row; it had an almost artistic significance, as though preserved for a post-modern exhibition. I assumed the management considered something to display was better than nothing and the display demonstrated an irrepressible desire on behalf of the shelf-stackers to make themselves useful. This was perhaps the only occasion when shelf-stackers could display their goods with an individual personal interpretation. Whether this impressed the shoppers was questionable, as they searched for non-existent sugar and bread, only to find pencil-cases and one make of jam.

Whenever something in demand appeared, it was rare for it to actually get as far as being displayed. A network of informers would have somehow discovered its arrival and the store would be besieged by demanding shoppers removing it as fast as it hit the shelves. It was possible for the goods never to reach the shelves, being instantly transferred from loading pallet to shopper's basket. An informal communications network appeared to become established to inform anxious Lusaka residents about the location of essential supplies. In many instances black-market hoarders intercepted even this communications route and stripped goods out only to sell them at inflated prices in their own premises.

Lusaka city centre. Long avenues of high-rise offices

When news of a long awaited product spread, queues formed at the doors of the store. The penchant for order in queues so thoroughly displayed by their colonial masters (but did they ever really queue here?) was absent. It more often resembled a mob with the premises under siege. The carnival atmosphere which is seen so much in African life, whether in bars, or in the bantering of groups waiting for a late train, was absent in this urban struggle. But this was not a natural order. Urban living and the necessities of a cash economy imposed harsh conditions that made life not only difficult in the city, but a tough struggle to survive in the surrounding townships. When their meagre income could not wrestle the necessities of life out of the system, it stripped away their dignity. There was no-one on their side. What they scrambled for was only obtained by someone else's loss.

On my own shopping expeditions along Cairo Road, I often came across police with long batons wielded to good effect to keep at least some sense of order in the shopping queues. It resembled a life and death struggle with shouting and threats between those latecomers struggling to get in front of the mob and the early arrivals keeping them back. The police inevitably tended to slowly lose ground as the throng grew in size. When the doors finally opened, it was a surge of humanity that clamoured for the scarce goods. Hours of pent-up frustrations were suddenly released, for the expectancy of obtaining a single loaf of bread! For so many, it was hope that the anxiety of such a long wait was worth it. There was scrambling and pushing as scarce commodities were grabbed before the supply disappeared. On occasions the doors were actually never opened, for fear of the crowds releasing their anger on the shop assistants. Goods were passed through the security bars into a sea of waving hands. There were casualties with people being trampled underfoot and babies were reported to have been crushed to death while strapped to their mother's backs.

Business on the streets of Lusaka

The tragedy in all this was that many of the products under siege were staple foodstuffs capable of being grown commercially. Why bother with growing locally when money was there to import so much?

But now foreign exchange cash was no longer available. Although initial shortages, which affected most people on a day-to-day basis were foodstuffs, increasingly the whole fabric of the industrial and service sector began to suffer.

Villagers in remote districts knew little about what was happening in the larger cities. They grew staple products for their families, with occasionally enough surpluses to sell at the local market. But even they were not so remote from the international price of copper. The precious metal was a global commodity and its falling price had somehow come home to shrink their cooking oil supplies and paraffin for their lanterns. Medicines at their local hospital started to vanish. How was the village headman to explain what was happening to communities who barely knew what copper was?

Garages ran out of spares for the average car; machinery seized up for the most basic of running repairs. Even the copper mines, the single most lucrative export earners in the north of the country were not spared. This was indeed expensive and essential machinery, but still resulted in two hundred ton ore moving trucks incapable of moving due to non-existent spares.

Good times for some

For some there were profits to be made from the misfortunes of the many. An underworld of thieves, hoarders, black marketeers and 'informers' grew up with the aim of gaining a percentage by either supplying goods or knowing someone who could deliver. Lusaka was both the administrative and business capital with every foreign embassy and non-governmental organization being represented. The Copperbelt towns of the north although smaller, still maintained a moneyed elite amongst the supervisory ranks of the miners. This resulted in many businesses and individuals with enough money to pay the premium demanded for hard to get goods. The embassies had so-called 'diplomatic bags' to bring products in by. Such methods could by-pass customs and get what in Zambia would be labelled as 'luxury goods'. The commodities that came under this heading made up a bizarre category and certainly included some genuine 'luxuries', but items such as vehicle tyres and car parts, were not exceptions.

But for many of the city's residents, it was the network of informers and tip-offs that supplied their needs. It seemed that if something was needed there would always be someone, somewhere who could get it - for a price. As usual it was always the average working person who lost out in the scramble for scarcities. They rarely had the money to pay a black market price and their free time would be spent scouring the markets for a scarce item that might have been overlooked, or waiting outside a store for hours at a time hoping that a delivery would arrive.

During the months of trauma when shortages of once commonplace goods brought long queues and black market dealers, I was never aware of any widespread public discontent. Apart from minor outbursts from small crowds outside a shop and newspaper headlines demanding an explanation, there were few acts of disruption. There were no street protests or even violent displays against political leaders, or those accused of profiteering. Perhaps most city dwellers thought they were part of a collective responsibility for the mess the country was in. Or more probably, the old African quality of acceptance in the face of adversity was keeping the rumblings of discontent in check.

Protesters did take to the streets in political action against the country being labelled a 'frontline' state and being a base for the so-called freedom fighters. Although many disapproved of involvement in a movement they believed was none of their business, it was the reports of scarce foodstuffs being diverted to the 'freedom fighters' that caused widespread resentment.

CHAPTER 22

The surreal world of currency corruption

T HE SHADOWY world of the 'hard' goods black market was paralleled by an even murkier marketplace that existed throughout Zambia, for the 'soft' goods of currency fraud. This was essentially an underground network by which quite large sums of local currency were invisibly exported in exchange for any transferable international currency, but especially the US dollar and sterling. It was not exactly money laundering, as money in the local currency (Zambian Kwacha), was largely earned by legal means, not via the drugs trade.

Whenever there is a shortage of something, no matter whatever it is, a price will be generated which reflects demand. What was illegal and what the government attempted to eliminate, were residents transferring their surplus local kwacha into their overseas accounts by selling it to (usually) expatriates for foreign exchange. The expatriates in return would not need to import foreign currency, which the government urgently required. It was the uncertain political climate that made many residents with more wealth than they could dispose of locally, invest their surplus in safer havens across the world. It was an extraordinary example of the distinction between the poor with barely enough money to buy even the basics and a growing minority with so much they could export the equivalent of thousands of dollars. A tragic example of what can happen in developing countries.

The amount of money that could be exported legally through the foreign exchange system was severely restricted due to extreme shortages of this golden commodity. There was a risk factor in doing this, but it had to be weighed against the ability to transfer funds whenever the seller demanded. What foreign exchange available in Zambia was certainly needed by the government for much needed imports. Foreign currency legally brought in by residents (and exports) was needed for the purchase of foreign supplies not available locally and desperately needed to keep the economy ticking over. These were indeed ripe conditions for a black market.

There was a remarkable set of conditions that made the system work. In a country with so much corruption, there was complete trust between the buyers and sellers of the currency. Without trust, the whole system would come tumbling down. Perhaps there existed some horrendous penalty for any such deception. I was never aware of any defaulter. The buyer of kwacha - usually a locally-employed expatriate or business owner - would agree a price and confirm the sum would be deposited into a foreign bank account in the specified currency. The bank could be anywhere in the world. After the deposit was made, or even before, such was the trust involved, the local kwacha in paper currency, would be handed over. No paper work existed, as this could have been tracked down and the business blown apart.

Even when on one occasion the British CID were brought in to investigate, all that happened was a quietening of the trade. Supplies dried up and prices declined as an atmosphere of nervousness reverberated around the principal dealers. No evidence to my knowledge was ever discovered, or any infiltration occurred of the groups involved. The problem in tracking down those who were traffickers of currency was not only the lack of any hard evidence, but the extreme secrecy surrounding the whole business.

Although the total amount of local currency finding its way outside Zambia was potentially large - although no-one could put an exact estimate on the sums involved - it was due to the relatively small amounts of cash, spread over a large number of individuals. There may well have been businesses selling up and transferring the proceeds overseas in large amounts, but to do this legally would have taken years and was relatively rare. The businesses involved would generally prefer to transfer their money piecemeal through the illegal market, as a means of spreading the risk and to avoid the suspicion large sums would attract. Setting up the funding for new ventures in the host country was a priority for many.

Hedging their bets

The individuals involved in moving their kwacha cash wealth were a mixed assortment of locally based Zambian businessmen, expatriates and numerous Asians. This latter group were certainly the merchant class of the country and accumulated vast amounts of cash. They were also the most vulnerable if the political climate changed and compulsory business take-overs by the government occurred. Past and recent history in Africa does not generate confidence for such individuals and their long-term livelihood. Better to hedge one's bets and jump when conditions demand. When that jump may become a push, a nest egg in a foreign country would be a valuable start-up capital. Of course there must be buyers of that cash and this group were largely composed of short-term contract employees, especially those working for the government. They would be paid the same scale as an indigenous employee, but would top up their spending ability by drawing on their generous home benefits. Exchanging their foreign currency for local kwacha was a useful alternative.

Other buyers formed a curious assortment, ranging from missionaries, voluntary service personnel, teachers and even bank employees. There were of course non-residents such as tourists who bought local currency, but this was strictly a cash exchange. Although it all had a cloak and dagger image with deals struck in darkened alleyways, in reality it was all done fairly openly, but with an assurance that everyone involved could be trusted. Just like the paying of bribes to get things done or obtain scarce goods, it was against the law, but few seemed to care. There were a sizable minority involved and everyone seemed to know the practice existed.

A rate for the job

The black market exchange price at this time was something like four or five times the official bank rate. This it was assumed, was a price those wishing to transfer their wealth were willing to pay. A curious range of nicknames was applied to local cash purchased in this way, such as 'funny money', 'monopoly' (from the board game) and 'snow' come to mind. All foreign currencies purchased would usually have to be 'hard' or convertible, i.e. US dollars and £ sterling, were the most popular, with German marks and French francs next in line, but also the South African rand was a frequently requested destination for deposits.

As in all things in Zambian life, middlemen existed between buyer and seller, for that little percentage which oiled the process. When dealing with middlemen, the rate was generally fixed. Individuals including professionals and businessmen would often strike their own deals and as there were no go-betweens, better terms were available.

This illegal means of currency conversion was so common it was more or less accepted as the norm by any individual who had to bring money into the country. The Zambian banking authority must have obviously known what was going on, but were seemingly incapable of controlling their runaway currency. Yet had the Bank of Zambia adjusted their official rate on individual transfers, more cash transactions would have gone through official channels. However this was never going to happen, as officially the black market for foreign exchange just did not exist and there was no way of estimating what the sums involved actually were. Such was the bizarre background involved in so much of consumer banking, the process stood normal conceptions of money transfers on their head. As for instance when I opened a bank account upon arrival and was told by the white expatriate manager:

"I would advise you not to import any foreign exchange through us. In addition, don't get any loan through us either. Go to one of the local traders. But just be careful who you deal with."

And who would distrust a bank manager's advice? So, along with the rest of the informal sector, I too set up my own 'banking system'.

By word of mouth information, I discovered my local dentist was anxious to do currency swaps. He was an Indian dentist with a busy practise in the city centre. I asked his receptionist for a private consultation.

"Hello Dr. Khan, I don't have a problem with my teeth right now, but it's possible you may want to buy some foreign currency."

Whatever hint of initial surprise there may have been, was instantly replaced by the business acumen seemingly built into every Indian, whenever a deal was to be made. After a little hesitation, came the reply . .

"Yes, it's just possible I might. How much are you thinking about?"

"Oh, I was looking at around K1,000."

He seemed to be doing some calculations in his head and he apparently reached a figure.

"Will K4 to the £ be alright?"

"Sure, it will do fine."

"Well, come around this Saturday after surgery hours and we'll get it settled."

So, after a few pleasantries and within a few minutes all formalities were confirmed. Whether in the meantime my currency credentials were checked out by some obscure rating agency, I had no idea.

I duly arrived with my holdall (large denomination bills were fairly rare and small bills much more common) and the process began. It was necessary for me to know all of my dentist's bank details, including account number and address, in order to transfer funds from my bank in England. His bank was in South Africa and I suppose one day, or when the local political situation demanded it, he would fly in and use this nest egg to establish another base.

The kwacha bills, all well used grubby examples, were bundled together with elastic bands in every multiple of denomination that existed. They formed a miscellaneous heap on the waiting room table, probably collected from the previous week's list of patients. It was a scene reminiscent of a clip from a movie bank heist when the gang empty their holdalls of cash on the table before dividing the loot and making off to distant locations.

Having counted out the various bundles they were loaded into my holdall, with a minimum of counting. All I had to do was promise to inform my UK bank to send the required amount in sterling to the account in South Africa. There were no receipts, no security, with everything being done on trust. It was an amazing example of personal integrity operating within the world of corruption, yet with efficiency and an ability to produce results. This operation contrasted with a government crippled with corruption and bureaucracy, possibly with members of its own body carrying out these very same transactions.

Large numbers of small denomination kwacha notes occupied a relatively enormous amount of space. They had to be kept somewhere. To deposit such relatively large amounts of small grubby notes at the local bank would be sure to arouse suspicions and questions as to where it came from. However, for the local dealers around the market or along Cairo Road, it would be in a normal day's business to go into the local branch with suitcases full of the stuff. At closing time queues formed as bags were emptied and paper money, much of it worn out and practically at the point of disintegration, was painfully counted out.

But for salary paid expatriates, leaving large sums of money at home could be hair-raising in a city rampart in house crime. Yet many did, but for me another secure depository had to be found. This dilemma was resolved by the same enigmatic solution that drove the whole process of currency fraud. Like a pirate with his chest of gold and by the blackness of night, I buried the whole contents of the cash-laden case in an obscure location in the garden. There was no map showing its location that could fall into enemy hands. My main concern was whether the ants would get to it first. This operation did justice to the whole bizarre transaction, where normal rules about banking could not apply.

CHAPTER 23

Surviving security

B EING RESIDENT in Lusaka produced an uneasy complacency with the ongoing sense of insecurity. Zambia was a so-called 'frontline state' with its government directing a moral duty to support and give refuge to 'freedom fighters' in their liberation struggle with Rhodesia, their wayward neighbour to the south. As with the rains, which were always due at a particular time of the year, but when exactly no-one was sure, so a security disaster was also waiting to happen. The on-going sense of insecurity never disappeared.

In the wealthy suburbs of Woodlands, two miles or so from the city centre, any home would be surrounded by two metre high chain-link fencing, with an added topping of razor wire for good measure. Even the houses of moderately well-off Zambians would follow the same pattern, except their fencing would not be quite so high. This fortification would generally be covered with dry elephant grass, so no-one could look in - or out. As most of the dwellings were of single level bungalow style construction, only the tops of the roofs would be visible from the road.

The view of the houses in these wealthy suburbs was not of white painted walls, but of mesh fencing with sun-aged grass challenging the topping of razor wire for supremacy. To gain entry, it was necessary to shout from the gate to gain the attention of either the house-servant, or especially at night, a security guard. The fear of attack from the outside world made any occupier of an executive home reluctant to move in unless security was provided. Advertisements for homes always specified the degree of safety apparatus that was installed - window bars and fencing were part of the essential qualities of the desirable home. Reliable night-time guards were a desirable extra.

Instant justice

The thieves in the market places of the city centre were not the only villains to suffer the wrath of the law-abiding public. In our last few weeks in Lusaka, we were care-taking a house while the owners were on leave. A night-security man patrolled the garden from dusk till dawn. One night in the early hours, a commotion at the fence gates, coupled with shouts from the guard, brought me baton in hand into the garden to investigate. A group of local residents had caught a burglar in the act and in true local fashion had meted out their own 'instant justice'.

The blooded and gasping victim had been tied to our fence for collection by the police. We were one of the only houses to have a phone and therefore the means to summon police assistance. It must be said that the majority of Zambians were law-abiding and theft was against traditional culture. Justice had to be seen to be done - and it invariably was. All knew the penalty of justice delivered by the public. When the police duly arrived, there was no report requested or questions asked. The victim was bundled into the back of their vehicle and with a curt "Good night, sir, we will take care of this", they sped off along the darkened streets. The police would indeed 'take care' of the culprit and their own methods were likely to be administered during statement taking.

The wealthy suburbs.
A house in the upmarket Woodlands district of Lusaka

The pursuing of those 'caught in the act' was commonplace in Zambia. The Central Market in Lusaka made easy pickings for the light-fingered. The shortage of the most basic of commodities drove many otherwise law-abiding individuals over the edge of desperation. It was quite a common sight to witness a speeding thief being pursued by a rampaging mob in the market's side streets. There was genuine terror in the escapee's face, as his fate would be decided by his ability to out-run his pursuers. For the rampaging mob on his heels it was not just a despised thief they were after. He represented the collective theft they were all suffering and the powerlessness they felt in a country that appeared ignorant of their needs, or at best unable to reconcile its conflicting moral duty in the liberation struggle, with providing the necessities demanded by its population.

Evading the pickpockets

The pickpockets along Cairo Road - the main shopping area - were a brazen lot. This was not a city for window-shopping even if there was anything of interest to see displayed. The risk of being surrounded by a gang adept at emptying your pockets was too great. I often took a zigzag route along Cairo Road at some speed to throw off would-be pickpockets. When I anticipated an attempt was being made at my pocket or bag and was able to make a sharp diversionary move, the thief would often look back from along the street and give me a wry smile. It was as if some cautionary game was being played out on the streets with the actors acknowledging and appreciating their role in it. In this city where rules were so often ignored or misplaced, theft could become a game.

Guns and security

The Soviets, in support of the war effort, had loaded the country with such a variety of weapons, it would make an arms dealer delirious with delight. It was easy to obtain small arms such as automatic pistols and of course, the weapon of choice for all liberation movements, the AK47 Kalashnikov assault rifle. For those who required weapons with more bite, there were always convenient middle-men who could obtain heavier and more lethal products, including rpg's - rocket propelled grenade launchers - heavy machine guns, anti-aircraft weaponry and even surface-to-air missiles.

Although all this hardware was meant for the liberation forces in their attacks upon Rhodesia, defectors sold their armaments on to the highest bidder and stolen shipments found their way on to the 'civilian' market. As with the supply of vehicle spares, there quickly became established a network of suppliers who could obtain such 'defensive' supplies for whoever needed them for whatever purpose. But so hazardous was security within the major cities, even newspaper classified advertisements featured weapons under their 'for sale' columns. Seek an automatic pistol and before long an advertisement would appear supplying the item. Such was the supply route for the more 'sophisticated' criminal element.

Outside practically every shop a watchman armed with a truncheon, either slept out a drunken stupor or sat out the night

Vehicles being stolen at gunpoint were common, especially at night when the driver stopped for entry at the gated house entrance. In the instant between the driver honking for attention and the gates opening, there was enough time for a hijacker to emerge from the shadows and take over the vehicle. Armed hold-ups in shopping car parks in daylight hours became ever more frequent. There were few African countries in this era that experienced such a rapid decline in public safety. But war and the breakdown of social order were to become commonplace in several African countries in the early 21st century.

Around many of the public buildings, entry was impossible without a permit and gates were patrolled by armed security. All employees had identity cards supplied by the national registration department, complete with photograph and their owner's basic details. In a country tense with insecurity jitters and infiltrated by saboteurs - both black and white - the more official looking documents which could be displayed the better. My official government employee pass plus my national registration card were essential items of armoury in personal defence against security checks, which seemed to gain in popularity as time went on. Without such innocuous, but essential documents, tense situations especially in a society seemingly under threat, could easily escalate out of control.

At night all the shop fronts in every street had steel bars or rigid mesh over their windows and an incredible array of padlocks decorating the doors. Outside practically every shop a watchman armed with a truncheon, either slept out a drunken stupor or sat out the night. The shop front verandas with their dim lighting revealed only their outline shapes as they walked around or turned over in their sleep. Guards were generally not known for their bravery in the face of opposition. Minimal wages and elementary defence were not worth risking their lives for. They represented a deterrent to only the most timid of thieves.

The shopping areas of Cairo Road and its parallel Chachacha Road became deserted in these twilight hours except for the output from the bars around the market place. The streetlights did not penetrate the gloom under the shops' verandas. These were designed for shade from the fierce noonday sun and few lights came from behind the barricaded shop fronts. Here the guards kept nervous eyes on cruising cars and sounds of footsteps from side alleys. The daylight bustle became a night-time of silent fear; the gangs struck indiscriminately and came armed to counter any opposition. Late night bars and the occasional police siren, mixed with the howls from distant dogs and constant chirping insects, now became the city sounds. Night-time swept all before it, emptying the streets and installing an eerie cityscape, which only the onset of dawn would remove.

Getting the message out. Buildings are a popular advertising site

CHAPTER 24

Zambia as a 'frontline' state
The carve-up of Africa

THE FUTURE of Zambia was always going to be influenced by the countries on its borders. The country was originally known as Northern Rhodesia as far back as 1911, at this time being under the control of the British South Africa Company. In 1924 it became a protectorate under the British Colonial Office. A larger grouping was eventually formed and together with Southern Rhodesia and Nyasaland, became known as the Central African Federation. This arrangement was put together in 1953 by the British conservative government as part of the colonial carve-up of Africa.

The European powers arbitrarily imposed borders, which cut across ethnic boundaries, and formed the borders of the countries we see today. Little did they realise what the trauma of independence - and its aftermath - would cause in the next thirty or so years. To the north the Belgian Congo occupied a swath of tropical jungle the size of Europe. The Portuguese held similar sized landmasses with Angola to the west and Mozambique to the east. In the south of the continent the equally enormous but well developed South Africa watched the big powers grapple with their unruly offspring. South West Africa was administered by South Africa from 1910. It was not until the formation of the South West Africa People's Organization (SWAPO) in 1960 that another struggle for independence seriously began. It would take until 1990 before the new state of Namibia was founded.

New countries emerge

The 1960s were to prove a momentous decade in the political struggles of southern Africa. Northern Rhodesia emerged as Zambia in January 1964 with Kenneth Kaunda as its first president. The same year saw the break up of the Federation with Nyasaland becoming the relatively tiny country of Malawi with the charismatic Dr Banda at the tightly held helm. The independence struggles of Zambia and Malawi were relatively peaceful affairs compared to the traumatic political jousting and widespread liberation wars that enveloped many of their neighbours.

In 1965 Rhodesia sought independence from Britain and declared its now famous 'Unilateral Declaration of Independence' under Ian Smith. This move was quite unique as it was a *white-led* country seeking independence. The drama of how Rhodesia moved from UDI to full independence became world news at the time and this story has been well documented in many books and journals.

The 'frontline' states

However, the territories of Mozambique and Angola were also developing their own independence struggles and these were to become sources of political intrigue in the years ahead. The term 'front-line' state was coined by President Kaunda and applied to all countries in the region who considered themselves to be actively involved in promoting the cause of black majority rule in Rhodesia and ultimately, South Africa. The countries giving themselves this title were Tanzania, Mozambique, Zambia, Botswana, and Angola. While it is true they were all involved in the struggle to some extent, it was the countries of Zambia, Mozambique and Angola who were the real protagonists, as they gave up their own territory for the training of troops. These states became known collectively as the 'Patriotic Front'.

New war names

The Patriotic Front states were to suffer the consequences of the position they took on, as they suffered the brunt of Rhodesian ground and air borne attacks. The PF as they came to be known, were generally considered to be Marxist orientated, due to their association with the Chinese, Cubans and Soviet training teams. It was always difficult to know what to call the troops of the Patriotic Front. The PF had the preferred name of 'freedom fighters' and also called its men *vakomana*, meaning 'the boys in the bush'. The Rhodesian Security Forces developed their own more colourful descriptions of this bush fighting force, generally calling them guerrillas or 'c.t's.' or 'terr's' - communist terrorists. As the war progressed, more exotic names became common, including 'gooks' or 'floppies', describing the way they fall when shot. As with most conflicts, a dictionary of war slang grew up in the military to cover practically every situation the forces were involved in.

Powerful backers

But these countries were not going to be left alone to form their own unique destinies. There were much larger players in the game who used the territories as extensions of their spheres of influence. The world's second largest power, the Soviet Union saw an opportunity to make puppets of Angola and Mozambique by supporting local leaders who already had socialist ideals for their countries. The Soviets had the military might and a seemingly just political cause, that of ousting an unpopular colonial regime and forging a truly independent country. They also had the strong Marxist forces from Cuba, who were no strangers in the strategies of guerrilla warfare. With their own friendly, communist-leaning leader in power, their influence in a fledging country would be forceful indeed.

But things were not to be as straightforward as this, if this could in any way be seen as a clear issue. Another socialist power was flexing its muscles in the region and targeting the same impressionable states. The People's Republic of China also had the armament, expertise and political will and its own selected black leaders who were struggling for leadership. As I have documented earlier, the Chinese were already an influential force in independent Zambia, having constructed the TAZARA railway to the port of Dar-es-Salaam.

The influences of communist powers over large swathes of newly independent states, including the future of Rhodesia, resulted in the United States rebalancing the political agenda. The USA was emerging with a bloody nose from Vietnam at the hands of these same Marxist forces and they were certainly not going to allow the Soviets to gain an impressive lead in these politically sensitive territories. And in the geographical centre of it all was Rhodesia, a staunchly old fashioned capitalist, frontier-spirited state, who had its own problems with the mother country.

Local politics and their supporters

There were two black liberation movements vying for majority rule in the independence struggle for Rhodesia, both known collectively as the PF or Patriotic Front. Zambia became host to ZAPU, the Zimbabwe African People's Union, formed in 1962 and led by Joshua Nkoma. Its army was known as ZIPRA - the Zimbabwe People's Revolutionary Army based in the vicinity around Lusaka. Like most organizations in Africa, it too was tribal based, affiliated to the *Ndebele* group with its spiritual capital in Bulawayo, Rhodesia. Its army had an estimated force of between 9,000-15,000 at any time, some in the training camps in Zambia and others engaged in the guerrilla struggle in the Rhodesian bush.

The Soviets and East Germans supplied most of its armaments and logistical support. But this came via Cuba, at that time a Soviet enclave, and not directly from the Russian military. This would have been seen as dangerously close to direct influence. But there were certainly Russian instructors in the background, training in the use of amongst other armaments, the SAM 7 Strela surface-to-air missiles, which they had supplied.

The other black liberation movement was ZANU, the Zimbabwe African National Union formed in 1963 after a break-up with ZAPU. It was led by Robert Mugabe and based in Mozambique. Its other notable member was Ndabaningi Sithole, who challenged for leadership. The two groups had an uneasy relationship, but were under considerable pressure to cooperate. ZANU had an army too, known as ZANLA, the Zimbabwe African National Liberation Army, with a force of around 12,000. It was essentially a Chinese trained outfit, generally regarded as young ruffians, with a Maoist-style campaign, which besides engaging in the liberation struggle, had an agenda to transform the countryside. There were other parties, but none with the clout of these major contenders.

Standing alone against this onslaught, the Rhodesians had their own major white political party, the RF or Rhodesian Front, lead by premier Ian Smith who certainly did not want black liberation movements within its own borders. When UDI was declared in November 1965 his famous statement: "I don't believe in black majority rule in Rhodesia, not in a thousand years", became almost a statute.

Despite the war, the residents of George Compound, Lusaka always appeared to have a smile

Rhodesia could argue it had its own black political party, the lesser-known UANC - the United African National Council. This organization was headed by Bishop Abel Muzorewa, and was brought into the first Rhodesian elections. The country could now boast that it included a black political party and this was expected to achieve a moral advantage within the international community. Elections were held on 10 April 1979 and the bishop was duly nominated the country's first black president. With the Patriotic Front still fighting a bush war, it was excluded from the elections. But the PF regarded a Rhodesian black political party as a sham and as the war raged on, if anything its tempo was increased.

Life, trade and the war

In Zambia, the effect of the bush war did little to affect the sensibilities of the city's inhabitants. They had already been hardened by shortages for several years and had learnt to live and participate with the endemic corruption. They regarded their country as being too involved in somebody else's campaign. There was not only corruption within Zambia, affecting scarce goods and illegal arms, but the involvement of the country had spread to an international level, amongst those countries engaged in or affected by the war.

An attempt by Britain to bring a conclusion to the conflict, resulted in a blockade of Beira, essentially sealing the sea route for Rhodesian supplies. However, the USA still bought Rhodesian chrome as a strategic commodity. South Africa contributed vital supplies of oil. And in 1978, Zambia's president opened the rail border with Rhodesia to export its copper and import Rhodesian maize. All this was happening at a time when the bush war was at its most vicious. Even when these essential supplies of maize arrived in Zambia via this dubious route, there were claims that the maize was bypassing their own shops and entering the PF liberation camps. This caused storms of protest.

Although the residents of Lusaka had experienced years of this conflict, continuing shortages of even the basic commodities, together with no end of the conflict in sight, caused increasing resentment. The war became even closer, when news was leaked of secret training camps for the ZAPU army of 'freedom fighters' around the perimeter of their city.

By 1978-9 the war was increasing in intensity as the PF applied pressure for their access to power in Rhodesia. The Rhodesian Security Forces countered by raids on guerrilla bases in both Mozambique and Zambia. These increased during 1979, with the aim of halting the infiltration of PF forces into Rhodesia and also to damage the economic infrastructure of these two countries.

Raids into Zambia

A particularly heavy assault took place on 26 June in 1979, with the Chikumbi ZAPU camp eight miles north of Lusaka targeted. From a clear blue sky, five Rhodesian Alouette attack helicopters swept in at tree-top level across the Zambezi, skimming the savanna plains, approaching Lusaka and the fighters' camp with lethal accuracy. It was totally unsuspected by the training camp, who considered it would be an impossible target from such a distance. It took the boldness of Rhodesian air strikes to a new level. They were well informed of their target. A smooth wave appeared over the horizon with their rota blades hissing like swan's wings as they swooped in on the camp, releasing their rocket armoury with pinpoint accuracy.

The explosions could be heard across many areas of the city and plumes of smoke added to the dry season's haze. The attack was a bombardment both relentless and determined, upon a victim seemingly secure from attack. During the fighting more than thirty ZAPU troops and one Rhodesian SAS captain were killed. The daring nature of this raid was only equalled by their swift departure. It was over before local residents realized what was taking place. The now awakened anti-aircraft armaments came into action too late.

The isolation of Rhodesia had made the cause they believed in a rock-hard resolution.

The attack on Chikumbi camp was not the end of the excursion in to enemy territory. It was during this raid that the helicopters dropped assault troops in the very heart of Lusaka in the Roma district. The target here was the ZAPU intelligence headquarters, just a mile from the locally famous Mulungushi Hall where the Queen was to open the Commonwealth Conference in a few weeks time. Apart from the destruction caused, caseloads of sensitive documents were seized.

The Rhodesian force were more than a paid army, who did their fighting because this was what they had been trained for and were good at. They were fighting for a territory they were proud of and which they themselves and their forebears had built with a frontier spirit. As such the Rhodesian forces were associated with many years of battle-readiness and the notorious Selous Scouts were recognized as possibly the best bush warfare troops anywhere. The isolation of Rhodesia had made the cause they believed in a rock-hard resolution.

There are still many questions over the local politics of this raid. Why were the air defence systems so unprepared? The Zambians had been trained in the use of the equipment. Some of this air defence mechanism had been installed under instructions from the British government who also supplied Rapier air defence missiles. Whether the military were so scared of Rhodesian air superiority they dared not defend PF bases, in case their own military were attacked, was open to question. Perhaps to show their readiness to action, the next day after the raid, ZAPU fighters fired on a Boeing 707 passenger airliner coming in to land at Lusaka Airport. Fortunately they missed, but Rhodesian newspapers made great play about their enemy needing to know the difference between a Hawker Hunter fighter-bomber and civilian aircraft.

The war comes closer

There was outcry and street riots by the people of Lusaka at the boldness of an attack on their city centre. Just how much should they accept in supporting a war they did not want? Demands for more leadership and positive action forced President Kaunda to ask for protection from the Rhodesian air raids. He went as far as requesting that British troops should occupy Kariba and that Lusaka be protected by jet fighters. Although no troops were sent, RAF Javelin fighters did arrive in Lusaka with the quite bizarre situation where the assistance of the Rhodesian authorities in Salisbury airport was used to guide them in. It was only days since this same airport was used to initiate the Zambia raids. Was this a solution only Africa would facilitate to convene a solution, or just the absurdity of politics?

The sanctions that were imposed upon Rhodesia were in fact broken by all of its former trading partners

However raids by the Rhodesian air force continued, resulting in mounting resentment against Britain. As a former colony, despite UDI, it was thought Britain should take its errant junior to task. For some days after the raids the city heaved with resentment, encouraged by nationalistic newspaper commentaries of retaliatory action. It was at times like these that indignation against Britain was directed at white residents. They were an easy target. The city centre was occasionally given a cautionary 'no-go' status for whites by the British High Commission, after there were reports of people being attacked.

In my shopping expeditions along Cairo Road, I did not personally experience any of these hostile reactions from the local residents. But during these turbulent times, it was not only the pickpocket opportunists I had to be wary of, but a new breed of political agitators as well.

It was generally considered Britain should bring influence to bear on Rhodesia. This meant an agreement to a structure that would sooner rather than later lead to majority rule. However, Premier Ian Smith had ruled this out back in November 1965 by declaring independence. Rhodesia turned its frontier spirit into manufacturing many of its own supplies, so successfully, the country became self-sufficient and relied even less on imports. But even as the war was progressing, the bizarre situation continued, with the PF attempting to destroy Rhodesian farmers' land while Mozambique and Zambia purchased maize supplies from the same Rhodesian farms, their own being so inefficient.

In an attempt to speed the settlement process up, Britain did make gestures by sending a naval blockade to the Indian Ocean port of Beira to prevent oil shipments to the land-locked country. However the sanctions that were imposed upon Rhodesia were in fact broken by all of its former trading partners. The USA continued to buy its strategic stocks of chrome; South Africa supplied oil and many other countries continued trading. Zambian air space continued to be notoriously vulnerable to attack and on one Rhodesian bombing raid in 1979, on guerrilla camps near Lusaka, Zambian airspace was taken over while the raid took place. In spite of this, the build up of armaments supplied by the Soviets continued. The *Times of Zambia* reported the acquisition of armaments on 13 August 1979:

Dr Kaunda told a Lusaka rally . . . some weapons had already been obtained following the recent visit to the Soviet Union, German Democratic Republic and Romania by chairman of Defence and Security Sub-committee, Mr Grey Zulu.

The outraged Lusaka residents considered the violation of their country's air space to be the last straw and acknowledged their disgust by attacking the British High Commission. I happened to be in the area when the attack occurred. A mob of maybe twenty or more were aiming stones and blocks of anything movable over the fenced perimeter. There was no route through this fracas, so I took refuge in the German Embassy around the corner until tempers cooled. It was not so much the relatively minor damage caused to the High Commission, but it registered the deterioration of relationships with Britain. All local Zambians could appreciate was that they were hosts to armies occupying their territory for the purpose of staging someone else's war.

The danger of living in such a volatile country, or more especially its cities, can surprisingly quickly be accepted as part of the deal when coming to live in Africa with its ferocious local politics. And therein lies the danger of being complacent in violent cities where lives appear to have a downgraded value. Zambia was a so-called front-line state, but whites were a kind of front-line ethnic group. This was the same identifiable group that was causing so much disruption across the southern border. The air-raids and attacks by Rhodesian forces for all their importance, were not widely reported locally, or at least not the full story for fear of destroying morale. But these were newsworthy stories back in the UK and letters arrived from anxious friends and relatives asking how we survived in this war-zone. The same situation occurred in Rhodesia for much the same reasons. In both countries true details of the progress of the war were difficult to get. Typical of the confused state of news, this item appeared in the *Times of Zambia* on 6 November 1978:

Police are holding 20 white and black persons for either being found in sensitive areas, having hand grenades, making suspicious inquiries or behaving strangely.

The PF forces within Zambia were not only well-armed but were reported to be receiving resources of food and supplies denied to the country's citizens. They were not only a force the people of Zambia would like to be rid of, but were causing infighting between themselves and the Zambian army. As the *Times of Zambia* reported:

The Ministry of Home Affairs denied rumours that there had been fighting between rebel troops and Zambian forces in the Kafue area on Saturday. A ZAPU spokesman in Lusaka described the harassing of Zambian civilians as a 'panicky reaction' by the rebels who had failed to contain the freedom war inside Rhodesia.

From western countries, Zambia appeared to be a war-zone, but for the people living there, including its expatriates, the raids started to become a normal part of life. Normality however, masked the ruthlessness of the war and when occasional reports of brutality and carnage did appear in the local media, the true horror of what was happening appalled an already war hardened public. There was nothing 'normal' in what was happening in this bush war.

Most of the aerial attacks were on the perimeter of Lusaka or several miles distant, aimed at the freedom fighters' training bases. With the arrival of the Rhodesian attack helicopters in the heart of the city it brought an urgent sense of the closeness of the war; it was no longer just out there in the vast wasteland of the bush, targeting remote towns or isolated farms. Now the war was near to their own homes and across the street from the local shops.

Audacious raids

About a mile from our apartment on the edge of Lusaka stood the rather grand accommodation of Joshua Nkoma, just across the road from the president's residence. He was the original leader of the ZAPU - Zimbabwe African People's Union - a liberation movement in Rhodesia formed in 1962. After being released from imprisonment in Salisbury, he was living in political exile in Zambia, having been given safe haven by President Kenneth Kaunda. All this time he was taking part in settlement talks with the Rhodesian whites and the other liberation factions. But Nkoma was also responsible for organizing his own liberation army in Zambia, which mounted attacks on its southern neighbour. The Rhodesian Army not surprisingly, wanted this irritation squashed and mounted an attack against the ZAPU leader. It was on the 13 April 1979 when a daring land assault was launched into the heart of Lusaka aimed at Nkoma's military command and his residential premises.

Under cover of darkness and apparently without being challenged, their forces crossed the Zambezi on one of the closed bridges using camouflaged four-wheel drive transport laden with surface-to-air rocket launchers. The high-speed convoy reached the outskirts of Lusaka within a few hours. There was an intense bombardment of Nkoma's Lusaka home. Within minutes their target was reduced to a smouldering ruin leaving only a jagged outline of what was previously an elegant residence. Before resistance could be assembled, this strike force disappeared as silently as it had arrived. To defuse the outrage of a Rhodesian invasion, Kaunda announced:

I am not so sure that those who bombed Nkoma's house are not resident in Zambia.

The remains of Joshua Nkoma's residence after the attack

It later emerged Nkoma had survived the attack, possibly he was not even present in his luxury mansion. When news of this event spread the following day, the reaction was politically explosive. The fact that a foreign strike force, travelling overland, could hit the capital city of a country on a war footing without warning, caused the highest level of criticism of the defence forces and intelligence sources. This resulted in a level of security consciousness in excess of anything experienced before. Road checks and alerts at any public building suddenly intensified with something of a knee-jerk reaction.

The white expatriate population were especially vulnerable. In the *Times of Zambia*, reports circulated of white Rhodesian spies in the vicinity of the training camps on the fringes of the city. Scare stories and rumours were rife in this atmosphere of fear and a heightened sense of tension engulfed Lusaka. As the newspaper reported:

. . . another man was arrested when police found him taking pictures of the Lusaka main post office.

It was in this same post office - a sensitive communications centre - I was taken in for questioning after enquiring about a post office box number. The over-zealous staff were suspicious I might be one of these notorious spies and may be attempting to plant explosives. Such was the nerve-jangling atmosphere in the city, anything was seized upon as a potential threat to security. Fortunately my civil servant status and relevant documentation that I always carried with me, provided an easy release. But this was not before the investigating police had been convinced I really was no threat to public disorder. This was not the case for others who lived around politically sensitive areas.

A fractious settlement

Towards the end of 1979 the war in Rhodesia was reaching a critical phase. On 10 September the now infamous Lancaster House talks headed by Lord Carrington and Ian Gilmour, with the PF, Ian Smith and President Muzorewa, were started as the final hope in bringing all the warring sides together. Initially very little was achieved, not even the lifting of sanctions, but the talks dragged on for weeks. In Rhodesia there was something approaching 20,000 guerrillas attacking vital installations. But their relations with the local people deteriorated as their demands for food, women and shelter increased. Many local people in the tribal lands were slaughtered on the pretext that they were informing on the PF. There were frequent clashes between the two armies of the PF with contradictory reports being sent back to their respective command HQ. This prompted FRELIMO, headed by Samora Machel in Mozambique, to send in his own troops as a morale booster.

While the heads of this mix of competing forces were arguing at the talks, the bush war continued with increasing ferocity. Each group saw the prize within its grasp. But the battle-hardened Rhodesian Special Air Forces were not idle either. They launched raids to within 160 km. of Maputo in Mozambique - a distance of some 800 km. from Salisbury. Additionally, raids continued into Zambia with several road and rail links attacked. But the guerrillas were becoming better trained and had increased supplies of Soviet and Chinese firepower. The Rhodesians captured some of this equipment during raids.

As the war went on, so did the talking by the heads of the warring factions. Almost every conceivable interested party took part in the talks. The British Prime Minister Margaret Thatcher talked with Pik Botha, Prime Minister of South Africa. From the USA, President Carter constructed an aid package for the region to break the impasse and keep things going towards a settlement. An ironic humour must have existed in these exhaustive talks, as a ZAPU spokesman remarked on the attempts to 'stampede' the PF. Sir Ian Gilmour the chairman retorted: "This must be the slowest stampede in history".

There was general agreement towards a cease-fire, but as the effects of the Rhodesian attacks on installations in Zambia reached the PF, they became ever more obstinate and obstructive towards the settlement. The Salisbury government reacted by stopping the supply of maize shipments into Zambia. Without such vital imports the country would be brought to its knees and Kaunda's position would become increasingly unstable. The now outraged Kaunda made threats of putting his country "in a full scale war situation". The blockade of maize shipments had knock-on effects. To the north of Zambia the increasingly corrupt Zaire would also be left short of food supplies. President Mobuto of Zaire was an ally of Muzorewa and although this chaotic nation had enormous internal problems of its own, it could still have brought yet more pressure on the Rhodesians to negotiate.

The chaos and infuriating political processes, which are so much of life on this troubled continent were seen repeating themselves all over again in the tangled web of discussions being displayed during the tense weeks of this conference. However, an official cease-fire agreement eventually took place on the 17 December, 1979.

The final signing was four days later on the 21 December, a long seven years after the hostilities had seriously started.

CHAPTER 25

A precarious city

THE CITY of Lusaka was an increasingly fractious place to live during the final stages of the war. Its citizens were becoming increasingly rebellious against the shortages of basic supplies and its attendant associated level of corruption. Lawlessness was becoming an endemic ingredient in the structure of their lives. Desertions from the ranks of disaffected freedom fighters added to the already swollen numbers of local petty crooks. Russian supplied small arms, sold by the deserters, found their way to increasingly violent criminal gangs. These outlawed elements of the PF had seen enough of the fighting and deserted the bush war, taking their weapons with them. It was generally believed the government had given shelter to these groups, some of whom were now involved in every sort of criminal activity. Added to this explosive mix were reports of so-called 'Rhodesian spies' combing the areas around Lusaka, supposedly to locate the training camps of the Patriotic Front.

The increasing accuracy of Rhodesian Special Air Service Squadrons in hitting these areas was believed to have resulted from their intelligence reports. Around these locations any appearance of white faces would spark a security alert. Lusaka developed an atmosphere of fear. Although the city had its share of bomb scares, actually the destruction was generally outside the city limits, in the PF camps. Attack helicopters hitting these camps could be heard from the main streets, but there were no terrorists lurking around the corner aiming rocket grenade launchers at the local police station. When this happens fear becomes associated with a society on or going through stages of disintegration; normal life ceases to exist. This was a war in the bush, but the PF training camps became an important target for the Rhodesian forces and brought the conflict ever closer to the city. Life in Lusaka was on the limits of normal, or what passes for such in so many of Africa's cities. The war was 'out there' and so long as that was where it stayed, it was as much as the residents were entitled to expect.

Residents were beginning to get used to the home-grown crooks and increasing levels of violence, or at least some kind of uneasy tolerance existed. But as the war became closer with attacks aimed at targets not only within the city, but also close to their own homes, it appeared that perhaps there were spies on surveillance missions. The city was now confused by what colour the enemy was. The Rhodesian whites had an additional black element to their army, so infiltrators into Zambia could not be identified on colour alone. News on what was going on was not only government edited but was not altogether trusted.

Meeting the militia - a personal encounter

It was late one night when I strayed by a training camp, or as far as I could tell, at least some sort of military post. I had taken a wrong turning and this was a dangerous move in a city sprung with tension. Streetlights were dim and few knowingly approach military installations. So it should have been of no surprise to be stopped by Kalashnikov wielding militaries.

I was delivering our housegirl, Beauty, home after a late-night baby-sitting stint. She lived on the city limits in one of the smaller townships called Chilenje, about four or five kilometres from the city centre. Upon returning, I must have strayed over the boundary into a restricted area. I was not sure of my directions and was driving slowly - not always a good idea in a city rife with thefts of cars taken at gunpoint from slow-down areas at road inter-sections. Apparently out of nowhere came shouts and the sounds of studded boots running after the car. Lusaka was able to infect its residents with a precursory disposition for assessing potential danger together with an ability of instantly deciding on tactics of flight and survival. It was something acquired, something which filtered through the living here without you even realising it was happening. Perhaps it became intuitive, borne of necessity. But whatever this reaction was, one must decide in a flash whatever the course of your next move should be, and in that split second know what to do,

In a briefest of moments this involuntary process worked its way through my system; whether to race for the next corner, not knowing whether it was a genuine military check, or a group of hijackers intent on easy pickings. Whichever group it may be, the outline shadows of their weaponry convinced me they would be aimed at my departing car. Within that briefest of moments, I decided the corner was too far and my government papers would adequately explain who I was. Government employees are held, for some reason, above the normal rabble of humanity. In the dim glow of distant streetlights, the pounding boots surrounded the car.

The figures now resolved themselves into camouflage uniforms with military-style berets carrying a selection of guns. I was ordered out of the car to explain who I was and what my motives were in what appeared to be a restricted area. Through the darkness I glimpsed the outline of a pick-up truck that had stopped with more rifle-toting militia on-board. As when dealing with custom officials, the essentials of cool and courtesy from the start are necessary life-enhancers. Lusaka was a city where life was cheap and disappearances could easily be explained away.

A torch surveyed my papers and gruff suspicious questions followed:

"What is your reason for being here? Why are you taking this road? Do you know this is a restricted area? Civilians are not allowed here. What is your name?"

My answers met the questions head on and appeared to slow the onslaught of any further interrogation. My car was commandeered by some of the rifle-toting camouflage-clad personnel, while the rest climbed into the back of the pick-up. By this time I had a distinctly anxious feeling about the whole scenario. I was ordered to drive back to Beauty's house in the Chilenje suburbs. By now there must have been about six or eight supposedly military or training camp personnel of some sort both in my car and the accompanying pick-up. The area was about a couple of kilometres away. I indicated the house. Without a word both vehicles emptied and the militaries took up strategic positions around the house under the protection of the garden shrubs. I stood by the car and silently watched the crouching figures through the semi-gloom of a distant streetlight. The group leader summoned Beauty to the door and questioning began. From my vantage point it appeared her story collaborated with mine, and with a signal from the leader, the troops abandoned their positions and assembled around the pick-up. The leader's tone was now lighter and friendlier:

"Please be careful in future when driving in this area. Here are your papers, sir, my apologies for any delay."

"I'm glad you found everything in order. Good night to you."

My reply was followed by the usual handshakes and smiles and more friendly parting gestures, including directions into the city, before the pick-up truck sped away into the darkness. Perhaps they were glad to go back to their barracks and relax once more without the irritation of an insurgent to deal with. The whole operation had been silent and I suppose efficient. To my relief the troops had turned out to be genuine military, whether from the Patriotic Front or Zambian Army I was never to know.

Through the darkness I could see the Kalashnikov rifles had now been slung over the shoulders of the camouflage-wearing troops. They stood around relaxing, and the whole atmosphere was now like having a cloud disperse.

Like so many situations in Africa, change can be swift and surprising. A few minutes before I had been a possible suspect spy for the Rhodesians, which could prove to be not just embarrassing but a seriously life-threatening situation. The knife-edge scenario could have switched by just an imperceptible change of word or even tone.

They were presumably under orders to detain anyone remotely suspicious of gathering details about their location. For a few moments I stayed by the car, the evening's extraordinary events playing over in my mind. It was as though I had suddenly walked into a stage play and had been mistaken for one of the cast. But I had to remind myself this was

Africa and normal rules are often on hold. You had to learn a new set and however extraordinary they may be, they must be lived by and can produce both gratifying and scary outcomes. My encounter with the militia had reminded me just how precarious life here could be and how life threatening situations could materialise seemingly without provocation and be diffused, simply by one's attitude and carrying the appropriate documents. The improbabilities of what life entails in living in this mixed-up city was not something I was ready to contemplate at that moment and I headed the car for the corner and away from the military base.

As with my encounter with the militia, there is always the element of the unexpected in so much of what happens in Africa. It is more a land of mystery than a continent with predictable consequences. It is a place where plans may mature with an outcome forged by the spirits of the forest rather than human involvement. Everything from the most ordinary bus journey can develop into an adventure or at least something that proves to be not as it was intended. Something as simple and spontaneous as a gang of enthusiastic children scrambling over themselves to plead for your last ballpoint pen, all smiles despite having so little. It's something which just happens and however insignificant, becomes a lasting image.

Whether it's one long nightmare of an event you thank good fortune to have escaped from and never wish to repeat, something is gained. It all fits into the chaos of a place. But it is destructing to see the grinding poverty and corruption and know something about how to put it right and yet be unable to do so. A demand is made - and it is a demand - to move one's life into another gear and to adjust. There is so much needing to be accomplished and so many simple changes that would make life better for everyone. But if everything could be changed most of the allure which brought you here in the first place, would be lost. But in the improvement of people's lives there is usually a cost, in the lost environment or something less tangible. Each individual must determine whether the experience of living here is positive or not. Any lasting impression is not easy to summarize. It is as colourful as the landscape itself.

The endearing happiness of a Lusaka resident

CHAPTER 26

Cinema and politics

MY INTEREST in the silver screen went all the way back to my teenage years. It was before television made an indelible impact and when film theatres were crowded and several could be counted along a typical high street. It was an age of double bills and B-movies with cheap entrances and charismatic stars who still remain iconic figures and maintain an enthusiastic audience, to this day. I must have seen as many films as anyone could fit into time outside school hours, and later, around a working week.

In Zomba, Malawi, there was a film society both Kathy and I regularly attended. It was the kind of thing reminiscent of village halls, held in a squat, anteroom of a local school with rigid chairs and benches. This was enough to rekindle my interest once again. The films were on a circuit that started their African adventure from South Africa, to be circulated around Rhodesia and goodness knows where else. Celluloid reels have only limited tolerance to extremes of climate. Yet these must have endured everything from dry heat to the dripping damp humidity during the storms of the wet season. They survived being thrown about on cross-country buses with dust storms swirling about their steel canisters.

When the reels arrived in the projection booths, I could imagine the sprocket wrenching trials of abused film, being forced through less than appreciative projectors, often devoid of the most basic of maintenance. Their endurance to destruction was taken further when the much-abused reels reached Malawi and their trials were to enter a more invasive stage. It was here that the reels encountered the legendary Malawian censorship organization and endured further ill-treatment. As a private film society, our titles escaped much of the censorship that was routinely metered out to the public circuit.

The zealous censors hacked into the films removing anything that hinted at corruption or what they saw as western degradation. The distributors, not surprisingly, restricted films to those considered 'safe' viewing and established their own form of censorship by prohibiting any title likely to attract attention and risk being attacked by the Malawian guardians of morality. Even for the films that did arrive, long footage of celluloid still hit the censor's floor before an alright to view certificate was attached. However the spools did survive such mistreatment and delighted their audiences, irrespective of numerous breaks and sound crackles during the showing. I never did determine by what means these cut pieces ever got back onto the reel in the correct order. The next audience on the circuit must have experienced some curious cinematic scenes.

Cinema Petit

My involvement with Cinema Petit, the Lusaka classical cinema society, started as a journey into an adventure, which was to have a lasting influence both on the society itself, and for me, it was an introduction in negotiations with an extraordinary range of people, from the most diverse backgrounds.

Will the reel break? The author as projectionist

My regular attendances and interest in its operation enabled me to take over in the projection room and generally help to keep things running. When my colleague Peter Jackson stepped down from his position as chairman, I took over. He was an expatriate architect who decided to make a go of it in the newly emerging Zimbabwe. The whole operation was on an entirely different level from the small outfit in the Zomba schoolroom. For a start it was housed in the rather prestigious Lusaka City Theatre, a 200-seat auditorium with excellent seating, professional screen and pretty good sound facilities, together with a separate purpose-built projection room with lighting controls. This theatre was one of the rare artistic legacies from when the rich days of copper supported a booming city.

The theatre had that dry smell of old fabric and mellowed paint undisturbed from countless sets stored backstage. The clear outside air never got into the auditorium and it remained sealed off from this world like a cave newly discovered hundreds of feet below ground. Even when the lights were at their brightest there remained an atmospheric gloom, as if the lights were about to suddenly dim in deference to those on stage. This cavern-like place had a silence that enveloped you as soon as you crossed through the swing doors and entered the auditorium. It demanded an urgency to get on with the next show or film. The projection room had its own environment generated by the air tainted with thousands of micro-bits of cinema reels, shed as miles of the stuff clattered over the projector sprockets and sound heads.

There was a ready made audience from embassies and the country's central offices, quite apart from a large base of expatriates, many of whom were looking for a better change of diet to that served up by the commercial cinemas. To attract this 'sophisticated' audience, it needed a superior quality of material than what was on offer from the public cinemas with their heavily censored, although popular 'circuit' films. Cinema Petit generally survived on the quality end of circuit films. I set out to improve its film programmes by cooperation with the numerous embassies and local cultural associations. It was the start of a journey of discovery.

The cultural centre of the city

Lusaka was an ideal place to realise these aims, as the infrastructure in the form of an audience was already in place. Most of the world's embassies and diplomatic entourage were located here, together with a host of non-governmental organizations and numerous United Nations bodies. Many wanted to impress with their country's cultural prowess by inviting touring artistic troupes and stage shows. But the obvious logistics of getting orchestras and the like into such a relatively remote land-locked country made this a fairly rare event.

Film however was an altogether different option. It was reasonably easy to transport - as long as you were able to get to the source of supply. The local cinemas were not really suitable. They were already taken over by the local towns people and generally survived on a diet of popular action and romance. The City Theatre had an up-market atmosphere to it and was a centrepiece of expatriate patronage, a sort of colonial club, but with a distinctive cultural feel to it. Its mainstay patrons were still the expatriate population, but with a minority of well-off Zambians who either used the bar as a sort of watering-hole or, a smaller number who participated in theatre productions.

However the old image was still well entrenched. I assumed the embassies would consider this a better venue to host their film events. They wanted to impress with their films and I wanted to post up a programme of interesting material. It was an ideal partnership, but it needed a kick-start.

Promoting the cinema

Through various introductions and also by simply putting my case to offices such as the American Cultural Services and British Council, I was persuasive enough to get an initial trickle of classical film material brought into the country. Film reels invariably arrived through the 'diplomatic bag' and were not subject to duty or censorship. With the programme now including pristine condition reels of such classics as *The Maltese Falcon* and *The Servant*, audience numbers started to escalate. More offers of films on a fairly regular basis started arriving, which made future programming far more predictable. I started to know the staff of the cultural institutions on a personal basis and film reviews often took place on their premises. A sort of momentum developed with further introductions to the embassy offices of countries from much of Europe. With an assortment of both English and foreign language films arriving in increasing numbers, it soon appeared Cinema Petit was starting to develop into a cinema society close to unique in black Africa.

To have access to such a range of quality productions was certainly extremely rare. As my connections with a diverse range of foreign cultural associations developed, I was gradually introduced to the enclosed world and the process of life within these often little known and potentially mysterious organizations.

Many of the films I would preview at home, with the society's 16 mm Bell and Howell projector, complete with wide-screen and sound system. I was fortunate to have a matt white wall extending the complete width of the living room. And so it seemed the business of film viewing and selection started to envelope as many waking hours as I could make available. The clatter of the projector started to become a backdrop to many pleasant evenings spent with committee enthusiasts churning through an ever-increasing pile of film canisters lodged behind the settee. It appeared the sunshine of Africa had no place in this world of film, which by its very nature demanded its complete exclusion.

The committee came from backgrounds as diverse as the films themselves. Not only from England, but also Holland and Finland, with occupations ranging from technicians, to staff working with the United Nations High Commission for Refugees.

The diplomatic connection

Many of the previews took place in the embassy or cultural association that had requested the film be brought into the country, usually with an invited audience. There were regular invitations from the splendidly named American Cultural Attaché, at his spacious mansion close to similar grandiose residences. Even a serious film preview, destined as a cultural promotion, was pretext for a boozy get-together. The double driveway led to a sort of neoclassical-pillared entrance. The film was a legitimate excuse to have an enjoyable evening with free drinks and a good reason to party. The lavish booze table full of imported varieties were a diplomatic entertainment allowance. As the host remarked: "Why go back to the US when there is a life like this here?" He had a point. And it applied to many diplomats who indulged a life of similar grandeur. Many informally admitted to the comfortable style of their life in a far-flung and sometimes forgotten, corner of the world. They had none of the stress that accompanied the local masses, facing the material shortages of the city they strived to make a living in. It was an extraordinary anachronism to be living in a city with so much poverty, with a bush war raging not far from the city limits, yet cocooned in a lifestyle of relative wealth.

I had little doubt that for many of the staff, life in Lusaka compared favourably with other postings in what could be more desirable places. It was perhaps this very isolation that gave the lifestyle such an abandoned air, as if the distance from home allowed, even encouraged such extravagance and made for its justification. Behind the smart entrances, I heard outrageous stories of chaos and inefficiency with the foreign staff brought in. There were those lacking language skills who could not converse with anyone outside the embassy. I was told tales about important documents being lost from an East European embassy, prior to a meeting with government officials. An inevitable scramble ensued as everyone from the ambassador down ransacked the building for the missing papers. I never discovered whether they were found.

Most luxuries arrived courtesy of the diplomatic service with 'luxury' extended to include car tyres and even household 'essentials'

One of the obligations of the diplomatic staff was to form relationships with their opposite numbers from other embassies. On special occasions like their national day, enormous numbers of invitations resulted in an official opportunity to combine a day out with a bonding session. For me it was an introduction to the life and style of a privileged section of overseas staff few got the chance to see and participate in.

Invitations to a cultural affairs event were not always the preserve of the rich and famous. Just being an expatriate from the appropriate nation would often be enough – provided you kept an ear open for what was going on. When Canadian premier Joe Clark arrived on a southern Africa goodwill tour, Kathy and spouse were soon placed on the reception list. Having her Canadian nationality, plus the scarcity of nationals, was to make attendance almost mandatory. Perhaps it was all about making up the attendance numbers, but it made for an illuminating evening. To be able to hold conversations with such leaders over complementary drinks and food were one of the perks of this lifestyle.

Most luxuries arrived courtesy of the diplomatic service with 'luxury' extended to include car tyres and even household 'essentials'. This included just about anything that could not be obtained locally. This often resulted in crates of 'special effects', including all the numerous film containers I requested. This secluded world epitomised the cocooned existence within the embassy walls, extending into the immunity from all sorts of prosecution, including traffic accidents and minor assaults, which was a normal part of life enjoyed by official staff. The now almost forgotten association with 'the long cocktail party' was certainly close to an accurate description of life enjoyed by its members, even though it was all part of the job.

According to one embassy member I knew, there was, "A continual round of socialising and partying on an almost daily basis, with either our own colleagues or with other embassy staff we knew well". The closeness of embassy personnel to world leaders (perhaps the lesser known) must have figured in the serious attractions of the job. A receptionist at the Italian Embassy I was friendly with, took all the telephone calls, even from President Kaunda, when he requested assistance from Italy in the importation of grain supplies. This closeness to those who were influential or important decision-makers was always a feature of expatriate life in relatively small communities. It was certainly one of the attractions of life in the embassy fold.

Even with my negotiations for an Italian Film Festival, the meetings were seen important enough to be chaired by the ambassador Dr. Cuneo. This charismatic individual had not only Roman features but left no one in any doubt as to who was in charge. He would verbally batter his subordinate staff who vainly attempted to come up with solutions. During the meetings I attended, it was difficult not to display a wryly smile as his gestures became increasingly close to body blows when his message appeared to be getting lost. But his inherent good nature would eventually make amends until the next inconsistency caught his attention. However this collaboration provided Cinema Petit with some of the best Italian classics.

The Soviet involvement

This was still the era of the so-called 'Cold War', and eastern bloc countries were notoriously difficult for me to gain access to. I had it on good authority that all these places were extensively bugged and elaborate recordings made, with surveillance kept of everyone who visited and who they were. The introductions I had to the East German and Romanian premises did not get very far. I was not sure anyway about which films these countries had lurking in their archives and in any case they appeared far too nervous about the prospect of letting me onto their territory. Likewise with the Chinese delegation, who would not let me on to the premises. I had to discuss my business through the main gate. It was therefore with some surprise I was introduced, completely spontaneously to the ambassador of the Soviet Union.

I had organised a film festival for the Swedish Embassy and while the guests were departing, I mentioned my interest in Soviet films. One of the Swedish delegation said the Soviet Ambassador had been invited and pointed out who he was. Dr. Vassily G. Solodovnikov had the title fitting to such a post. His visiting card read 'Ambassador Extraordinary and Plenipotentiary of the Union of Soviet and Socialist Republics'. Instead of forcing my way through either security or a ring of support staff, I introduced myself as he was making for the exit. He wore a formal dark suit, with a fit instantly recognisable, as only the Soviet Union could have produced. He had a patch of the same matching colour over his right eye. With the relaxed style of dress common in Lusaka, his appearance had something of the 1950s about it, or reminiscent of a grossly undersized security official.

He was courteous and brief and seemed genuinely interested in my suggestion that collaboration between his government and Cinema Petit would be advantageous to both of us. It was my only chance to tackle the highest authority of the Soviet Union in Zambia and I intended to put my case firmly and directly. Perhaps he would use his influence to get the best Soviet made films and we would put them into our programme. This would be, I pointed out, a great advertisement for Soviet films! It was not to turn out as easily as I had planned.

My argument seemed to have had an effect, as I was officially invited to the Soviet Embassy to discuss details. This I found to be extraordinary, even in a city with a reputation of having a socially relaxed atmosphere. The Soviet Union was still seen to be a huge and formidable world force with a tendency towards secrecy and a questioning attitude to anyone outside its own borders. This was to prove an important opportunity.

Close encounters with the embassy

This was to be my only personal encounter with Dr. Solodovnikov. I was to learn some time later of his supposedly close involvement and influence with the guerrilla forces fighting for control of Rhodesia. I made frequent visits to the embassy, usually supervised by Rashid Ibragimov, who carried the slightly less grandiose title of 'Second Secretary'. The whole complex was high-walled and from the outside, apart from a distant view of the tops of roofs, only the silhouette of communication masts could be seen. Its size emphasised the importance the Soviet Union had of itself and its influence as a world force. It had set out to impress. As I was escorted through to my meeting place, I passed vast rooms suitable for banquets or for receiving dignitaries. The wood panelled walls and floors were decorated with deep red carpets. Ornate chandeliers added an extra touch of luxury. Gilt chairs were placed at strategic points along what seemed endless corridors. There was an atmosphere of size and opulence, perhaps intended to induce some intimidation and astonishment in the minds of guests. Intentional or not, I was impressed by the grandeur of it all. Our meetings were always at a low coffee-style table with a carefully placed glass bottle of a soft drink and soda water, creating an atmosphere of detail and formality.

My discussions with Rashid took the form of finding which, of an immense library of Soviet films, would be suitable for showing. It quickly emerged these were not going to be released lightly and the embassy had their own ideas of the material they were to haul in from Moscow. Although I had my own list of requests, their intention was to show not only a well-known classic from the legendary director Sergei Eisenstein, but also a children's film and examples of modern, popular wide-screen material. In short, there was to be a selection of recent material virtually unheard of and not yet seen outside the Soviet Union. The intention was to stage a festival lasting a complete week, commemorating sixty years of Soviet cinema. This presumably was to show-off the country through its film achievements to a captive audience of embassy officials and to many in influential government roles. With an assembly from all over the world, it was intended to be a grand propaganda exercise.

I made several visits to the embassy to preview films brought in especially for the festival. These took place in a fully equipped auditorium, with a gently sloping floor and cushioned folding seats. The wooden panelling, so much a feature of embassy décor, continued the full length of this showpiece theatre. It was only interrupted by two giant portraits of Marx and Lenin, strategically placed either side of the screen, with a grand chandelier in the centre of the hall. The projection room overlooked the scene with twin 35 mm machines housed behind glass panels. It was a set-up that would be prized by any facility open to the public. But this was for exclusive embassy use and presumably selected guests. By the time I arrived everything would be in place; the projectionist would be waiting, the list of film sequences ordered and listed. I was expected to come away impressed at their efficiency and they were right.

The Soviets had their own special way of organizing things. The festival opening film was to be the Eisenstein classic *The Battleship Potenkin*, and the venue of choice, the film theatre used by Cinema Petit. Even though Zambian workers were available, the embassy used only their own personnel, all their own technicians and equipment, and even their personal drivers. Their two massive 35 mm projectors were transported from the embassy and somehow manoeuvred onto the upper gallery of the theatre. Invitations to the opening event were sent to embassy staff, every international organization in the city and government officials. A special reception was laid on in the theatre bar/lounge immediately prior to the showing, for all the great and the good of the city. There were even such Russian delicacies as caviar included –

something never experienced in Lusaka. As organisers, both Kathy and I fell into that category!

An extraordinary opening

The theatre was full on the opening evening. But it was not without incident. It was the time of the Soviet Union's controversial occupation of Afghanistan and while the welcoming speech was being delivered, an outburst from a few individuals in the audience against what they saw as Russian hegemony, drowned the words. My predecessor at Cinema Petit, who was intent on showing his political credentials before leaving the country, led this outburst. The ambassador and some of his staff who were sitting close behind me appeared unperturbed and sat motionless throughout. Perhaps they were used to outbursts concerning their nation's involvement in the affairs of other states, but a trump card was waiting to be displayed in the propaganda events of the evening.

Before the lights dimmed and before any reactions to the outburst could be registered, either for or against, a Moscow television crew, unbeknown to me, suddenly appeared with glaring studio lights. The normally subdued illumination of the auditorium erupted into the brightness of a sunny day as the cameras scanned over the rows of seated guests. Many of those present, I recall, attempted to conceal themselves with whatever came to hand. It was a politically sensitive time and their being shown on a Soviet television channel could have been embarrassing. By displaying such a variety of international guests at a private invitation could at least be assumed to demonstrate the Soviet Union was not isolated when some of its policies were being questioned. The next day I received a barrage of telephoned complaints about this event, accusing me of complicity in what was seen as a set-up.

The Soviet Embassy and its influence

The involvement of the Soviet Union in the affairs of southern Africa at this time was of pivotal influential and central to its operations was its ambassador Dr. Solodovnikov. He has been described as the *eminence grise* in Africa, as the Kremlin's lead man in its preparations for armed intervention in Rhodesia. It was claimed he was instrumental in assisting a Cuban led assault with Nkomo's PF forces into Matabeleland, Rhodesia. This would have been Russian financed with both armaments and supplies shipped into Zambia. His involvement has never been factually proved, but certainly Cuban troops and Russian equipment were fundamental in the whole campaign. In his book *Bear at the Back Door*, General Sir Walter Walker described the ambassador's policies:

He was told the continent must be cleared of whites within five years of his appointment. (Dr. Solodovnikov) is one of the leading experts in the Soviet Union

of African affairs and one of the KGB's senior officers. He is a former director of
the Africa Institute of the USSR Academy of Sciences and one of his publications
. . . is the basis for Soviet designs in Africa.

General Walker goes on at some length to describe how the
ambassador was directly involved in the terrorist campaigns of the
Patriotic Front against Rhodesia. By doing so he was influencing President
Kaunda to enter the Soviet area of influence.

I had no idea or suspicions about the nature and influence of the
person I had been introduced to. I was simply trying to persuade the
ambassador it was going to be a good idea to obtain a few reels of film to
keep our programme going!

It was no surprise for me to learn that all the embassies from the old
Soviet regimes and communist Eastern Europe were careful to scrutinise
anyone visiting their compounds. And once inside all sorts of recording
devices were used as surveillance for what went on. I was told on good
authority, even the private accommodation of the staff was similarly
wired up to keep a final check on anything that could be remotely
associated with deviant behaviour. There was little doubt my comings
and goings at the embassy were similarly recorded. I put these points to
several experts on intelligence studies in England. It was generally
considered not only the Soviet Embassy would have such information on
file, but also either MI5 or MI6 would have details of all visits to such
embassies. There would without doubt, be surveillance by the Russian
Ministry of Foreign Affairs or the KGB, who were notorious in the detail
of their own records. To gain access to records is often difficult and
extremely time-consuming, occasionally protected by a considerable
number of years for security purposes. But somewhere in some vast
underground labyrinth in Moscow, I can imagine sparsely illuminated
corridors of files and on a dusty shelf, the records of my comings and
goings in the Soviet Embassy all those years ago.

In researching material for this book, I exchanged some lengthy
correspondence with (now) Professor Solodovnikov. He described how:

. . . the western powers disliked me but I did my best to be useful for (to) African
people.

I also met the Professor Solodovnikov's colleague at the Institute for
African Studies, Dr. Vladimir Shubin when he was in England for a
lecture at the London School of Economics. Although he filled in a lot of
interesting background material I was interested in, he went to some
lengths to put the case that the professor was definitely not a KGB agent
and at no time did he knowingly bring in armaments to fund the rebel
movements. The professor told me he is now working on his memoirs, a
reflective process which often reveals much about the past and can restore

forgotten facts. Perhaps his memoirs will answer questions concerning these clandestine operations.

Films, culture and propaganda

The chance opportunity of being able to visit such a variety of cultural organizations and embassies, more or less at will, was really just good fortune. It was something not planned, but grew out of my involvement with Cinema Petit. After all, organizing a classic cinema club, was just my part-time occupation and at the time I had no idea it could lead to regular invitations to various embassies and involve discussing their cultural affairs programme. I was chairman of an organization set-up to show films and these places wanted its facilities to promote their own film achievements to a wide audience. It was a partnership brought together by the particular circumstances existing in a developing country at this time in history. Fortunately for me, these institutions wanted the world to see their films. These were the conditions that made the whole thing possible. I am without doubt, technological and political changes would make this almost impossible in today's world. However this may be, it was an extraordinary opportunity to observe how these rather closed and often secretive organizations worked. Few outside this restricted circuit get to obtain a glimpse of daily life behind their closed doors.

Many visitors to exotic and distant shores often assume their problems with local bureaucracy will be solved by a visit from the local embassy

Some of the embassy staff I became close colleagues with and learnt something of what was for them a daily routine. In the main I found little to be surprised about. However, to meet staff who were either involved in clandestine operations, or close to their superiors who were, was something I was not prepared for. There is intrigue and mystery presented to the masses on the outside; about what they do and the processes they set in motion. They are centres of influence, few get to see behind their guarded entrances. The comfortable and often lavish life-styles of their personnel and the cocooned safety of their existence are only compromised when they step outside the doors.

For the general public, embassies present an institution still seen to employ cloak and dagger methods akin to the best of the 'cold war' era. Ask the general public what their work is and answers range from their organizing 'James Bond' escapades, to the boring job of simply stamping visas and passports and the equally mundane task of arranging trade commissions. Of course all this is done, but I saw lots more besides and just as importantly, a few of those who pulled the strings.

Many visitors to exotic and distant shores often assume their problems with local bureaucracy will be solved by a visit from the local embassy. Getting someone out of prison or intervening when a national becomes fouled up in some political mire is mostly a chancy business for those running foul of the local system. If a big enough fuss is made, which results in a newspaper story, then some wheels may be made to turn. But this is not something that can be counted on. Embassies are there to smooth ruffled feathers, not shake them up.

But these places do have power and influence. It travels around unseen like in cables, and it can be used to prop up or bring down a regime. This could be any cause that benefits the home country and preferably their host country too. It might be a political or military group with the right agenda that needs funding. These delegations are still out there in the world, doing the same kind of things, still attending those cocktail parties and for all I know showing classic films to an invited audience.

What I saw in the Russian embassy is now a part of history. It was the centre of power and influence in southern Africa and its strategies started to shape the future direction of nations freeing themselves from colonial powers. The majority of the people who were caught up in the fighting, for a supposedly new and improved future, knew little about the power struggles, even while the bush battles were raging. And even since the regimes have changed, the lives of many are still no different. For many it is worse. The legacy from those struggles still lingers in the background, even though those who were major players are long gone. My part was just to get hold of and show some entertaining film reels, but along the way I was able to see a part of that history as it was happening.

Embassy of Italy

and

Zambian - Italian Cultural Centre

in co-operation with

Cinema Petit

cordially invite you to

A festival of films by Italian Director

MAURO BOLOGNINI

Hindu Hall

7-12 June, 1980

SWEDISH EMBASSY/
CINEMA PETIT

We will be showing the
Swedish Film Classic

"WILD STRAWBERRY"
by Ingemar Bergman
in the Hindu Hall
Tonight at 20.15 hrs
ALL ARE WELCOME

CINEMA PETIT
IN CO-OPERATION WITH
THE SWEDISH EMBASSY
SHOWING THE CLASSIC
FILM
"SMILES OF A
SUMMER NIGHT"
DIRECTED BY
INGMAR BERGMAN
starring
EVA DAHLBECK.GUNNAR
BJORNSTRAND AND
HARRIET ANDERSON
IN HINDU HALL ON
TUESDAY, NOVEMBER 27th
at 20.15

00655/d-26

USSR embassy and cinema petit,. present a Soviet film festival to commemorate 60 years of Soviet cinema, proceeds to Child Care Adoption Society of Zambia, Tuesday 26 February at 17.00 hours, "your paw, pet", children's film, Wednesday 27th February at 20.00 hours "chapaev", 1934 classic film by the brothers Vassiliev, entrance 50n, Friday 29th February at 17.00 hours "The Dear Boy", modern children's film, Saturday 1st March at 20.00 hours "The Right to Jump", life story of Brumel, world champion high jumper, entrance 50n, Monday 3rd March at 20.00 hours "Doctor Ivens' Silence", science fiction drama, entrance 50n, shows at: — Lusaka Theatre Club, (Playhouse), Church Road.
5198/d-22

Newspaper advertisements for Cinema Petit

CHAPTER 27

Safe or dangerous

EVEN WHILE the hostilities raged, many of the people in the remote heartland of Zambia, in villages at the end of dusty trails, far beyond the military training camps, barely understood the processes supposedly being waged for their ultimate good. News was a scarce resource; few had radios and many could not read. They had but the basics for survival and when the rains did not come, even survival was a basic need to be prized. It had to be strived for and fought after with an acceptance and endurance. Their lives changed little despite the passing years and the changing of politicians. Often their only contact with the processes of power was the occasional pep talk given by their local MP on a flying tour of the region. Villagers in remote regions wanted the war to end, and the bush armies to disappear. Their problems were immediate in the here and now, not with those in power many miles distant.

Visiting a strategic site

I applied to visit the Kafue Dam hydro power station some 60 km south of Lusaka. It is a giant project where a dam blocking the Kafue River straddles a strikingly scenic gorge. The site is in a politically sensitive area and to get permission to visit here was up to the whim of whoever in the Zambian Army happened to be giving out stamped approvals. It was not just because of its obvious strategic importance, but it is sited only 60 km from Chirundu at the border crossing into Rhodesia. The army maintained strict control of the whole area and even the suspicion of possible insurgencies would put the whole place on high alert. Things must have been quiet at the time, for after some lengthy negotiations I achieved the prized permits with their emblazoned official stamps and requisite signatures.

Together with Kathy and son Lloyd strapped in the car's back seat, we descended the sandy road towards the gorge. The surprised military checkpoint demanded that a soldier accompany us at all times. From a quizzical group of soldiers, one was ordered to the task. Possibly glad to be relieved of the tedium of patrol, he climbed into the back, his AK47 Kalashnikov assault rifle slung over his shoulder.

Whenever we were allowed to briefly stop momentarily to get a view of the area he carefully placed his Kalashnikov on the seat next to Lloyd and alighted too. He seemed blissfully unaware of the child's itchy trigger fingers and it took some persuasion to get our guide to move the rifle to a safe distance. We toured the whole installation, our presence turning a routine day into an occasion for the army to be proud of the installation they were looking after. We even had a chance to see the immense turbine generators supplying power to Zambia's cities.

The visit had an unreal atmosphere to it. This was a strategically important installation only a few kilometres from a border that could be a prime target for an assault on an essential installation. It could also be an easy crossing point for the Patriotic Front to stage a hit and run strike into Rhodesia. The gorge is located in an isolated area making it difficult to defend. The fact that it was possible to be sightseeing in a high-risk, strategic location appeared a contradiction. But no-one here seemed concerned. This war had many contradictions. At this very moment Rhodesian maize was being shipped to hard-pressed Zambia who was giving shelter to the rebels who were determined to see their enemy overthrown. Whether our guard reflected on this I didn't ask. The army was happy to draw their pay and whoever it was out there fighting in the bush they didn't much care. They wanted an end to it all. When it was all over, whatever the outcome and whoever came to power, for an ordinary villager, little was likely to change. They wanted better wells, improved roads and higher prices for their products. They could only hope for all these things.

The legacy of the liberation struggle

The last few chapters have had the bush war as a backdrop. Much of what framed life during this time in Zambia and Rhodesia was a consequence of this conflict. I have attempted to put this in context and show how life becomes routine even when a war is not far away. Life takes on a normality simply because the conflict becomes 'normal'. The war becomes part of people's lives and they get on with day-to-day living, even though their lives are in danger. Even though villagers could be innocent bystanders, they could not ignore the casualties occurring on their territory.

There are accounts of this war by generals and politicians who were either directly involved or were, in a variety of ways, capable of affecting its outcome. They were capable of moving men and machines from places in another continent, for example, from Cuba or the Soviet Union. Other nations were influential bystanders. The larger than life politicians who had direct control over the liberation forces struck deals with the powerful countries involved, often backed with weapons and promises. The fighting forces were equally as diverse. They were fragmented and struck deals of their own. This is Africa and nothing is as straightforward as it seems.

For the white Rhodesians it was their home, perhaps for several generations, and they had built a unique or at least comfortable way of life. It was a similar situation in Mozambique and Angola. The liberation forces wanted the land – and power – they saw this as their birthright.

Once the conflicts started, there was no going back. Yet in remote villages there were those who knew nothing about the war. They did not want to know. Politics were not something the elders approved of. Their life was difficult enough already.

When the conflicts ended, the powerful backers discovered problems in their own homelands and disappeared. The liberation leaders remained in their hard won territories and had their own internal squabbles. But the ghosts of the past linger on. Local strongmen, like Mugabe in today's Zimbabwe, still hold on to power even though many of his citizens and certainly some western nations would like to see him go. His status as a liberation leader from the 1970s still gives him clout and the African Union remains supportive and respectful of those achievements.

It is only in the 21st century that these same countries, especially China, have returned to do deals with whoever is in power. The old days, when they fought side-by-side with local armies in the liberation struggle are long gone. Whatever their policies were then, all are now warmly invited, as they bring armfuls of cash and start major infrastructure projects. They all want the oil and mineral deposits this continent has so much of. These now independent nations of Africa can strike new deals, not for politics, but for the wealth beneath their feet.

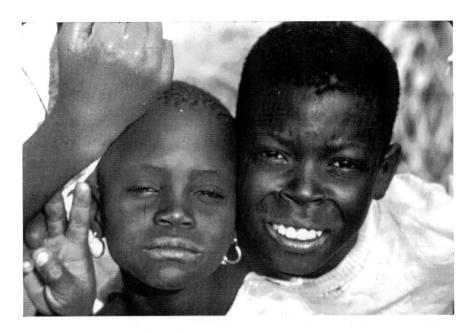

Children from the townships. They are the future

CHAPTER 28

An alternative life

IN THE late 1980s with Kathy and Lloyd, I visited Leonard Kapusa in the northern province of Malawi. I had grown to know him well during my time in Zomba. He had married Katrina, a girl from Australia he had met while studying there, under a sponsorship arrangement. He was then working at a government mechanical engineering unit, as head of their training school. He had run foul of some high government officials and had fled with his growing family back to his traditional homeland in the north of the country. He was one of those individuals you felt could always be trusted; it is something which comes across in the tone of voice, in small gestures and in a warmth of personality. He was honest and spoke his mind. But speaking one's mind was a dangerous occupation in Banda's Malawi. Besides this, the northern ethnic groups were known to be fiercely independent and perhaps this had something to do with his ill-fated entanglement with authority.

Their home was on land given by the local chief on an isolated but beautiful location some eight miles from the town of Mzuzu in the Northern Province. It was off the road on the escarpment leading to the lakeshore town of Nkhata Bay. An earth road ran beside a small village leading to where they had set-up home. Their two daughters were now at boarding school in New Zealand and three boys were at home for the school holidays. The Kapusa household was self-contained. The land provided all the maize needed for basic food and dried fish came from the village. Lake Malawi was not many miles down the escarpment. Chickens and goats roamed around the enclosure. A couple of dogs woke up in the cool of the night and kept watch. Local charcoal burners provided the cooking fuel needed and paraffin for the lamps must have come from some general store out near the paved road. The track past their house did not really lead to anywhere, therefore both wheeled and foot traffic were rare.

The block-brick walls of the house were set in a levelled-out side of the hill. Our visit was in July, the cool season and the terrain was still lush with vegetation. A maize field was drying out before the cobs could be picked. Chickens scratched around the dry earth and the two dogs would stretch out in the early morning sun after a cold night under the stars. There was no electricity and no piped water - as we would know it. A mountain stream flowed by the house and a pipe directed a crystal-clear stream into a concrete storage bath. The soft gurgling of the water and the breeze rustling and waving the nearby bamboo branches created the only discernible noise.

Leonard said that the local people avoided the area, as they believed the place was haunted by spirits. Perhaps there was something in this as there were no casual interlopers in the two weeks we stayed. There were two workers who helped around the place, doing odd jobs here and there. As far as I could tell they were just happy being around and if they could make themselves useful, so much the better. I doubted whether they got paid, but probably room and food was sufficient.

The days passed in the sort of way they would in a modern health spa, where you are sent to detox; except it would have some sort of regime to coach you from one relaxing treatment to another. Here there was no regime or defined structure to the day and without a watch, hours lost their meaning and even the passing of days became difficult to define. It was an island with only the minimum needed to sustain life; it was as though anything else brought in to change this would be a misguided attempt, something akin to corruption. There was no pretence about this being an escape from the outside world. The life here followed a natural order and interfering with it would make it something it was not intended to be. Everything seemed in balance with a timeless quality and an atmosphere of peace and serenity. Perhaps indeed the spirits did live here and had chosen the spot for themselves and for a chosen few. The outside world was a distant place.

Tranquil days

Mornings started early, as the first rays of the sun crept over the hillside and warmed the early dry season air. Slowly life stirred into our small group. There was no kitchen or at least a location that could be reliably identified as such. Katrina had put this development on permanent hold. Things here will take time. But to me, breakfast and indeed the evening meal, taken in the corrugated shelter was a delight. At the centre was a charcoal fire, over which a pot was hung for cooking the maize meal. A few chairs and a couple of planks supported on old tin drums provided our seating, which half surrounded this centrepiece. Before the fire was stoked-up in the morning, the two cats would be curled-up like two Cinderellas, on the edge of the warming cinders.

Leonard had acquired an old Volkswagen Combi, from a Dutch couple in Zomba, who had intended to make an overland crossing in it back to Europe. But before they had covered the first two hundred miles, the engine exploded and with some coaching it amazingly limped back to base. Leonard breathed some life back into the stricken machine and it once more ventured on to the local roads. When the move north was needed, its cavernous interior provided ideal transport for all his *katundu* -

baggage and possessions. Now it backed into the kitchen shelter and with its rear door opened provided the storage needed for all kitchen paraphernalia. Old vehicles in Africa are rarely discarded without being stripped of just about anything that could in any way prove useful. But as far as I could tell everything on this old Combi was still intact, with more parts to it than many vehicle restorers in Britain would start with.

The kitchen was always the centre of life

There was only one link with the outside world and this was from an old short-wave radio that could pick-up foreign transmissions. From this remote location, where newspapers rarely reached, it would be useful, even essential, to know what was happening. Political events with the inevitable rival take-overs can occur with frightening speed and local knowledge of who is in control can be a lifesaver. It is sometimes faster to learn about potential upheavals from remote broadcasts than rely upon distorted local interpretations. Life in the outside world can reach even the remotest of places. The radio was battery powered and like so many other commodities, batteries are rarely discarded. It was common practice to store perhaps ten or more in a card tube with wires at each end, extracting the very last ampere of power for a torch or radio. But in addition to this, a nearly exhausted car battery was also wired-up in the power cycle. This display of household batteries, coupled together with a car battery, its trail of wires entering the connections of a small transistor radio was an extraordinary sight. It delighted Leonard to be able to apply his electrical skills in a challenge not to be found in any textbook description. The preparation to power-up took some minutes, but once connected, a crackly BBC Overseas Service was an unreal background to our breakfast.

All our meals, breakfast included, were essentially the same. The variation of dishes according to what time of day it was, which is so much part of the western world, does not exist in traditional African life and was not part of our menu. Maize porridge - *nsima* - which began with every meal is either eaten on its own or preferably with relish, which is essentially a mixture of vegetables, usually including tomatoes. Maybe, if times are good, some meat or dried fish will be added. With a giant lake bordering most of Malawi, fish is found in many markets. As with the early surveyors who dressed for dinner and used crisp table linen, even in the most remote of locations, Katrina displayed the same drawing room manners.

But for those early pioneers, their table etiquette was more of a challenge against the harshness of the environment, a statement announcing that their culture would not be diminished at any cost. They were not prepared to go 'bush'. Maybe without realising, something of that determination had established itself in our household. But at our mealtimes there were no bone china displays, only well-used plastic. All the same, it was still given the same respect and care as though it really was part of a fine china table setting. The charming table manners in our camp-side atmosphere complimented our rustic surroundings and brought an order and ritual, which was both welcoming and reassuring.

Every late afternoon I would organise a run with the two boys along the mile or so of track, past the village and out to the main road. This was partly for fun and exercise, but also to visit the grass thatched *Chibuku* beer stall and soft drinks stand just across the road junction. It came to be a regular daily ritual with the villagers turning out to see not only the rare sight of a white person in the area, but a running one - something quite extraordinary. They gathered around the village entrance and smiled approvingly while the children jumped up and down clapping and shrieking with delight, following us to the next corner until we disappeared. We carried back our carton of *Chibuku* and soft drinks as a reward for our exercise and entertainment to the village children. The drinks would be mixed and sipped as we sat around in the gentle warmth of the cool season sun. Leonard discussed his plans for turning his land into a chalet stopover for tourists and Katrina told us her dreams for the next stage in her kitchen renovation. And then tea would be served.

No need for the outside world

There was a sense of timelessness in the Kapusa household, a 'lost world' where everything needed to sustain life was below one's feet: the soil for crops and the endless clear water stream from the hills above. It may well have served as a showcase for the modern trend of environmental living, where sustainability from natural resources is so influential in the design of western homes and the environment. Perhaps the environmental lobby would have devised a small hydropower unit driven from the same stream to charge up the deflated batteries on the transistor radio. Would it really have enhanced this life to install a radio aerial for greater coverage, or even (today) a satellite dish with television and world news coverage? The intrusion of these modern technologies may well have eroded a way of life sustained by its remoteness and isolation.

The outside world seemed out of place in this sanctuary. A warning of a change in local power politics was essential, but there was little apart from academic interest in what was happening elsewhere. It would have interfered with the kitchen routine and disturb the discussion about the maize crop or how to fix a leaking water pipe. These local concerns dominated our breakfast and seemed appropriate as we sat on the planks around the stirred embers of the kitchen fire.

Perhaps this knowledge of the outside world should have been welcomed. But with these changes would undoubtedly come others. Maybe even a desire for the trappings of an urban life. It is a delicate balance between a somewhat romanticised world of rustic living and the slow encroachment of the outside world. When I look back, it seems this household did have the right balance and any encroachment from 'outside' had to be viewed with suspicion. There are many today who strive to turn their lives into such a simplified style. This effort requires determination and it is ironically, difficult to achieve a 'simple' life, or whatever this may mean. Yet here on the slopes near the lakeshore, this ideal was found, honed from necessity and achieved by accident.

Nkhata Bay market. Fried kasava is always popular

A reflection

THROUGHOUT AFRICA, the contrasts of life for the rich and poor have changed very little over the years. Since the period I have been documenting, life has improved for the fortunate few. But in the small towns and villages, where the majority of the population live, little has changed. Look at the paper statistics and you will find most countries have indeed become richer, but it's generally the already well-off who have benefited and for millions poverty is still a way of life, with little changed since independence.

The colonial wars have passed, to be replaced by inter-ethnic conflicts, some that are still raging. Misguided land re-distribution schemes have turned Zimbabwe from the breadbasket of the nation to a food importer. The wealth of the continent was once held in the rich farmlands, owned by generations of white farmers. However controversial the new black owners claim to the land, many of them care little for the prize dropped in their lap. Many of the new owners are tenants and care little for the wellbeing of thousands of farm workers who have been displaced. Much of the land is destroyed as well.

The old political protagonists from west and east have gone. Now the countries that once tried to sell ideologies, come with cash, sometimes to buy farms, but mostly to negotiate long-term arrangements to acquire the vast mineral wealth being discovered in ever-increasing quantities. The new wealth from below the surface is being rapidly exploited with China, India and wealthy Middle East countries leading the way. Infrastructure projects such as power stations, are built to smooth the acquisitions . These buyers do not care who is in control, and will buy from anyone who has the goods they want, no matter how corrupt. No wonder some dubious leaders hang on to power.

Now it's easier to travel on the new roads that have appeared, but in many rural areas, the same pot-holed tracks that get impassable in the rains are still the norm. There are bigger and brighter cities boasting an urban elite. But look closer and not far from the supermarkets selling smart, expensive consumer goods, the shantytowns are still there. Many of those with ordinary jobs live in these places because this is all they can afford and many will barely make enough for life's essentials. They have grown up to a life no different from a generation before.

Part of the fabric of life is the endemic corruption I lived with for so many years. This is still as entrenched as ever and has become an essential part of the process of doing business. For petty officials and those whose job it is to hand out government licences, some who may not have been paid in months, it can be understood. But as ever, it is the poor who suffer. They cannot pay the bribes so necessary to get things done.

There are sinister consequences of wealth and poverty. They breed corruption, which can extend from politicians all the way through to those running market stalls. It is common to find those with access to power, position or simply something in demand, to exploit those in need. It is a tragedy that those who are the most vulnerable, the poor, are affected the most.

The rural areas, so often neglected and forgotten, still farm in the traditional way. However, the modern world has caught up in surprising ways. Mobile phones bring in information about prices and where the best places to sell goods are to be found. But the well-trusted bicycle and over-loaded bus are still relied upon to get their products to market.

Progress in small steps. Village wells are replaced by piped water

The new politicians have promised change, but the challenges are immense. Street protests by the poor demanding improvements now occur, but Africans are an accepting people and still smile and appear happy despite their deprivations. The contrast with the have and have-nots is still as distinct as ever. Probably the contrast is even more visible. As in all developing countries this gulf is difficult to ignore. Those with plenty contrast abruptly with those who only have the means to exist one day at a time. However unfair this is, international agencies or government action have made improvements, but so much more needs to be done.

Some countries have made rapid strides since independence and are destined to grasp the better standard of living so eagerly strived for and deserved. Yet other countries have spiralled into chaos with inter-ethnic rivalry. The spill over into refugee camps for thousands of misplaced innocents is as great a problem today as it ever has been.

The search for a job is still as demanding as ever. It is still a tragedy that many countries have a skills shortage while thousands cannot get a job. Those with the necessary skills so often leave for a better life in distant lands, often to western countries, despite being trained at huge expense at home. But who can blame them, as the recipient nation is morally complicit in the international struggle for the best manpower, often cheaper then training their own people.

The scourge of AIDS has fallen with devastating effects on many sub-Saharan nations, often resulting in the deaths of many breadwinners. The over-stretched health services cannot cope and large numbers of people have had to rely upon the generosity of the extended family. Many diseases are still inflicting tragedy on the lives of the rural poor. The tradition of help within the family provides so much, but ignorance and lack of basic resources cause much of the suffering.

Despite all the problems, there is much to be positive about. One thing never changes. There is so often an overwhelming sense of happiness in people who have so little. Many schools do not have nearly enough books, let alone computers and science tools. But the kids are willing learners and always smile. Just visit one and be impressed. People are not content with their lot, but are willing to make a go of whatever opportunity comes their way.

Transient expatriates still blend in and out of the landscape like migratory birds. There are not so many, as aid budgets are trimmed and local people increasingly fill the top jobs. In the old expatriate clubs, new local managers and those that can afford the fees now prop up the bars. There has always been a white resident population, especially in South Africa. Despite the political changes their life-style has barely changed and they still hold good jobs and have access to private hospitals and the best schools. Their life has changed little, except they have been joined by the new rich blacks who are increasingly taking the lead in start-up companies and becoming the new managers.

The colours of Africa are reflected in the people as much as the landscape. It can be a violent place with inter-tribal battles raging for years and innocent victims part of the cost. The causes can be obscure, but struggles for land and resources are increasingly behind many conflicts. For those not involved, these war-zones and the battling tribes and clans, are confusing. Government forces, militias that suddenly seem to have appeared out of the jungles, and even armies from neighbouring

countries, increase the mix. Added to this complexity are the rivalries even within the groups.

As with the sudden onset of the rains, reconciliation takes effect and peace once more reigns. But laws and treaties have little effect and old scores are waiting to be settled. It's as if the struggle for existence against the demands of the elements was not struggle enough. An extra harshness of life must be enlisted, as though human war has a more predictable outcome.

A dhow is still used as traditional lake transport

In Africa it is essential to adopt another life-style. Many of the services and infrastructure are always likely to breakdown with frequent power-cuts. But it is helpful to remind yourself that many in the towns and practically everyone in the vast savanna have no piped water and no power lines nearby. The water supply may be a mile away and a free hospital a day by bus, but with only basic facilities. What these villagers achieve is by their own efforts. There are no cash handouts and government help usually has strings attached. Self-reliance by using their muscle power is not new.

For the traveller, the 1980s will still have been the best time to cross this huge continent. Colonial wars had largely ceased and many of the local strongmen had yet to flex their muscles. Tourism had yet to take off and the foreign traveller was a curiosity. Some parts are still like this today, but it is generally a more dangerous place. Life is still considered cheap.

Living in Africa is a life-changing experience, which only becomes apparent when you move away and reflect on the continent you have left. It has nothing to do with leaving something of yourself there, but bringing something of the place away. Africa has a vibrant life where, given half a chance people will seek by their own efforts, to improve their lives, despite the chaos going on all around; despite its stifling bureaucracy and corruption. It does not pretend to be anything different from that which it is. Values can take on a new meaning and you find yourself examining issues in a different way. You realise how so many exist with so little.

Elephant grass for new roofs

Living in a country where so much runs counter to what has been learnt from the western world is always confusing and demands a change of outlook. And, if you are changed, and it brings some elements of understanding then it is for the better. But when you return to your home country, it is quite common to find the majority of people know little about the Africa they see on their TV news. Worse, many are simply not interested in making the effort needed to understand such a bizarre place. There appears little to compare to life in the developed world. It's too far away and little good news ever seems to appear. By living in Africa you have the opportunity to better understand what is happening and why, on such a large landmass containing so many cultures and customs. This may still be one of the best reasons for having lived there.

The visual images of the landscape are always striking and something never forgotten. One will always remember the intensity of the light and how the mid-day sun paints vivid colours whether it is in the rains or dry season. The sights, sounds, smells and colours are always there, however much development has taken place.

Just one instance brought this home when we were camping in a remote part of Zimbabwe, high up on a mountain plateau. The air was crystal clear as the altitude was above any possible dust clouds. There were no towns or even villages for miles and no matter how far I looked into the distance no glimmer of light was discernable. It was as if all human life had disappeared. The air was so still the silence became noticeable. As evening fell the darkness became impenetrable, but in the heavens, a magic lightshow was just beginning.

I laid down and simply watched, as though I was being drawn into the centre of the universe. I thought to myself:

"I've looked before, but have never realized the majesty of what a night-sky can bring."

The sky was like a thousand fireworks all ignited at once, with no sound and only a trace of colour. The more I looked and my eyes became tuned to the background, even greater numbers of stars appeared. I became spellbound by the grandeur of it all. Yet it must occur somewhere almost any night of the year. This was an extravaganza I dare not look away from, in case it all disappeared. It was simply a beautiful spectacle, like coming over a mountaintop and finding Shangri-la shimmering in the distance. Perhaps tomorrow night there would be clouds, or I would descend to the dust and smoke-filled plains. But high up here, above the clouds, this sky would be waiting to be discovered all over again.

Africa is a land of contrasts and has come a long way in a short time. There is so much opportunity. Only the people can make the changes necessary for a better future. This will take time and will not be easy. It will be like waiting for the rains and the renewal of life.

Bibliography

A guide for Returning HMOCS and Aid Personnel
    Ministry of Overseas Development 1969
Bear at the Back Door by General Sir Walter Walker
    Dialogue with Professor Vassily Solodovnikov former USSR
    Ambassador to Zambia and Dr. Vladimir Shubin,
    Institute of African Studies, Russian Academy of Sciences
Living in Malawi Ministry of Overseas Development 1969
Livingstone's Lake by Oliver Ransford
Preservation of Health in Warm Climates
    published by Ross Institute of Tropical Medicine 1969
Time Magazine 15 July 1966
Times of Zambia, 1978-79